THE KEY
TO A HAPPIER ME

OPENING THE DOORS TO LIFE'S TRUE TREASURES

Nadia Wong
♡

BY
NADIA WONG

First Printed in United Kingdom 2021

Published by Conscious Dreams Publishing
www.consciousdreamspublishing.com

Edited by Madison Whitehead and Elise Abram

Cover by Nadia Wong and Madison Whitehead

Key design by Maia Wong Astarita

Typeset by Oksana Kosovan

ISBN: 978-1-913674-65-6

Dedication

In loving memory of my beautiful niece Angelica Biancaniello.

28/11/1982 – 17/2/2021

Thank you for being a source of love and light in this world.

I dedicate this book to anyone who has ever felt unloved, unseen, unheard, unworthy, unappreciated or powerless over their life and happiness.

I see you, I hear you - I was you.

I'm not only here to remind you of the beautiful light that resides within, awakening you to the truth and beauty of who you really are; I'm also here as a source of love and inspiration to help you embrace the fact that your life truly matters.

Love is always the answer.

Much love

Nadia x

CONTENTS

Introduction

Have you ever had one of those serendipitous moments when life has called you away from what you are doing and led you on an exciting new path?

Well, that is how this book was born.

It was Christmas morning, 2018, when I woke up early, feeling exceptionally grateful for my life. I was on holiday in Sorrento with my family. My kids and husband were still asleep while I lay in bed, thinking about the journey I had taken to get me to where I was. The joy I felt was spilling over, and I knew there and then that I had to share that joy with whoever needed it. Only four years earlier, I had been completely lost in a pit of darkness and despair, wondering when the misery of my life would end. And yet, there I was, happier than I had ever been. Nothing in my outer world had changed, but *I* had. It didn't seem fair, somehow, that I was blessed with a joyful heart when there were millions of people all over the world still suffering and enduring their existence like I once had. So, I decided to share how I created my own joy.

I'm not a patient person, so I immediately set about creating a free five-day course that I could run online in the new year as a Christmas gift for my Facebook family.

I ran the course at the start of the year, which ended up being a great success. It opened the hearts and minds of all the people taking part, bringing about a lot of breakthroughs. Increasingly, I came to realise just how powerful this work was in creating positive change in the lives of others. So, it seemed natural to set about turning that course into something more to enable me to widen my reach and have an impact on many more lives.

Because I was in the middle of writing a book at the time, I decided that when the book was complete, I would begin creating a new one based on the foundations of my course, but the universe had other plans.

I'm the kind of person that likes to complete whatever I set out to do, and as such, I knew I *had* to finish the book on which I was working before I could start on this one. However, strange things started happening to me that undeniably led me in an alternative direction. I tried to ignore the whispers within my soul, but the signs were so powerful that I could ignore them no longer. I have been a spiritual person for most of my life, not so much religious, so it was clear that a force greater than myself was leading me to a higher cause. I knew within the depths of my soul that I had to listen, so I abandoned my current book and started on this one.

I hadn't given the book's title much thought, but as I began writing it, I considered what to name it. While reaching into my bag for my keys one day, I found a key. Not just any key, but the one on the cover of this book.

How on earth could that kind of antique-looking key just appear in my bag? I had never seen it before in my life, but there it was, in the inside pocket of my bag into which I reach every single day! I have been through all possible scenarios, trying to figure out how such a key could have appeared in my bag, but it is still a mystery to this day. My only explanation was that it had somehow fallen into my bag, but for it to be in an inside pocket that I reserved for my keys was mind-blowing. I felt that, perhaps, it meant that I was to call the book *The Key*, but I googled it and discovered that another book of that name already existed, so I let it go. As weird as it was, I thought perhaps I'd placed too much meaning on the 'key' incident, and I let my idea go. However, a week later, while I was out for my daily walk, right outside of a house in the village, I accidentally pulled out one of my gold earrings as I was removing my earphones. I felt it falling out, so I knew for sure that it couldn't have gone far. I got down on my hands and knees and began searching for it there. My sister then called and said she was in the village for a walk, so she came to help me look for it. After 45 minutes, we decided to give up and let the mystery of the lost earring go. There was nothing strange there, but the next day, as I walked by that house, I decided to have another quick look. I glanced along the garden wall of the house to see if someone else had seen it and placed it on the wall at eye level. Can you guess what I saw? No, not my earring but another key, not hidden away, but sitting there in plain sight! I was a bit spooked when that happened, to be honest, and I asked the universe for a sign that I was on the right track. From that day until I completed my book, I saw a new white or light-coloured feather on my daily walk – not the same feather in the same place, but a different one *every single day*! To top that off, when I met with my friends for my birthday, without knowing my 'key' story, they had bought me a pendant with a heart and keyhole in it. That was it for me. Shivers went up and down my spine, and I just knew it was no coincidence. For me, there couldn't have been a more prominent sign from the Universe unless, of course, God Almighty Himself had come down to tell me, face to face.

You may think I'm crazy, but I can assure you that I'm a normal(-ish) human being with my feet firmly on the ground. Still, I have to say that I believe this book wasn't all my doing, I had Divine help!

****

If you are still here, congratulations; welcome to the first day on your journey to living a happier life! I'm afraid I can't wave a magic wand to help you, but I can give you this key to open the door to a happier life for yourself, one in which you are the pilot, the navigator, and the decision-maker. You can choose to fly beneath the clouds and endure the ever-changing weather or soar above them to clear blue skies, regardless of what is happening in the atmosphere below. You are the creator of your own life and your own story.

Your happiness is in your hands, not anyone else's. You have the power to create the kind of life you desire, whatever that is. The choice is all yours. Your circumstances do not determine the quality of your life. You do!

Lasting happiness doesn't just happen by chance. It is made, just like a delicious cake is made. We need the right ingredients and method before getting to work on our creation. We can decide to create whatever we want – be a cake or the lives of our dreams – but it takes conscious awareness and action to get started, so let's begin today with a single step.

One quote I use time and time again is that of Chinese philosopher Lao Tzu: 'The journey of a thousand miles begins with a single step.'

What he says is so true, and it makes perfect sense. In order to go anywhere in life, we first have to move forward, even just one step in the right direction. We can't just sit around and expect a wonderful life to land in our laps. We have to take steps towards it to live, love, and create that wonderful life for ourselves.

Each step we take in this book will be a step closer to understanding how to create a happier life for ourselves, but reading about it alone is not enough – we must take action!

It's not what we know that makes us successful in our endeavours; it's what we do with our knowledge that counts. I'm here to show you the doors to life's true treasures. I have walked through them myself, but you will also have to step through to claim your own life and joy. I can't do it for you.

This book contains ten doors that, when opened, will allow more love and light into your soul, making your life brighter, enabling you to see, feel, and embrace life's true treasures. Once inside, you will learn something new about who you are and the actions you can take to ignite the light within your heart. It is a journey that will take us deep within and that we cannot rush. It is not a race to get to the finish line or the end of this book, it is about gaining a clear understanding of who we are as individuals. So, we have to take time to ponder each concept and be completely open and honest with ourselves as we answer each question. Taking one step at a time means we can consistently move forward in all areas of life that will get us to where we want to be, whether we are working on our bodies, minds, or souls. The joy of life is in the journey, taking in new experiences, meeting new people, and enjoying time with those we love, and not racing to get to the end. There is so much more to life than enduring pain and suffering. It is a journey of discovery and adventure to accurately understanding who we are and how we can make a difference in this world.

We are all meant to be here – right here, right now – and we are all blessed with free will. We can either choose to endure the time we have on this earth and make do with what we have, or seek out the treasures of life and truly live. We reap what we sow. Therefore, we get out what we put in. We can only harvest happiness if we first plant the seeds, but it also takes time and patience to reap the rewards.

When we learn how to play a musical instrument, it takes time and consistent practice. We may find it challenging to begin with and consider giving it up as we wonder if it will ever feel natural to us, but in time, we become competent enough to play with ease and flow.

If we apply the same principle to life using this book as a guide, our new way of thinking will become natural and flow with ease. It's about putting what we learn into practice daily, taking the time to learn how to play the beautiful instrument of life.

Think of it as a fascinating adventure into your mind, heart, and soul that will help support you on your journey through life as you take the scenic route to admire all of the breathtaking views as you go.

We often go through life at superspeed without taking the time to look around, but in doing so, we miss out on all the beauty surrounding us, so we have to enjoy the ride as we rediscover who we are to understand our true worth.

To create anything extraordinary in life, we must first have a vision of it in our minds. All inventions and engineering breakthroughs begin with a thought. The Wright brothers had the foresight before they were able to create the first powered aircraft, but they also had to *do the work* and fail time and time again before they succeeded to make their first flight in 1903. It wasn't a one-day, one-week, or one-year project – it was a work in progress with the determination to realise their vision. The Wright brothers knew it was possible, and they never gave up. How do I know this? Because they succeeded. Without believing in their process, they would not have spent seven years making it work. The same goes for every invention ever created. They all began with an idea in the mind of someone who followed through. Imagination alone doesn't make them inventors – it's what they do with their thoughts and how they put their ideas into practice that transformed them into a reality. And the same goes for us.

For us to create happiness, we need to visualise joyful versions of our lives in our hearts and minds and take the necessary, consistent actions to get us there.

Before we begin opening the doors to some of life's true treasures, let's first understand where you are right now. Are you content with where you are in mind, body, and spirit?

When we set our satellite navigation systems, we first need to know the starting point so we can work out how to get to our destination from where we are. So, where are you?

By answering the following questions openly and honestly, you will be able to gauge where you are, not only as a starting point but also as a reference to look back to on this journey to see how far you have come.

If you find yourself back at the starting point, you will know that you are moving in circles and have strayed off course, which will remind you to re-align yourself with your soul. We all get lost from time to time – that isn't the problem. The challenge is knowing what direction to take, whether to keep moving or give up and stay where we are. The destination isn't where the joy is – it's through moving forward one step at a time, growing, learning, and connecting with the very source of our love, one day at a time, with a peaceful soul, knowing we are exactly where we should be.

So, please answer the following questions honestly:

- *On a scale from one to ten, how happy are you in your daily life at the present moment (one being you are desperately unhappy and feel as if you have no control over your happiness, and ten being that you are one of the happiest people you know, and you understand that your happiness is due to your state of mind)?*

- *What number do you want that to be and why?*

_____

_____

_____

- *On a scale from one to ten, how much time and effort are you willing to put into getting yourself to the level that you want to be (one being as little time as possible as this is not important to you, and ten being that you know this is essential inner work that will transform your life and that of your family, so you will give and do all that it takes)?*

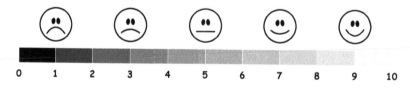

- *Now, rate, on a scale from one to ten, the quality of each area of your life listed below (one being it is in desperate need of change, ten being that you are happy in this area and it needs no improvement):*

- *My personal relationship*

- *My family*

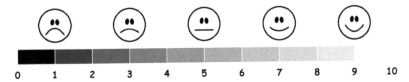

- *My work*

- *My health*

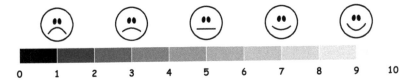

- *My finances*

- *My personal fulfilment*

0   1   2   3   4   5   6   7   8   9   10

- *Which three of the above are the main priorities in your life at this moment in time? Write them down in order of importance, and explain why they take precedence over the other areas.*

1. _____

2. _____

3. _____

- *How much time do you spend day-to-day on your digital devices, watching TV, or doing similar mindless activities that distract you from concentrating on your personal growth and wellbeing? How does that make you feel?*

_____

_____

_____

_____

_____

- *What do you hope to gain from reading and applying the teachings of this book to your life?*

_____

_____

_____

_____

- *What do you truly want from life?*

_____

_____

_____

_____

- *On a scale from one to ten, how much love do you have for the person you are right now (one being that you hate yourself and don't feel you are of any value, and ten being that you believe you are here for a purpose, and you feel comfortable saying that you love yourself as a human being)?*

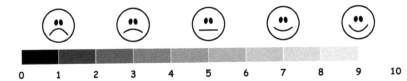

GRATITUDE

Happiness Flows with An Attitude of Gratitude!

One of the greatest lessons I have learned in life is the power of gratitude. It is an essential step towards living a happier life and is the answer to dealing with most of life's challenges. Even in times of great difficulty, we can always find something for which to be grateful if we truly look for it. It reminds us of what and who we have in our lives at any given time, giving us the hope and strength to keep moving and keep loving. Being grateful for all that we have and are without comparing ourselves to others allows us to see the value in each day and in each person that crosses our path.

Most of us go through life waiting to be happy, expecting to reach fulfilment when we find our one true love, when we have more money, when we have comfortable houses, when we have children, when we retire, when we lose weight, and so on, but *now* is the time to be happy!

No one knows how much time we have here on this earth. We could live on for many years, but we could just as swiftly go tomorrow. So, let's not waste a single minute of it and be grateful for every day that we can spend with those we love.

Gratitude is the very essence of happiness. It's about focusing on what we *do* have instead of what we don't. Whatever we put our energy into expands. Therefore, when we are focused on good things, more good things will appear.

I do this little awareness experiment with each of my clients and write about it in every one of my books because it is so powerful, and I'd like to do it with you now. Whether you have done this in the past or not, it is always good to remind yourself just how significant your focus and awareness is to your life.

> *Wherever you are right now, for ten seconds, take a good look around you and seek out everything that is the colour brown.*

Now, once you've got a clear picture of all the brown you know is around you, close your eyes and say out loud all the things you saw that were red or blue.

Please, don't read on any further without doing this experiment. It will only take a minute, but the effects can last a lifetime, and they will change your whole perception of life for the better. Don't just take my word for it – you must experience this for yourself for you to reap the benefits.

Now that you have done the experiment, how did you do? How much red or blue did you see? If you are in a room you know well, then you may have been able to name a few things from memory. Now, take the time to look around carefully, and you will see all the red and blue you failed to see before. It may be in a picture, a painting, a book cover, on a label, or in the pattern of a cushion – the more closely you look, the more you will find, but why didn't you see it before? It's because you weren't looking for red and blue, but brown.

This is what life is like.

When we go through life focused on all the beauty and that which is right we will see exactly that. Alternatively, if we are focused on our problems and what is wrong, then that is what we will see, no matter how many beautiful things are surrounding us.

I did this experiment with a client, and she failed to see the big red door sitting right in front of her. How on earth did she manage to miss it? It couldn't have been more obvious, but she was simply unaware of it. It may sound crazy, but this is how the majority of us go through life. We tend to focus on what is wrong and not on what is right.

As children, we are not taught how to think, so we don't realise the power we have over our thoughts and our lives. We were asked 'What's wrong?' time and time again as children, but how often were we asked, 'What's right?'

By integrating gratitude into our lives, our hearts begin to open as we focus on how truly blessed we are already for having a home, a family, a bed to sleep in, eyes to see, legs to walk on, and so on. So many people do not have these blessings, yet we take what we have for granted. Once we open our hearts and minds and truly appreciate the small, seemingly insignificant stuff, happiness will begin to flow in abundance.

My path to happiness began with a daily gratitude practice, which ultimately changed my life. It took me from a place of despair and pain to discovering the key to an abundance of happiness. It is my go-to place in my heart and mind that sustains me on a daily basis, and more so when times get tough. We would be foolish to think that once we attain an understanding of how to live a happy life, we'll be in a state of constant joy. We are and always will be works in progress. Our good daily habits can sustain us, but if we begin to adopt bad daily habits – which is just as easy to do – we can lose our ways again. It is paramount that we consistently apply good habits in all areas of our lives to sustain our sense of peace and wellbeing.

We desperately work on bettering our external world to improve our lives, but nothing outside of ourselves can bring long-lasting love, peace, and joy within.

Imagine if your car wasn't running smoothly and kept breaking down. Would you buy it a new sound system or treat it to some fancy alloy wheels to make it perform better? Would you give it a makeover in the hope of it running reliably again? No, that would make no sense whatsoever. To get your car up and running at optimum levels again, the first thing you would do is look under the hood to see what the problem is, right? We first have to look at the inner workings of the car to understand what is going on and then find a solution. We can't maintain the health of our engines by seeking quick fixes on the exterior. Yet, in our own lives, so many of us think that changing our outer appearances will solve the problems that come from deep within.

Only by opening the hood of our minds and hearts and looking deep within ourselves are we able to identify what prevents us from thriving in life. When we understand what is going on, we can then find solutions and take the necessary steps to get ourselves running at full power by diving inwards and tapping into our souls.

We all know what gratitude means: giving thanks for and appreciating what we already have. But do we understand the *power* of gratitude and its effect on our lives? I know I didn't. It was when I began writing about and wholly filling my spirit with that for which I was grateful that I realised its abounding power in creating a life of joy. Many aspects of life changed because I focused on what was good about myself, my life, and my surroundings. I started to see all the outstanding people with whom I was surrounded instead of seeking what was wrong.

In the Bible, it says, "Seek and ye shall find," and from my experience, that is accurate. When we look for what's wrong, we find it, because we are consciously seeking problems, but when we look for the good in people, things, and places, we find exactly that.

Two people can go to the same event together, one can love it, and the other hate it, but that says nothing about the event itself. It all depends on what each person looks to gain from the event. For example, imagine going to your partner or spouse's family's party, and you don't really want to be there. You can do one of two things: you can decide that it will be fun before you enter even though you really don't want to be there, or you can resign to having a terrible time. If you decide to enjoy it, you will find people and things you like, and you will have fun. Alternatively, if you are dead set on not enjoying yourself, then guess what? You won't enjoy yourself. When I first began practising gratitude, I had to work really hard at finding things for which to be grateful (other than my children, of course). I had allowed life to get me down, and I found myself at war with the world and with myself. I had been so focused on what was missing in my life, everything I wanted but could not have, that I had blinded myself from all I already had. Previously, I had managed to dig myself into a dark pit of fear, anxiety, and despair in which, quite frankly, I had lost my will to live. I was in a hopeless and horrible place from which I felt there was no escape, but gratitude turned that around.

I think we all have a calling and a reason for being. I also believe with all my heart that I had to go through the darkness, pain, and despair to lead me to my true calling. If not for the struggle, I would not be here right now, reaching out to others, helping people turn their lives around, too. It is my divine destiny to be a life coach and writer, to be the guide that holds others' hands and leads them to joyful hearts. I didn't choose this work for myself; it chose me. As well as bringing my life purpose and meaning, it allows me to tap into my inner joy. I cannot keep in this desire to share my knowledge and wisdom as it flows to me and through me so naturally. Because I know how it feels to be lost and powerless over my life, I am now able to help others. I could've done with someone like me and this book back then, so I now spend my life *being* the person I needed in my life. If I had not suffered emotionally and just plodded through life, I certainly wouldn't be living such a joyful existence now. I am the happiest person I know, and when I don't feel cheerful, I know what I need to do to turn that around. I live each day with a peaceful heart because I know I am doing all I am destined to do by living this moment and being grateful for all I have now and all I have ever experienced, good and bad.

When we are in the midst of pain or turmoil, it isn't always easy to be grateful for our horrible situations. However, if we cannot change them, we have to accept that we have no control over that particular area and still be thankful for the other blessings we have. We *will* learn and grow from this, and it, too, shall pass.

For example, I nearly died in my twenties due to living with chronic asthma, but because of my near-death experience, I realised the value of my life. I had previously taken my life for granted and hadn't given my health very much thought. In the same way that we don't prioritise our health and wellbeing, we don't always value the people in our lives. Only when we are at risk of losing them do we see how much they mean to us.

After my near-death experience, I radically transformed my lifestyle. I learned about what I needed to do to get well and rid myself of chronic asthma for good, which took me on a holistic path. I stopped eating sugar, refined foods, dairy, and all processed foods and began eating clean. I took a breathing course to retrain my brain to breathe correctly to deal with the asthma attacks. I had regular acupuncture treatments and put my health and wellbeing first. I also gave up my hairdressing business as it hindered my healing. It didn't bring me joy anymore, so giving it up was a part of my healing process. I eventually moved to Italy, where I have lived for the past 18 years.

All of this came about from my chronic asthma and near-death experience. I can say, hand on heart, that I am grateful for the suffering I went through then and for the reminder that life is for living. We have more power over our lives than we think we have, but because we live in fear of the unknown and stay safely in our comfort zones, we do not empower ourselves to use it. We end up living a mediocre existence even when we are not happy.

When I say mediocre, I mean in measure of the lives *we* desire to live, not in comparison to others.

For most of my life, I have lived modestly. I had no desire to gain fame or fortune or to have my name in lights. I am a simple lady with simple needs; all I needed for many years was time with my loved ones, especially my two beautiful children. But as my children grew, I began to feel invisible and insignificant to them. I had made my family my world, and I felt settled for life. In doing so, I had naively failed to foresee the emotional detachment that naturally occurred as my children became more independent. I got so wrapped up in being the best mummy I could be that I overlooked myself and what I would do in the future.

There I was at 45-years-old with no clue as to how I was going to spend the rest of my life. My children still needed me, but I knew it was time to get back to work. I had lost all of my confidence, and just the idea of getting back to work filled me with anxiety, fear, and self-doubt. I hadn't worked for 15 years, and the world had changed so much that I had failed to notice living in my perfect little mummy bubble. When I began to think about re-immersing myself back into the reality of life, the world looked so scary to me. I had no computer skills, I mean zero. Other than doing a Google search, I was baffled by technology and scared to death of not being able to catch up to the world. I had lived happily in my bubble for many years, but when it burst, I fell with a hard thump, immobilised with fear and dreading the rest of my life. All I could think was: "What now? Is the best of my life over? Is it time to wait out the rest of my life for old age? Is this *it* for me?" That is where I found myself for the next few months, in that deep pit of darkness.

Because of my holistic journey back to health years earlier and my search for a better way of life, I eventually turned to the books that had sustained me then, and I retraced my steps back to me again. I worked hard on myself by looking within and getting to know who Nadia Wong, the woman, was, not Nadia, the mother and wife. As I looked deeper, I reminded myself of the power I'd previously had over my health and life. If I applied the same determination and energy to the state of my mental health and depression, could I overcome that, too?

I had beaten chronic asthma and was living a healthy, medication-free life after years of hard work, having given my life an overhaul, and I was determined to tackle this, too. Refusing to let this break me after everything I had been through, another new journey into my mind, heart, and soul began in which gratitude played an enormous part.

It was the fuel I needed to keep me focused on the value in my life, within my soul and also in the world around me. I opened my eyes to more than I had ever seen before. I compare gratitude to putting on seeing glasses for the first time. I have *literally* been short-sighted for my whole life. I was too vain to wear glasses, but when I started driving lessons at 17, I had no choice. The safety of myself and others depended on it, and of course, it helped me to see where I was going. So, when I first put on the glasses, I was blown away. Just…wow! I had missed out on so much. I had spent my life blind to the world around me.

The same goes for gratitude. When we seek it, feel it, and express it daily, everything becomes clear, and we wonder how we could have missed such beauty in the first place. We can't see what we can't see, can we? Through making a conscious effort to wear our gratitude glasses, we enable ourselves to see a whole other world that had always been there in front of us the entire time.

Set yourself a daily task to help you to see things that you were not aware of before. For example, if you walk down the same street regularly, set yourself a challenge to count as many different types of flowers you can see. Unless you are usually aware of your surroundings or you are a flower lover, you will most likely realise that you don't see flowers often, but once you begin to seek them out, you'll be amazed at how much you miss day-to-day. If there are no gardens or houses around, look for beautiful features on the buildings or perhaps, trees. When we have our eyes and awareness fully open, we are able to find what we are looking for with renewed zeal.

Seek out the good in life, and you will see it. When we seek out ways to be kinder, we will find them. When we look for good qualities in ourselves and others, we will also find them.

Think hard about what you want to see in your life: happiness, love, friendship, fulfilment, meaning? Seek, and you will find, but be aware of your focus. If you are looking for reasons as to why your life is unfulfilling, you will find them. If you look for what you don't like in people, you will find that also. By looking for the good in all things and all people, life will start to be brighter, and joy will begin to enter your heart.

GROWING WITHIN

At the beginning of my gratitude journey, I committed to finding things for which to be grateful and recording them in a gratitude journal, which I write in every single day. As soon as I wake up, I thank God for giving me life, another new day, and for all that I have and am. When I get up, I go straight to spending a few minutes writing in my gratitude journal and writing a wonderful day into existence. What does that mean? I write down how I want my day to go. For example: "Today is a wonderful new day, and all good things and people flow with ease and love into my day."

Our minds are like sponges, so whatever we fill them with first thing in the morning becomes the base of what we carry around all day. When they are full of positive, feel-good thoughts, we are less likely to absorb anything negative. I choose to show up as my best self every single day, so I fill my heart and mind with gratitude that sustains me throughout the day.

Just as breakfast is the most important meal of the day – providing our bodies with clean and nourishing fuel to sustain us – feeding our minds with wholesome stimuli in the morning is essential to keeping them functioning at their best.

In this world of technology, we are never far from devices that eat away at our time, distracting us from what we value most. Often, hours can pass without us even noticing as we get sucked into other people's lives and their ways of thinking. We begin by comparing the worst parts of ourselves with the best part of others, yet so many people reach for their phones the minute they open their eyes, exposing themselves to this comparison game, filling their minds with unhealthy food. Because we cannot control exactly what comes into our news feeds or inboxes, we cannot control what goes into our minds the first thing in the morning.

What works for me is switching off all devices around seven pm every evening and dedicating that time to my family. They stay off until I have completed my morning ritual to give me the best chance of having a joyful day. I cannot control what happens around me during each day, but I can prepare myself physically and emotionally to deal with whatever life throws at me.

To introduce yourself to gratitude, begin by writing three things for which you are grateful in each of these categories:

People

For example,
1. My husband for his support and love.
2. My son for the love he brings to my life.
3. My daughter who brightens my days with her joyful presence.

1. _____

2. _____

3. _____

Possessions

For example, my car for giving me the freedom to go where I please.

1. _____

2. _____

3. _____

Physical

For example, my eyes that enable me to see all the beautiful things in the world.

1. _____

2. _____

3. _____

COUNTING MY BLESSINGS

We all have "off days". I am no stranger to darkness, and I have had my fair share of off days, but now I face them by taking control of them instead of allowing them to control me. How? By counting my blessings. When we focus on what we have, it helps us to break a negative thought pattern and allows us to free ourselves from the chains that restrict us.

During the time in my life when I found myself in that deep dark pit, I had very few good days, and the rest were off, but as I began to practice more and more gratitude, my good days slowly increased, and the off days became fewer. The off days then turned into half-days, then a few hours, then an hour, all the way down to minutes, but that didn't happen by itself – I had to make it happen. It had to begin with a desire to change the negative thoughts and take my happiness into my own hands instead of just waiting.

Understanding our emotions and learning how to deal with them, just like you are doing here in this book, will allow you to recognise your thought patterns and help you to help yourself out of a bad day and back to living more joyfully.

I may be the happiest person I know, but there are still moments in which I catch myself falling into old thought patterns. Perhaps when I am tired or faced with negative situations or sadness, I use my tried and tested tools to get out of that space as soon as I recognise it and move back to a place of gratitude.

One "off" evening on my growth journey, determined not to go to bed with a heavy heart, I came up with the idea of counting my blessings to get me back on track. I knew that practising gratitude worked because I was feeling so much better, but my daily gratitude practice just wasn't cutting it on that particular evening, so I decided to step it up a notch. I sat down with a blank piece of paper and wrote at the top of the page, "Counting My Blessings". Then, I opened my heart and wrote down all the things that I am blessed to have.

Once I started, it began to flow so effortlessly; the words were like weights falling away from my heavy heart. In ten minutes, I had managed to write down 100 blessings, and I felt lighter and brighter with a heart full of gratitude and love.

Because I was consciously looking for blessings, I found them. I began as usual with my gratitude, people, physical, and material, and the list went on. When we take the time to think about it, we all have so much.

The fact that I can write these words and that you can read them is an enormous blessing. The ability to communicate with potentially millions of people through using words and letters is incredible when I think about it, sincerely.

On my 'Counting My Blessings' list that evening, I started with the simplest of things, and I was truly humbled when I realised how fortunate I was to have this life, this body, this home, these people, eyes to see, ears to hear, a mouth to eat, a tongue to speak and communicate, teeth with which to chew, skin to protect my flesh, a heart, lungs, kidneys, and liver, all doing their jobs by making this body of mine run smoothly.

Of all the things that were going right, my focus was on the few things that were going wrong. That evening, I went to sleep with a peaceful heart and a joyful soul. Counting my blessings became an off-day practise on which I could rely when I found myself slipping back into my old way of thinking. These days, I very rarely need to use it, but life still throws me a curveball from time to time, and I am grateful for this tool that I used to help me find peace again. We cannot control our life's circumstances, but we can control how we deal with them and how they affect us. Use the space below to start counting your blessings today.

Counting My Blessings

REGULAR DAILY PRACTICE

Buy yourself a notebook and begin each day by writing down 'TODAY IS A WONDERFUL DAY, AND MAGICAL THINGS ARE GOING TO HAPPEN' to affirm in writing that each day will be a good one, followed by at least three things for which you are grateful. Try not to write the same few things but to find new things in different areas of life.

It is beneficial to do this at the end of the day, too. Before I go to sleep, I write down at least three things that went well during the day to enable me to sleep more peacefully, focusing, again, on what is right and not what isn't. Just as we fill our minds and bodies with nourishing fuel for breakfast to get us through each day, we also have to think good thoughts before bed to reinforce our positive mindsets as we sleep.

A negative thought at night can be likened to a bloodstain from a nosebleed on a pillow. The longer it stays there without getting washed out, the harder the bloodstain will be to remove. It will become ingrained into the fabric as we sleep, just as negative thoughts become ingrained in our minds if we do not replace them with peaceful ones.

KNOW YOUR SOUL

'HE WHO KNOWS OTHERS IS WISE. HE WHO KNOWS HIMSELF IS ENLIGHTENED.'

– Lao Tzu

To live happier lives, we have to develop a certain level of inner peace and love our sacred selves deeply, but to love ourselves deeply, we first need to know our souls. Do you know who you are?

You may say, 'Of course, I know myself,' but do you, truthfully? You may know your physical self and your external likes and dislikes, your capabilities and potential, your body and how it responds to outside factors, but do you know your soul?

If you do know who you are, the question is if you are living as the real you, your authentic and sacred self, or are you following or being influenced by others in the world around you and living the life you think you ought to live? Do you make your life choices from the depths of your soul, or do you make them according to an ego that wants to be liked, fit in, be valued, and accepted by others according to society's standards?

In the fast-paced world of today, we are all becoming so busy but often getting nowhere fast. We are busy chasing after more of everything with the belief that more is better, but do we even know why? We all too easily get sucked into other people's versions of a happy life without realising it. We find ourselves asking, 'How did I even get here? This isn't the life I had planned.' We may feel like we have to keep striving and chasing what others are chasing due to the fear of missing out or being somehow left behind, but we fail to stop to get to know who we really are and what we genuinely want to gain from the precious time we have here on earth.

We don't *need* fame or fortune, fancy titles or awards, big houses or fancy cars and the like to be happy; we only need to know ourselves, love ourselves, and be ourselves.

We already have everything we need to live abundantly happy lives, so all we *need* is to connect back to our source of love within and live in alignment with who we are, but we have to make conscious efforts to do so.

Worldly riches are not bad by any means, and they can bring us lovely moments and experiences, but again, we don't need them to be happy. Whereas, we *do* need to know and love ourselves to feel that inner peace that enables us to live with joy.

It is a futile pursuit to seek happiness outside of ourselves; it is a state of heart, mind, and soul. The only way to embrace it entirely is to do this inner work of knowing your soul and loving your sacred self.

When we reconnect with our true selves and become fully aware of our worth as a 'soul being', we then realise our values as 'human beings'.

So, why don't we know our soul selves?

I believe the first thing we should all learn as children is that we are not who we 'think' we are – this is the one universal truth that so few of us understand. We don't teach it because so many of us identify ourselves through who we 'think' we are, but we couldn't be more wrong. Our thoughts are simply that: thoughts. They are merely a collection of our past experiences that we believe make up who we are. Let me explain.

We are all conditioned from birth by our well-meaning parents, relatives, siblings, teachers, friends, and all the people and media who surround us. We learn that if we say and do things we are not supposed to, it will make us naughty or unkind, or if we eat a lot or don't share, it will make us greedy or selfish. We also hear our well-meaning loved ones telling others all about who we are, and we begin to assess our self-worth through others' opinions of who we are. No one is exempt from this, but this is when we begin questioning who we are, and self-doubt begins to creep into our growing hearts. We start labelling ourselves as good or bad, kind or unkind, cheerful or grumpy, pretty or ugly, intelligent or stupid, fast learners or slow learners, athletic or clumsy on our feet, and the list goes on. We either live up to these labels or live our lives inherently striving and fighting to prove ourselves and others wrong.

The older we become, the more labels we wear to make us into the people we *believe* we are today. We continue to define ourselves by what we have or haven't done, what we have or haven't achieved, what we have or haven't experienced, or what we have or haven't accumulated in wealth, and we continue to wear these labels throughout our lives, which unmistakably influence our decisions. The more we define ourselves by the false labels we wear, the harder it is to connect to our soul selves. These imposed labels take us further and further away from who we are until we find ourselves lost in the fog of the world without our souls to light the path. Our soul selves are our guides through, leading us to lives of joy and meaning, but because we unwittingly allow ourselves to hide beneath all the labels that mask our true natures, we lose our ways and find ourselves wandering aimlessly through life with no idea of why we are here.

Once we reconnect with our soul selves, we will hear the still small voice within that will lead us back onto the paths of our true destinies. Our paths will become clearer as we rid ourselves of all the false labels as we go.

When we become still and quieten the ego-mind by taking time away from the busyness of life, perhaps spending time alone in nature or prayer and meditation, for example, we can reconnect with the truths of who we are.

Whether we call it the voice of the spirit, intuition, or just a gut feeling, things become evident to us, and the truths of who we are will come to light. We just know without knowing why. We inherently know when something or someone is right or wrong for us, but we all too often ignore that voice as we allow our egos to take over and make our decisions for us, which, in turn, leads us away from inner peace and love.

When I briefly worked in network marketing, I learned that an attitude of 'monkey see, monkey do' was the way to success. In other words, follow and imitate what successful people do, and you will be successful, too, but looking back now, I realise that this wasn't the best advice because success exists in different forms for each of us.

To be successful in any area in life, we first have to define what success looks and feels like for each of us.

Yes, there are a lot of apparently 'successful' people in the world, but you never know the full picture. Perhaps they have:

- Highly successful businesses but poor health.
- Millions in the bank but lack loving relationships.
- Fame and fortune but are time poor and have no personal lives.
- Flawless bodies but are unhappy within their soul selves.
- Beautiful homes and family lives, but they hate their jobs.

The question is then, if we do everything we are supposed to do to 'succeed' in the material world, how will we end up *feeling*?

Don't get me wrong – I fully believe in having a mentor in life that can lead and guide us to the lives we choose, but we also need to choose our mentors wisely. If we need to work on strengthening our marriages, for example, we should consider advice from someone who has been happily married for many years and not from someone who can't hold down a relationship.

I coach people to create love, inner peace, and harmony in their lives. That's just who I am, and honestly, I am happy that way. I write books because I want people to get the benefits from my work as a coach but in such a way that every single person can have access to it. I am the happiest person I know, and if I do not share my knowledge, I cannot be at peace with myself, knowing that others out there are feeling powerless over their happiness.

So, seek out those that have succeeded in life in the area in which you want to excel, but ultimately, this inner work has to be done by *you* to enable you to create joy in each area of your life, be it business, health, relationships, or in anything else.

However, if we listen to the wisdom of those whose lives are not in alignment with our values, we risk being sucked into a different world than we desire for ourselves, again leading us further away from who we are and our inner peace. It is not a matter of whether coaches or mentors are good or bad; it is more about finding those that are in alignment with our soul selves who are good matches for *us*. We do not align with everyone, and that is okay, but we cannot judge others for not being like us. We are all different but equal in value, no matter who we are.

We have no idea why people do what they do. We may judge others for being unsuccessful or for not doing much with their lives, but we don't know them. They could be living their ideas of dream lives. We all have reasons for the way we live our lives, and we cannot judge others for their life choices either.

Perhaps some financially successful people are striving for success to mask a whole other painful world that exists within themselves. Perhaps some are driven because they came from a poor background and vowed they would never go back. My point is that we cannot know what is in the hearts, minds, and souls of others. We cannot look into their lives and understand what makes them tick, be it good or bad in our eyes. No matter how their lives look on the outside, we can never know what is going on within another human being.

In this world of social media, we only see the best parts of other's lives and compare them to the worst parts of our own, but we don't *know* these people. We only see what they want us to see, and we make up the rest of the story in our minds.

We are all guilty of reading between the lines from time to time or making unfounded judgements about others, but when we barely know the souls inside ourselves, how can we believe that we know anything about the souls of other people?

Those of us who have known people who have taken their own lives often wonder why we didn't recognise they were feeling so desperate. We say to ourselves, 'If only I had known, maybe I could've done something.' They may have seemed perfectly happy on the outside, and none of us could've known of the incredible pain or suffering they had to bear. We may think we know other people, but the truth is, we honestly cannot fathom what is in their souls, no matter how close we are to them.

The previously mentioned monkey see, monkey do attitude is not the way to live life with joy. The only way to find joy is to look within because everything we need is within ourselves. No one else is responsible for our happiness, and no one can *make* us happy. We are accountable for our own health, wellbeing, lifestyles, happiness, and the quality of our relationships.

We are here in life to support each other, love each other, and hold each other's hands through life, but we are not here to compare ourselves with others or compare our lives with theirs. We are all unique, so it is impossible to duplicate a happy life.

Take a set of twins, for example – two identical-looking bodies, yet two separate and unique beings. They are not one person split into two, but two beings with two minds, two hearts, and two souls. Granted, twins have a special bond, and we hear stories about how they share pain at times, but it is impossible for them to share thoughts, and one twin does not know the essence of the other's soul, no matter how close they are.

We cannot *copy* success, and the same is true for happiness. Rather, it must be *created* with a process of inner work that allows us to know our souls and live in alignment with who we are. What do *we* truly want from life? Is it money, fame, beauty, love? When we start comparing ourselves and our lives with others, we turn away from who we are and get sucked into the world of 'never enough', which stunts our happiness and growth as soul beings.

When we were small children as pure, innocent beings, we did not discriminate. We saw everyone we met as people, not as men or women, rich or poor, black or white, or educated or uneducated. We played with everyone. Our soul selves led us to see love in all people. Our souls interlocked as we shared ourselves with the people we met. As we grew up and away from our natural selves, we started listening to the opinions of others and began ignoring our inner voices. Our egos took over our thoughts, which led us away from our true natures. We got sucked into other people's ideas of what we should and shouldn't be and do and found ourselves following the crowd into the fog. Essentially, we became who we 'thought' we were.

Some people spend their lives just waiting and hoping – waiting and hoping to be happy; waiting and hoping for love; waiting and hoping for inner peace; waiting and hoping for an opportunity to come along to lead to success in all areas of life. Hope is an admirable virtue to possess, but hope alone is not enough to bring us the lives we desire.

It may take a shock or fright to awaken us to the truth of who we are. Perhaps only when we are amid trauma, affected by a grave illness or accident, or maybe a near-death experience, might we stop to take notice of where life is taking us. These metaphorical slaps in the face can knock us off the treadmills of monotonous lives to awaken us from the disconnection from our souls.

We can become so used to the treadmill of life that we don't notice that although we are working hard, we are getting nowhere, that we are no longer growing but living day to day without meaning and purpose.

We may reach the end of our lives, look back, and realise that instead of living 70 years, we have lived the same year 70 times over.

These life traumas are, therefore, essential to our growth and progress, even though they feel as if we are being punished or cut down while we are going through them.

We may feel that life has been cruel and left us beaten or broken physically or emotionally, but because of our pain, we begin to question our existences and feel the need to seek out the meaning of life.

The problem, however, is that we seek answers outside of ourselves, but just like I mentioned in the *Gratitude* chapter, we need to look under the hood of the broken-down car rather than change anything externally. Ultimately, the answers we seek are already deep within us. By taking the journey inwards to understanding our soul selves, to know the sources of our love, we begin to unravel the mystery of who we are. In doing so, we come to realise that life's heart-breaking traumas and events turn out to be the blessings essential for us to identify our purposes and reasons for being.

Personally, one of my greatest life's blessings was a near-death experience. Why? Because it was the pivotal point that awakened me to how fragile my life was, and it changed the trajectory of it. In the midst of a severe asthma attack, I felt my life slipping away from me, but the strange thing was that I was not scared. All I could feel was pure and perfect peace. There was an absence of any fear, and I felt surrounded by a perfect source of love and light. It brings me to tears writing about it now, but that moment changed my life forever. I just knew there was more to life than meets the eye, and my quest for answers had begun.

Every traumatic event in my life has taught me a valuable lesson, and I refused to let them break me. Instead, I used them to strengthen myself. There were times when I thought my heart was so broken that I could never put it back together again, but here I am today, teaching you what I learned from my inner pain and how I got through it.

Contained in the pages of this book are components that make up the keys I used to unlock the joy within myself. I can show you the doors, but *you* have to choose whether or not to walk through them to claim your love, inner peace, and joy within yourself.

Everything that happens to us happens for a reason, even if we don't understand it at the time or even later. It sounds cliché, but we have to trust that this is how it is supposed to be. I can tell you, hand on heart, that I would not be sitting here now, writing this book, if I had not suffered in my own way.

We cannot compare suffering, and we are not exempt from challenges, but we can learn the lessons that will teach us to become wiser and more compassionate beings. I do what I do because I hate to see people suffering in any way – it breaks my heart – and I know that my work can ease this suffering for others on some level. It is the calling of my soul that I cannot ignore. I do not write to sell books but to share my love and energy to ease suffering. Doing so allows my soul to be at peace, knowing that I am not wasting my time chasing after a life without meaning.

This work is my life's purpose and my reason for being.

Life's experiences often force this growth within us, but sadly, some people don't come to this realisation until it's too late, when they are about to leave this earthly realm. To 'come out', so to speak, to reveal their true selves. They spend their whole lives conforming, being and doing what others expect of them, never having dared to have lived life being authentically themselves, following their souls, dreams, and aspirations. Many people find themselves at the end of their lives filled with regret. Doing this inner work on yourself now, building new and reinforced foundations on which to base a well-grounded life will pay off. When the storms of life come – and they *will* come – these foundations will sustain you.

I aspire to reach the souls of every one of you reading this book, to support you in awakening your soul selves before it is too late, so you can live life joyfully *now*, being you, realising you have the key to a life filled with true treasures. Inner peace, love, and joy are your birthright, but for you to attain them, you need to reach within yourself to reclaim them.

So, where do we begin the journey within to know our soul selves?

We can begin the process of understanding who we are by eliminating who we are not. We have already established that we are not who we 'think' we are, but let's be more specific:

- We are *not* defined by what other people tell us we are.
- We are not our age.
- We are not what we do for a living.
- We are not what we look like.
- We are not the religious group of which we are members.
- We are not where we were born.
- We are not our ethnicities.

- We are not the colour of our skin.

- We are not our social status.

- We are not the labels society puts on us.

- We are not the size of our bank account.

- We are not the number of followers we have on social media.

- We are not our success.

- We are not the qualifications we have gained.

- We are not what our sexual preferences are.

- We are not how intelligent we are.

- We are not our genders.

None of the above define who we are; they are external labels we use to describe our lifestyles and bodies. They can detail our external physical forms, but not the essence of who we are. So, who are we, then?

We are the soul that was miraculously placed into our mothers' wombs at our conceptions and left to grow until our bodies were formed into vessels to house our souls during our time on earth. After nine months, we were born without labels, without striving to be anything other than ourselves. We are love, the very essence of the source of creation. We are spiritual beings, experiencing life as human beings, and we are here to experience all aspects of life to grow our souls. Our bodies are temporary vessels we use to undergo this thing called life, but we are not our bodies. Who we are runs far deeper than that, and this is why we need to know our souls to live happy lives. When we disconnect, we feel lost, alone, and fearful of life and death, but once we become aligned with our soul selves, we know there is nothing to fear, and everything becomes a lesson from which to learn and grow. When we realise that we are not our bodies or our minds and see ourselves as parts of the nature of life itself, we begin to see that deep down, we are all the same, we are all equal, and like every cell in the body, we all have parts to play in the evolution of the human race. We could delve deeply into discovering who we truly are as soul beings, but let's keep it simple to help us gain a straightforward understanding of who we are.

When I explained the concept of soul beings to my children when they were small, I used the analogy of a glove. Our bodies are like gloves, and we are the hands. When our formless selves (hands) enters the gloves (bodies), we work together to experience life. The glove alone is merely a lifeless, empty shell, but its purpose is to allow the hand to participate in the physical aspects of life. I explained that when we die, we just remove ourselves from the glove that contained us. We may only wear these gloves for a few years, or we can wear them for 100 years. They serve us for the time that we need to be here, to learn what we need. In time, the gloves become weathered, and they eventually cease to exist, but the essence of who we are does not die. We cannot die because we are sources of energy. Another way to think of our life forces and life sources is to imagine our bodies as digital devices, like a smartphone. Without an energy source (soul), it is useless. Our bodies are the most complex pieces of engineering that exist on the planet, but without souls at their cores, they cannot come to life.

When they work together and the glove yields to the hand, all is well and harmonious. If not, we feel a sense of disharmony and inner conflict.

If you find this whole concept hard to believe and you are thinking to yourself, 'What nonsense,' this is the voice of your ego-mind talking, your thoughts trying to use your past experiences to verify this truth. If there are no experiences, it disregards what it hears. If, on the other hand, something within you feels right, then that is your true self. Personally, when I come across something new, I stop and listen to my body and how it feels always leads me in the right direction for that particular lesson. For example, if it feels right in my gut, and I feel warm and centred, I know I am getting somewhere, but if I feel uncomfortable and sick, I know it's not for me at this time, or I'm not ready to understand.

When the body does not listen to the soul, there is disharmony and unease.

The Ego

The ego is the well-meaning protector of our bodies and a part of our gloves, our outer shells, but not who we are as soul beings. Some may say that it is the thinking part of who we are, there to remind us of the dangers, there to urge us to step up to defend ourselves or honour our places in the world by fighting, striving, pushing, fearing, competing, and comparing in an attempt to protect us from worldly harm. Our souls only know and desire love, peace, and harmony for ourselves and others. Again, our souls are the loving energy sources within us that can never die.

When we understand the difference between our *soul selves* and our *ego selves*, we can calm the inner conflict. Being aware of our thoughts and recognising that our fears are not a part of our soul selves is enough in itself. When we face choices in life, we will always know which path is the right one by listening to and following our souls instead of our fearful minds. Our inner conflicts aren't the result of what is happening around us but about the misalignment between body, mind, and soul, which arises when we go against our natural soul selves.

If we do allow the ego to take command of our bodies and shut out the voice of the soul, we create inner turmoil, which can manifest as imbalance and distress. We seek to escape from life and our tormented hearts, but it is the battle within ourselves that causes us harm, and no outside factors can change that.

Because we are unaware of who we are, we may use alcohol, drugs, sex, and other thrill-seeking activities in an attempt to numb the turbulence within, only to discover that when the effects wear off, we are faced with anguish once again. We all have the power to escape this inner turbulence, but we have to look inwards and heal from within by listening to our souls and silencing our egos. Once we go within and connect back to our soul selves, we begin to understand that we are spiritual beings having a human experience and not the other way around. It isn't an easy concept to grasp as there are so many unanswered questions that follow, but when we profoundly connect to our souls, we *know* without knowing. A deep feeling of inner peace grows within us when we listen with our souls and not only with our ears.

I felt the weight of this truth when I went to see my mum's body after she died. I hadn't seen her for a few months because we lived in different countries, but she died only a few days before we were finally going to be reunited. I'd been so desperate to see her, but sadly, I didn't get the chance to see her alive again. I was scared to see her lifeless body, but I wanted to take one last look at her and touch her skin. After all, this would be my last chance to see my beautiful mum. Four days after my mother died, I found myself at the funeral home, standing outside the door to the room with her body inside, and I mustered up the courage to enter. Because she had died so suddenly, I was still in shock and had mixed emotions. Half of me was excited to see my mummy again after months of being apart, and the other half was full of dread because by seeing her, I would know there was no denying she was gone. So, one half of me wanted to run to her, and the other didn't want to see her at all so I could pretend she was still in my life and living somewhere else. After a time, I edged my way numbly into the room to look at her, laid in the open casket from afar. I experienced a surreal mix of emotions, still not sure whether I was in the midst of a nightmare or if it was happening for real.

I eventually went closer and saw and touched her cold, lifeless body, but she was not there. Her body laid before me, and I felt her hands and face, naively hoping she would become warm again, but she, her essence, and her spirit were gone. It was the weirdest feeling. I just knew without knowing that she was not her body. I didn't cry or react. I was strangely still and unfeeling. As I walked away from her, I looked back one more time, and it was at that moment that I felt my mum close to me in a wave of love, not in her body at the back of the room four meters away, but within and around me. I sensed her warm and beautiful presence and love, which touched and lifted my soul. I came out of that room perfectly calm, knowing my mum was at peace. I can only try to explain how I felt. Unless you have had your own similar experience, it may be hard to grasp.

Because my dad, sisters and family were with me at the time, they all looked at me strangely as I bounced out of the room, recounting what I had felt. I told them that Mum had passed through me, that her soul had touched mine for a passing moment to communicate that she was at peace. I could tell by the looks on their faces that they thought I was having some kind of mental episode because by then, I was elated and smiling.

I was enlightened by what I felt, and I knew from the depths of my soul that even though my mum's body was gone, her spirit still lived, somehow and somewhere, not in a scary or spooky kind of way, but with a deep knowing and trust within my soul that she was happy.

This story may sound crazy to you – even as I write it down, it doesn't seem completely sane – but it happened to me. I can assure you I hadn't taken any drugs or medication of any kind if you were wondering.

We all have our ideas about life and death, and I am not here to tell you what is right or wrong but to open your heart and mind so you can begin to seek your truth. I do have plans to write a whole other book on this area of understanding, but for the purpose of this particular book, I have only just touched on it. The truth is, we don't know anything for sure. I share my insights and stories with you in the hope of opening your heart to the infinite possibilities ahead, to shine some light on the source of our existence.

Who are you?

When we understand who we are, look deep enough within ourselves, and tap into the love that lies within us all, we begin to see that we are all made of and given life from the same source of divine love. We are who we are, and we decide how to show up in life. Whether we show up as our true selves or as our ego selves, the decision is ours.

We can't completely understand who we are in one day. The most we can do is take a step forward by asking ourselves, 'Who are we really?' and begin this journey of self-discovery, opening our awareness to ourselves as soul beings as well as human beings.

So far, we have established who you are not, so now it is time to define who you are, to identify what labels you have placed on yourself in the past to mask your true self. Doing this will open your eyes to all the false labels that you or others have placed on you since birth. For example, I grew up with the belief that I wasn't a good girl. Why? Because I refused to eat properly before the age of seven. I refused to eat with my family at the table, I refused to eat what they were eating, and I refused to eat at the same time as them.

I remember hearing clattering plates in the kitchen and thinking that was my cue for locking myself in the bathroom until it was all over, and that is what I did every single day. My eating habits became a daily battle in my childhood home. I can only imagine how stressful that must've been for my poor mum, but because of my refusal to join in the family meals, I had labelled myself as being a bad girl.

My sisters ate everything put in front of them, and for this, my family praised them. Therefore, in my mind, they were good, and I was bad.

People also told them how beautiful they were, while they said that I was too skinny. So again, in my mind, I was the ugly one. To add to that, I remember my sisters had beautiful long, silky, black hair, whereas I had a short back and sides because I was 'too thin for long hair.'

Of course, being a real girly girl, I naturally dreamed of having the same long, glossy locks as my beautiful sisters, but by never being allowed to, I felt further set apart, not *beautiful* enough to merit lovely long hair.

Though it was no fault of my parents, these were some of the labels I wore from such a young age and that I have carried with me throughout life: ugly, skinny, not pretty enough, naughty.

I remember my mum being close to tears, gently asking me, "Why can't you be more like your sisters and eat a bit more?" I knew she was worried about me, but I honestly can't remember why I didn't eat. Perhaps it was my way of getting more attention – attention is attention, for better or for worse.

The labelling begins for all of us in our childhoods, and every single one of us uses these labels to define who we are. It makes no difference whether we receive positive ones or negative ones; labels are labels. For example, my sister grew up believing she was a good girl because she always ate all of her food. The more she ate, the more they praised her (which was probably to encourage me to eat), but my sister grew up to be overweight and has struggled with her weight for her whole life. That particular label defined her as being a good girl, so whenever she felt down, she ate to feel good about herself again.

Another example is of someone I know being told by her very proud father every day how beautiful, clever, and perfect she was. She was a happy and confident child, and she would perform for anyone who asked. She was beautiful, kind, clever and adorable, and she knew it because her father constantly reaffirmed how special she was, but as she grew up, she was continually looking for praise and attention from everyone that never came. She always fell short of the expectations she had put on herself as she was no longer the prettiest, smartest, and most adorable. When she no longer got the praise to which she had become so accustomed, the truth sunk in that she was like everyone else, and it hit her hard. She didn't always win, get the part, or get picked to play on the team. The older she got, the more she closed herself off. She also used her labels to define her, but to her, life became a disappointment. She achieved a lot by society's standards, but she has struggled with depression for a lot of her life due to comparing herself to others and never feeling as if she was *enough*.

We can't blame our parents or the labels because that is a part of life and growth, but we have to understand that we are *not* our labels – they are only judgements and opinions about our physical selves, not who we really are.

Even though others label us throughout our lives, it doesn't mean that anyone has meant us any harm. We have the choice of whether to wear these labels or prevent them from sticking, so ultimately, we are in control of them. Just as we are responsible for our own happiness, we are also responsible for doing the work to peel back all of the labels life has placed on us over the years to reveal who we are underneath. We don't have to completely stop using them, as they are part of how we interact with life, but we *can* stop identifying ourselves by the labels we wear. Everything that happens in our lives is a lesson for us from which to learn, so this work is essential to our growth and understanding of who we are and why we are here.

Even as adults, we continue allowing labels – old and new – to define us, but once we truly know who we are, they will no longer stick. For example, if someone were to call you blue-faced, would you be offended? Would you wear the label?

No, because you know for sure that your face isn't blue. True?

Well, imagine if someone were to call you ugly – would you be offended? Most likely because you would, on some level, believe there is some truth in their words, no matter how you look. If they were to call you selfish or unkind, would you be offended? Again, you most likely would, but once you get to know the true you, and you know that there is no truth in their words, you will not be offended, no matter what they say.

If, on the other hand, someone calls you unkind, and you know you have been unkind, then you have to take responsibility for your actions and behaviours. There's no right and wrong way to be, but when we are living in alignment with our soul selves, we will be at peace.

We have full power and control over whether to live with this inner turmoil or let it go and rid ourselves of these limiting beliefs about who we are and what we can or can't do in life. You have the key, and it's up to you to use it. The more you live in alignment with who you are, the happier you will be.

Labels may hurt us or puff us up momentarily, but they do not define us.

Growing Within

So far, we have established that we are not our labels and not what we describe. Now, it's time to put that into practice by starting to look at the labels that we *do* wear. Let's say, for example, if I were to describe 'the glove' part of me (my physical form). I would use the following words:

My Physical Form:

- Female
- Middle-aged
- Mother
- Wife
- Author
- Life Coach
- Chinese/Italian UK born
- Married
- Dark hair
- Slim
- Healthy
- Recovered asthmatic
- Sister
- Friend
- Cheerful
- Energetic
- Hard worker
- Determined
- Enthusiastic

The list goes on, but these words don't tell you who I *am*. They describe my physical form and personality and not my soul. By listing these labels and ideas of who we think we are, we separate our egotistical physical selves from our soul selves.

Because of the extensive work I have done on myself over the years, I have fewer negative labels, but at one time, my list would have included words such as fearful, anxious, dependant, indecisive, and shy. When talking about my appearance, I would have found it hard to find positive words describing myself, but the negative ones used to roll into my mind and off my tongue easily and effortlessly, which you will most likely find, too. Regardless of whether these labels are positive or negative, they are not me; they are merely words and opinions that describe my physical form and not my soul.

When I talk about self-love, the characteristics above are irrelevant. To love yourself is to love your soul, your true self that was born into this world as a pure and beautiful being. Life has shaped your body, your mind, your personality, and your character, but you are not any of those things deep down.

Once we do this inner work and know who we are, we not only move forward with more love for ourselves, but we will live life with more compassion and love for others as we begin to see everyone as soul beings. Our eyes and hearts will open, and we will see that the people by whom we are surrounded are also on this journey, seeking their souls to bring them inner peace and love. We will become more forgiving, more compassionate, less judgemental, and more tolerant of other people's behaviours as we understand that they are being led away by their egos and from their natural loving spirits.

Even though we are all unique and have our own personalities, each and every one of us comes from the same source of love, and we are all taking this journey together. Some of us find the path to joy, and others go through life chasing their tails, desperately seeking that inner peace outside of themselves but getting completely lost in the fog. We are each responsible for our own journeys and the quality of our lives as no one can do this work for us. Our happiness is in our hands, and we have the free will to choose whether to do this work by delving deep within or continuing to chase our tails. The decision is entirely ours.

To help clarify who you are as a soul being, first, make a list below of labels you use to tell yourself and other people who you are as a physical being. By first establishing who you are physically, we can work to differentiate your body from your soul, using my list above as an example.

Your Physical Form:

_____

_____

_____

_____

_____

_____

_____

To give you an idea of who we are as soul beings, we could use the following words to describe our higher selves, but to be honest, they cannot sufficiently reflect our souls as they are the essences of our divine natures. Still, this will give you an idea of what I mean.

My Soul:

- Awareness
- Loving
- Compassionate
- Kind
- Empathetic
- Joyful
- Knowing

- Faithful
- Aligned
- Humble
- Unbiased
- Trusting
- Consciousness
- Peaceful

We cannot *think* these qualities into existence; they are simply who we all are at our cores. Many of us have lost touch with our true essences and have allowed our ego-minds to take over our lives, but fundamentally, we are all the same. How each of us acts and behaves in life is dependent on how aligned we are with our divine natures. The more aligned we are, the more at peace we are within. It really is that simple.

*Now, list who you **know** you are as a soul being.*

Your Soul

_____

_____

_____

_____

_____

_____

_____

_____

With inner conflict, we find ourselves having an internal conversation, perhaps asking ourselves things such as What are you doing? What were you thinking? This battle indicates a division between our ego-mind and our soul selves, but who is who? Well, your soul only knows love, so if the words you hear are loving and kind, they are your soul. If they are critical or fearful, they are your ego. Another example of how to know your soul is to understand that your soul is the observer. When you can look at yourself with loving eyes and be aware of what needs to change, that is your soul. The trouble is that this is often when the ego steps in to stop us from taking the necessary action. However, through knowing your true nature and observing the internal dialogue, we can make better choices that will bring us a sense of inner peace. We cannot control the outcome of our actions, but when we know that we have made the right decisions, the internal conflict dissolves.

COUNTING MY BLESSINGS

No matter how well we know ourselves, we can all fall back into old thought patterns and allow negativity and labels to seep back into our lives and our hearts. We can feel disconnected from our souls, perhaps saying and doing things that will hurt others or ourselves even though it was not our intention to do so. Perhaps, we have allowed the words or actions of others to bring us down. We all say things we don't mean at times and do things we wished we hadn't, which ignites the inner conflict. Guilt can start creeping in to make us feel unworthy, but we have to *stop* right there and forgive ourselves. We are *all* worthy of forgiveness, and we all make mistakes. Not one of us is perfect, and the sooner we realise this, the kinder we will be to ourselves and others.

For us to learn and grow, we must experience difficulties and learn the skills to pick ourselves back up again. We can fall time and time again, but remember that it's not about how many times we fall. Rather, it is about how often we get back up, brush ourselves off, and get back into the game of life. We can build strength and resilience with purposeful action and by consistently moving forward, in other words, never giving up on ourselves as soul beings.

Our egos will continue to rear their self-righteous heads from time to time and fight for power over us, but by being consciously aware of it and daily reminders to connect with our souls, we can tame the ego and keep our soul selves at the forefront of our lives, leading the way.

To silence the ego and connect with our true natures, we need to spend time alone – switch off from the confusion around us and escape within, tapping into the peace of our souls.

How do we do this?

There are several options available:

- Daily meditation and/or prayer.
- Taking long walks in nature.
- Sitting and observing the beauty of nature.
- Yoga practice.
- Qi Gong practice.
- Breathwork.

And this is just the start. In truth, there are so many ways we can learn to switch off or quieten our overthinking minds. It is essential to do what feels right to you. Only you can know when you feel at peace, feel that wave of serenity flowing through your mind, body, and soul in the midst of difficult times.

I find that running out in the open fields around where I live, observing the sky, clouds, and birds, connects me to my soul, and I feel an intrinsic sense of freedom and connection to all of God's creatures. In the summer, I love to lie in the sea, allowing my body to float in unison with the gentle ripples of the water while feeling the warm sun on my face.

These are my personal moments of bliss, and you will find your own.

I also meditate every day and evening, emptying my mind and releasing any emotional toxins I have accumulated throughout the day.

There are hundreds of free tools and guided meditations online to assist you if you find it hard to tap into your bliss using my suggestions. Try different ways until you find the ones that align with and lift your soul.

Think about what might bring you peace to enable you to switch off and feel connected to your soul. I'm not talking about when you come home from work and sit with a glass of wine or use distractions such as TV or social media. I'm talking about when you feel as if you are living in a beautiful world. What are you doing when you feel that perfect peace inside yourself when you feel compelled to stop and appreciate how beautiful life is? Is it when you are walking in a forest, communing with the trees? Swimming in the sea? Cycling on a warm day? Is it lying on the grass looking up at the clouds? Sitting by a stream or river, listening to the sound of the water? Is it sitting in your garden amongst the flowers, listening to the birds sing on a summer's day?

As we have already said, remember the adage "Seek, and ye shall find".

By seeking your moments of bliss, you will inevitably find and enjoy more blissful moments.

MY MOMENTS OF BLISS

_____

_____

_____

_____

_____

_____

Regular Daily Practice

When the list of who you truly are as a soul being is complete (in the section _Growing Within_), rewrite it and put it somewhere where you can see it daily. Read it often to affirm who you are. By constantly reminding ourselves of who we are to stay in alignment with our true selves, we will begin to feel more at peace, be kinder and more forgiving, and treat ourselves with the love we deserve. When we confront our choices, we can ask ourselves, 'Will this feed my soul or my ego?' and our choices will be made easy.

LOVING RELATIONSHIPS

IT'S THROUGH SELF-LOVE, INNER PEACE,
PERSONAL GROWTH, AND GRATITUDE THAT LOVING
RELATIONSHIPS ARE BUILT.

No matter what people say, I believe that when we are not in a good place in our personal relationships, we are not in a good place, period. Of course, we can distract ourselves and become busy enough in other areas of our lives to avoid focusing on our problems, but as soon as we relax, our relationships are at the forefront of our minds and hearts once more.

We can get by, temporarily ignoring the ache in our hearts with the hope that things will change, but if things don't change, the stress eventually takes its toll on us physically and emotionally, which can cause us tremendous pain.

If we carry on as if nothing were wrong, we are at risk of causing ourselves long term damage, emotionally *and* physically. But the good news is that *we* have the power to change it.

In all types of relationships – family, friends, spouses, partners, co-workers, neighbours, and so on – there will always be differences. The only way to avoid disputes would be to have no human contact at all, so we can assume that we will all experience moments of some kind of stress due to our relationships. As soon as we realise that our happiness and emotional states are *our* responsibilities and no one else's, then no matter what goes on around us, we can use that wisdom to minimise emotional distress.

I could write a whole book on relationships alone, which may be in the cards in the future, but for the sake of this particular book, I have only touched on a few areas on which we can begin to work to bring more love and peace to our existing relationships. By opening our awareness of how we think and recognising the power we give other people over our lives, we can work on ourselves, change our thinking, and get back into the driving seats of our lives. *We* can decide on the quality of our relationships, how we react to life's circumstances and the actions of others. *We* decide whether to choose happiness. *We* decide whether to play the leading role in the movie of our lives or give it to others and sit back and play extras. It is entirely in our hands.

I don't know about you, but I refuse to play an extra in my own life. We were all born to shine, but we can only shine from within, so as we journey through these doors of loving relationships, we delve deeper into who we are and how we can improve the quality of our relationships through understanding our own behaviours.

TAKING RESPONSIBILITY

Perhaps the single most important lesson I learned that completely turned my life around was that I was in control of my happiness. Regardless of how people behave around me, I can still be happy. When I learned this, my first thought was, "What nonsense. If the people around me treat me poorly, how could I possibly be happy?"

I was tremendously unhappy with my life and relationships at the time, but the truth was that I was dissatisfied with myself, even though I was not aware of it.

I used to believe I couldn't change my life unless the people around me changed, so the concept of being in control of my happiness was quite alien to me. Once I decided to try to live by what I was learning and apply it to my relationships, my life got a whole lot better. I could hardly believe how my life had turned around, and the only thing that had to change was *me*. Not only did I feel more in control of my life and emotions, but happiness began flowing in abundance. *I* changed my life, *I* had the key, and *I* made a happier me.

I am here to share with you how I was able to change my life by changing my mind, my way of thinking, and by letting go of my limiting beliefs. I had been so immersed in my misery that I was oblivious to the power and potential of my mind, leaving me powerless. I do this work to help open the awareness of others, to encourage them to open themselves up to learning and personal growth in order for them to take control back over their lives, just as I did. Nothing that I teach is beyond the realm of what you already inherently know, as it is a part of who we are as soul beings, but as we journey through life, we lose these precious nuggets of wisdom. They become tangled up in a web of confusion, comparison, worldly success, and accumulation. What we know doesn't improve our lives. However, it's what we *do* with what we know that makes the difference.

For example, we can study how to drive a car in books and courses, but until we actually get into a car and drive, our studies will be futile. We will know *how* to drive a car, but we won't be able to do it until we put our knowledge into practice.

I can talk until I am blue in the face about how to create more love, inner peace, and joy, but unless you apply what you learn here or from anyone else, your life will most likely stay where it is. You cannot drive your life forward in the direction you want it to go by reading about it. You have to get into the driver's seat, turn on the engine, and put the knowledge into practice before you can move forward. It makes sense, right?

Everything I ask you to do in this book, I have done myself. I would never ask you to do something that I had not already tried and tested on myself. I can teach it because I have experienced it and got the t-shirt, so to speak. I simply write to enable you to understand how life works from a different perspective, to show you how to gain control of your life, your emotions and your wellbeing, to help you to create more happiness within.

What made me so unhappy was the feeling of powerlessness over my life and relationships, so knowing I had control of my happiness played an enormous part in regaining my freedom.

IT'S NOT PERSONAL

When it comes to personal relationships, we tend to take everything far too personally, but in fact, everything does not have something to do with us. This may sound harsh, but we are not the main focus of other people's lives, and why should we be?

We tend to look for reasons to be offended by other people, perhaps the way they speak to us, the tone of their voices, the words they use, their lack of respect. We are also offended by their actions, what they do or don't do for us, what they say or don't say to us. But if we think about it realistically, do we expect our loved ones to have our happiness and wellbeing as their primary concern at all times?

They are living their lives, dealing with their own things, problems, thoughts, and emotions that have most likely got *nothing* to do with us whatsoever. We expect them to treat us with the utmost care and attention, but let's be really honest here – do we treat our partners and family members with that level of care and attention? Well, do we?

At work, we may have to treat our clients, customers, co-workers, and bosses with such care, but when we are not working, we want to relax and be free from pressure with our nearest and dearest. If we have to watch what we are saying, be polite, and handle our families and friends with the same kid gloves as we do with our clients, for example, would that be sustainable and form the basis of a healthy, long-term relationship? I don't believe so.

We all want and have the right to be open and free to be who we are, to be given the space to be ourselves, warts and all, but that doesn't justify or give us the right to be unkind. It does mean that if we need the space to chill, we are entitled to grant ourselves that space. Therefore, we should also permit our loved ones that same space and liberty.

Do you have friends or family members who are overly sensitive or easily offended, and you have to tiptoe around them? If you do, you will know how exhausting that can be. We have to always be on our toes, watching our every word to avoid upsetting or triggering a negative emotion in them. If we are honest, when we are tired, we avoid them as much as possible, not because we don't love them, but because they can drain our energy, and time spent with them becomes a chore instead of a joy. Because of this, it is necessary to ask ourselves if we are those people. Perhaps we are the ultra-sensitive ones, or we are insecure within ourselves. We may even be the needy ones who are hard work to be around. Although we might think of ourselves as big-hearted and label ourselves as sensitive because we love so much, is it possible that we could be that way because we don't love ourselves enough? Are we, perhaps, looking for others to validate our worth and love us instead of finding it inside ourselves?

We may think that the more love we give, the more we will receive, which is how the law of attraction works. It is also in accordance with the proverb "[We] reap what [we] sow", but the reality is that we can only give away what we already have for ourselves, which means that in order for us to share an abundance of love, we first have to hold a constant source of love within ourselves for ourselves. For example, we can't give away food to the poor if we have no food to feed ourselves. If we have a small amount of food, we can share what we have, but then we are left with nothing and will be unable to sustain ourselves. Well, the same goes for love. We can only give that which we have within ourselves.

When we have none, we have nothing to give. When we have a little, we can share it and will, of course, create more love, little by little, but by doing this inner work, creating a constant source of sustainable love within, we can share our love freely and openly without putting pressure on the people in our lives to be our constant sources of love. We will free them from the responsibility of making us happy as we take our happiness into our own hands.

People are said to be either radiators or drains. They either radiate loving energy to warm people, or they drain them. All of us naturally gravitate towards people who emit energy and light and avoid having our energies drained by people that suck the life out of us.

Who can blame us?

We naturally desire to feel energetic and have vitality in life, but the question we have to ask ourselves is if we are radiators or drains.

If we are truthful with ourselves and discover that we are drains, all is not lost. The fact that you are here means that you are ready for change and growth, and this will not disappoint. Once you start to take your happiness into your own hands, life will get a whole lot better for you and those around you, I can promise you that.

I have experienced both sides of the spectrum. I am now a radiator of love and light, but in my darkest times, I was a drain. As I lay helpless in the depths of the cavernous dark pit into which I fell, I became an ultra-sensitive, insecure, needy person who sucked the life out of myself and others. I had lost my true identity, closed myself in, felt that I could not cope with life on my own, and needed others to validate my worth. I relied on others to love me and make me happy. I lacked self-love and worth and was desperate for some love and attention from the people around me. I had become my own worst enemy, and I allowed myself to be sucked into a negative downward spiral. Although I desperately wanted to be rescued, I was the only one who could save myself. It was *my* responsibility to climb out of that deep dark pit. It was *my* responsibility to make myself happy. It was *my* responsibility to learn to love and value myself. The truth was that no knight in shining armour was going to rush in to save me from my unhappy existence. I had to step up to become my own hero.

FORGIVENESS

Forgiveness plays a major part in creating happiness in our relationships. We cannot go through life carrying the weight of our own and other's wrongdoings as we will be weighed down and become immobilised. If we were to keep hold of every unkind word or action that has been fired at us, we would not move freely through life. Imagine carrying a backpack filled with the pain of all unkind acts from the past. Each one of these is represented by a stone. The size of each stone is relevant to the amount of pain you suffered. How far could you carry this weight on your back before giving up?

The older we get, the more symbolic stones we add to our backpacks to slow us down, but we can, at any point in our lives, stop to remove these stones, letting them go, allowing us to be free from the weight of our past pains. We do this through forgiveness, making a conscious decision to let go of the stones and laying them down to rest.

Once we recognise and acknowledge that the pain of the past continues to weigh us down in the present, we owe it to ourselves to let it go. When I did this work on myself, the following exercise worked for me:

Close your eyes and imagine yourself standing at the edge of a beautiful and peaceful lake. The sun is shining, and there is a lovely cool breeze on your skin. You take in the beauty of the moment and decide that you no longer want to hang onto the pain, anger, or resentment that has eaten away at your life up to this point in time. You reach into your pocket and take out one of the biggest stones that burden you. Briefly acknowledge the pain it has caused you and throw it into the lake, releasing your attachment to it, and allowing the negative energy to wash away as the stone sinks into the water. As you do this, take a few deep belly breaths and mentally release the pain as you let go of the memory from the past. Continue to do this with every one of the stones you carry with you that weighs you down. The more stones you throw into the lake, the more peaceful you will feel. As you walk away from the lake, you will feel lighter and freer than you have ever felt, cleansed of the past with a deep knowing that life will now flow with greater ease.

I found that this worked for me, but you may like to set a variation of this scene in your mind with which you better connect. I recommend you do this practice as often as needed, depending on how tightly you carry this resentment and the lack of forgiveness around with you. Whenever you start to feel that same pain creep its way back into your mind and heart, return to the lake to offload your burdens yet again.

We are all in need of forgiveness as we all make mistakes. If we want others to forgive us, we also need to forgive, regardless of how badly they have hurt us in the past. It is less about letting the wrongdoer off and more about freeing ourselves from the chains or stones that steal our freedom and prevent us from living joyfully.

We cannot change the past, but we *can* decide whether to let it destroy our quality of life *now* and in the future. If we do not let go and forgive, we become prisoners to our thoughts, and we can remain trapped there for our entire lives. We all have the keys to freeing ourselves from the chains. We can either use them or continue to stay chained to the pain of the past. We can choose. One of my favourite quotes describing a lack of forgiveness and its damaging effects on our lives is: "Holding onto anger is like drinking poison and expecting the other person to die." We tend to think of forgiveness as an act towards those who have hurt us, but it is actually about gaining freedom from our inner torment and not justifying the behaviour of others. Forgiving others means that we take full responsibility for our happiness, as we know that no one besides ourselves has power over our emotional wellbeings.

I MAKE ME HAPPY

If someone were to ask me if my husband made me happy, I could honestly say that he does not. I make *myself* happy. My happiness is not dependent on him, my children, nor any other human being. I am solely responsible for the quality of my life and my state of joy, as are you for yours. That does not mean I am not happy with my husband or my children – it means that my happiness is not dependent upon anyone or anything except me.

Once we comprehend that we are in control of our happiness, we will stop expecting other people to make us happy, and therefore, begin to take full responsibility for the quality of our lives. Blaming and complaining will diminish due to our newfound wisdom that ultimately *is all up to us!*

Not only does this knowledge liberate me from my limiting beliefs, but it also gives me hope and a sense of freedom in my soul, as if someone had handed me the keys to a better future to unlock the door to a happier me. I now have the power in my own hands, and it is my choice what to do with my newfound power and wisdom. I no longer have to wait around, hoping and praying for life to get better. I am back in charge.

The beauty of this understanding is that we are also able to release our responsibilities to make others happy. It allows us to stop tormenting ourselves about whether we are good enough or being and doing enough to make our nearest and dearest happy. No matter what we do or how we behave, in the end, it's up to *them* to find happiness within themselves, and we can do nothing to change their internal thoughts and feelings. We cannot make other people happy; however, we *can* make them smile. We can be loving, kind, and thoughtful towards them, but their happiness is ultimately down to *them.*

Naturally, as a parent, I want my children to be happy, but nothing I do can make that happen. Of course, I can spoil them and give them what they want when they want it, but how can that possibly serve them in the long term? At that particular moment, they will be happy, but will that help them to become happy adults?

Giving our children everything they want teaches them that if others give them what they want, they will be happy, but how will they feel when they don't get what they want? Do we want them to create their own happiness or spend their lives looking outside of themselves for someone or something to make them happy?

We have to ask ourselves if spoiling our kids – or spoiling anyone, for that matter – running around after them, trying to *make* them happy, is about *our* need to please, our need to be loved, our need to be significant in their lives...or is it about them?

We all know that we do not always get what we want in life, no matter how much we desire it or even deserve it. There is no guarantee that we get to spend our lives with the person we want to spend our lives with, either. Life doesn't always go in our favour, so we also have to learn to deal with disappointment and come to terms with the fact that certain things were just not meant for us.

Ultimately, if I give my children everything they want by spoiling them, doing everything for them, or even overprotecting them, they will always need me to be happy. They will never learn how to deal with real life, to be self-sufficient, to be self-reliant. Life in the real world would be a constant struggle for them without their mummy. Love isn't always about giving; it's about sharing love, wisdom, affection, and most of all, being fully present.

One thing I am beyond grateful for in my life (that I did *not* appreciate at the time) is that my mum loved me enough not to give me everything I wanted.

As a mother, it is my duty to guide my children – as I do you – through each of these doors, but *they* have to take the necessary steps to move forward to create a happier inner world. Just as I cannot eat healthy food in the hope of nourishing them, I cannot do this inner work for them and expect them to be happy. I can only teach them *how* to become self-reliant, physically, emotionally, and spiritually, and the rest is up to *them*.

Once we fully understand that each of us is responsible for our own happiness, we also realise that no matter how much we desire it, we cannot change others to think as we think, do what we do, and behave as we do. We may believe that people should live life a certain way, but that doesn't mean that ours is the *only* way. It just means that we have found a way that works for us.

We come to understand that every single one of us is a whole individual soul being, capable of making our own choices, whether they are good ones or not in our eyes.

Even if we believe that we know what is best for our children, they are in charge of their lives. They are complete soul beings that came into this world through us, not for us. They don't belong to us, and we do not own them or anyone.

Neither our children nor our spouses are our possessions, so it is essential to stop trying to control them and leave them to be free to make their own choices and their own mistakes. I know it is not always easy letting go as our children grow into young adults because we are so used to being fully responsible for their wellbeing when they need us, but as they grow, so does their ability to make the right choices.

I believe most conflict within the family unit is either about taking everything too personally or a need for control. So, to avoid conflict, it is essential to work on ourselves first. For example, we all know that teenagers are notorious for going against their parents as they fight for independence. With their growing hearts and ever-changing hormones, they can turn into unrecognisable monsters that storm into our once peaceful homes. If we take their actions and words personally, we can end up in battles of the will, demanding that they treat us with more love and respect. So, instead of expecting them to change, we have to change how we respond and react towards them to create peaceful resolutions. That does not mean we are giving in, but we are creating safe spaces to clarify the situation. It may take practice on our part, but when we choose to respond to these situations differently or not respond at all, the storms can pass by relatively quickly with minimal collateral damage.

Now, this is no easy task, especially if our verbal abuser is out of control, and we begin to feel attacked. We go into defence mode to protect ourselves and often hear ourselves shouting back or saying the wrong thing, no matter how well-meaning, but in doing so, we throw fuel on a burning fire. The best way to deal with hostility, in this case, is not to react at all initially, to keep quiet and let the fire burn itself out. Without fuel, the fire will die.

Now, when I am the recipient of unpleasant behaviour and find myself being upset by people's actions, I try to remind myself that it's not actually about me. It's about facing their lack of inner peace, not mine. Knowing this, I can deal with the situation with more ease.

I am in control of my emotions and thoughts, and *I* get to decide how I react. Nobody else has that hold over me unless I permit it. Only I can allow words to hurt me, and only I have control of my happiness. Admittedly, it takes constant practice to start, but the daily reminders about which I will talk at the end of this chapter will help you reprogram old thought patterns.

The old adage "Sticks and stones may break my bones, but words can never hurt me" is true, but we also know that, at times, words can *hurt* as much as a punch to the face. With practice, however, we can train our minds to let those words slide off, leaving only a scratch. Some sharp words may initially pierce the surface, but the more emotionally balanced we become, the more efficient we become at shielding and protecting our hearts. If a person harms us physically, we cannot stop ourselves from being hurt, but with words, we do get to choose if they hurt us or not.

Earlier in this book, I also said that if we know our souls and listen carefully without the input of the ego, unkind words cannot hurt us. Knowing and loving ourselves is the invisible shield that protects us from pain inflicted by others. Unkind words tell us absolutely nothing about who we are; they tell us more about the person dishing them out. They tell us that our verbal abusers follow their ego selves and are not at peace with their soul selves; therefore, they feel the need to express their opinions about who we are or what we do, but their opinions are not who we are – they are merely their opinions. Most people don't even know who *they* are, never mind knowing who we are. So, why would we listen to them? Under no circumstance should we be offended because if the words *are* untrue, our souls knows it. It is when we allow our ego to step in for us that we become offended. When we live as our soul selves, there is no need for us to defend ourselves or to play their ego battle game. Understanding that we can choose to let hurt in or let it slide is a huge step towards living a happier existence.

76

We are all human, and we all lose our cool once in a while. No matter how much energy we put into being our best selves, no one is perfect, and we all make mistakes. So, when our loved ones are unkind to us, we have to remember not to take their words and actions personally. They, like us, are not perfect, so we also have to cut them some slack. If they are acting up, it is about their internal frustration and their feelings, and *not about us*. When we stop taking everything so personally, we begin to empathise rather than criticise, and start to see things from a more loving perspective. Perhaps, they are temporarily out of balance within themselves. Perhaps, they cannot sufficiently manage their emotions and are temporarily lacking a sense of self-control. As we come to know who we are as soul beings, we become more forgiving and can make more sense of our behaviours and the behaviours of others. I am not saying that unkind behaviour is acceptable, but at times, it may be understandable. When we remind ourselves that it's less to do with us and more to do with their present inner torment or their lack of understanding, we can refrain from reacting, allowing the hurtful words and actions to bounce off.

Another area that can be an issue when we take things too personally is when any of our family members want to spend time alone or with people other than us. If they choose to spend time outside of the family unit, it isn't necessarily about them choosing *not* to be with us; it's about them listening and connecting to their own personal needs.

We may take it personally and ask ourselves why, but it could just as understandably be about their need for space and time alone and not about avoiding spending time with us. We may want our loved ones to want to be with us as it feels good to be cherished and needed, but we all need time to be ourselves. In my opinion, one of the biggest reasons couples break up is because they feel smothered and lose their sense of freedom within the confines of marriage. I'm not talking about being free to date other people, but the freedom to just be themselves, freedom to be and do as they choose instead of what people expect of them, freedom from responsibility, even temporarily, freedom from the monotony of everyday life. Marriage itself does not cause this lack of autonomy, but it is the desire to control each other within that marriage that destroys it. Just because we said, 'I do', does not mean that we have to give up our free will.

I never wanted to get married as a young woman because I had big dreams. I had my heart broken as a teen, so somewhere in my mind, I had decided that life wasn't all about love and relationships, and I didn't want to settle down. My friends would talk about their dreams of getting married and having children, but I just couldn't see that for my life. That all changed when I was in my mid-twenties, the day my nephew Natalino was born. I took one look at that beautiful baby with a full head of black hair and fell instantly in love with him. That single moment changed my heart, my mind, and ultimately, my whole life. My desire to become a mother was a calling from my soul, and in my socially conditioned mind, marriage was the first step towards my new dream life.

I believe that fear of marriage and making a commitment is essentially a fear of being trapped, but when we are in monogamous relationships anyway, what changes? It puts a label on our relationships, which, perhaps, in our minds, imposes limits on who we are, but we can absolutely be married and also be free to be our true selves.

One of my closest friends, Karen, has been with her husband Davie for over 30 years; they have been married for over half of those. They are the happiest couple I know, yet they live their own lives and have retained their own sense of identity.

They are together, but not trapped, monogamous by choice and not duty. By living life the way they choose as individuals as well as a couple, they don't need to ask permission from one another or feel obliged to conform to each other's ideals. Granted, they sometimes have to go to events they would rather not, but they do it happily because they want to support each other. Now, I am not saying that they never have disagreements because, as I said before, every relationship has its conflict at times, but overall, they are happy. Their relationship is made stronger by the fact they are two individuals taking a journey through life together, hand in hand and not two half-empty souls looking for one to complete the other. They are not demanding or needy of attention and love. They have absolute love and respect for each other as human beings, lovers, and husband and wife. Some people might look at this couple and wonder how their relationship works as they do their own things a lot. They each go away on holidays with their friends, spend weekends away with family, and work away from home at times, but I have never known a more stable and secure couple. They have complete trust.

When having a heart to heart with Karen one day, I asked her, "Are you still truly in love with Davie after 30 years?" I was blown away by the way she responded. She looked at me, straight in the eyes, and said with intense surety, "Nadia, *I would die for him!*"

Because of their unconventional marriage in which they are free to be and do what they choose, at one time, I thought that they lived that way because they were happy enough but not passionately in love, but I was so wrong. Karen explained to me that they missed each other when they are apart, but it didn't stop them from living their own lives as individuals. They like different things, like all couples, but they would never dream of holding the other down or demand they be anything other than themselves to suit the other. In my eyes, this is unconditional love in the purest form.

If we are unhappy in life, no one other than ourselves is responsible. No matter how others treat us or how much we feel they are to blame for our unhappiness, we are the ones who have to change.

We can change our situation, our ways of thinking, our actions and reactions, even our whole lives, but one thing I know for sure is that if we wait for others to change, we can trap ourselves in this state of unhappiness indefinitely.

We expect our partners to be more like what we want them to be, to be more attentive to our needs, but they are not mindreaders. If we do not ask for what we want from them, how are they to know? Communication is the key to all happy relationships, but fear, hurt, or anger can often hold us back. I have done it myself, and I admittedly still do it from time to time. I expect something from my husband or children, and when they don't do it, or they have been insensitive to my needs, spoken or unspoken, I get hurt. I let the hurt build up, keep quiet, and tell myself they do not care or value me.

When I was a teen, I remember my mum behaving in the same way, but she would eventually explode in anger. My response used to be, 'If you needed something from me and had asked me nicely, I would have been happy to help, but if you are just going to huff around muttering under your breath, I will not help you.

Talk about throwing fuel on the fire.

So, let's get honest here and ask ourselves whether we *ask* for what we want from the people in our lives and our relationships, or do we *expect* those close to us to know what our needs are? This goes for all of our relationships. If we were to ask a friend for a favour, our sisters to babysit, our spouses to cook a meal, or our mothers-in-law to pick up the kids, would it kill us? No! So why are we so reluctant to ask for what we need? Is it because we don't want to come across as being incapable, lazy, weak, or needy? Is it because we fear rejection or humiliation? Is it because we are too proud? Whatever our reasons, the truth is that if we were secure enough within ourselves and felt valued in our role in our relationships, we wouldn't feel quite so vulnerable. A "no" would simply mean no, with no backstory as to why.

When our families and friends don't offer their help or come to our rescues before we even ask, let's not take it personally. We all have different priorities in life, and what is important to us isn't necessarily top-of-mind for others, but it doesn't make them mean or heartless, just different from us.

If we expect too much from our partners or put pressure on them to make us happy, they will eventually feel worn out and become unhappy themselves, but would that make us any more content? Love isn't about trading in our happiness to please others, is it? They are both infinite and plentiful, existing in abundance within us all, so we don't need to divide them to share them. We have to generate them within ourselves, taking charge of our lives, and leaving others free to be themselves.

The happier they are, the happier we will be, too, and vice versa.

Each of us is trying to find our way, our peace, and love within, so let's support each other as we take this journey together. Some of us need to talk through our feelings. Some may like to deal with them in peace and quiet. We are all so different, so let's be open and honest about what we need from our relationships and support our loved ones when needed, as well as offer them time and space for themselves.

We are not here to live each other's lives but to have a companion with whom to live our individual lives, to share our joys and wins, to have someone to support us when we are weary, to share incredible moments, to grow a family together, and to hold hands as we journey through life together. We are not here to carry the weight of each other's burdens but to share the load of the difficulties. Our life partners are not there to be our other halves because that would imply that alone, we are not whole.

We did not come into this world as half beings but as complete beings whose love is limitless. If we love someone openly, we should not expect them to fill the emptiness within us or *be* the light within us. We understand that we are two loving souls who have chosen to walk the path of life together, side by side.

All of us are entitled to our physical and emotional spaces to let go of our mind chatter and stresses of day to day living, such as work, family, finances, and other commitments. Time by ourselves is essential for maintaining and sustaining our wellbeing. In the fast-paced life that we lead in the 21st century, we can often become overwhelmed and crave freedom from it all. We all need personal space and moments of silence, reflection, and stillness to tap back into our souls, but do we allow our family members that space?

Craving alone time is in no way a reflection of how we feel about our families but a longing of our souls to be free and connect with ourselves.

We also need time away from our roles in the home just to be ourselves for a time, not mothers, fathers, husbands, or wives – we need to shake off our labels and just be. When our life partners feel free to be themselves within our relationships, we will know that they are with us and around us because they choose to be and not because they feel they should be. For example, I don't want my husband to stay with me out of duty or because he has made a commitment to me. What I desire for him is to be happy, with or without me. I would not want him to waste his precious years being unhappily married to me, dreaming of escaping the confines of marriage. If his heart is somewhere else, he is free to flee, and he knows that. When I agreed to marry him 20 years ago, that was my one condition: if one of us felt unhappy, we would not cheat but be honest and let each other go.

Because I am happy with myself and have learned to love myself, I am content, regardless of the condition of my marriage. I no longer rely on my husband to make me happy, love me for me, or be my other half to make me feel complete. Like all marriages, we have had our ups and downs over the years, but we are happy with the life that we have created together. We are two complete individual beings who are walking through life side by side and hand in hand, experiencing the joys and trials of life together.

Have you ever had the thought: "I know I can make them happy"?

I can only speak for myself here, but I used to believe that I could make people happy. I was sure that by showering people with my love and opening my big heart to them, I could make everyone happy. I was completely delusional, of course, but thankfully, I came to my senses. I didn't learn this truth in a book, nor was I offered words of wisdom from a friend – I learned the hard way. If I had only known then what I know now I would have saved myself a lot of heartache over the years, but I have no regrets – I am who I am. Perhaps, once upon a time, I naively believed that I could make people happy, but I would rather be naive and open-hearted than have a heart of stone.

Because I learned the hard way, I can share this wisdom with you with the hope of saving you future heartache, but it often takes a broken heart to open our eyes. Perhaps you are wiser than I was, but just in case you haven't fathomed it all out yet or you need another reminder: *"You can't make anyone happy!"*

I know this will neither be the first nor the last time I tell you this truth because, for me, it is one of life's biggest lessons that have to be set firmly in our minds and hearts. Of course, we can love, we can serve, and we can take responsibility for caring for others, but if we take responsibility for someone else's happiness, we will always fall short.

We have this romantic notion that we can swoop into another person's life to rescue them and make them happy, but this can be more about our need to be needed. When we see people who are unhappy, insecure, or feel unloved, we foolishly think that if we give them enough, love them enough, and be with them enough, they will feel loved and complete, but no matter how much we love someone else, the only way for them to feel fully loved is for them to fill their cups from the inside and know their worth. It is impossible to fill that emptiness within from an outside source.

If we enter into relationships with the notion of making them happy, when *they* are happy, *we* are happy, but when they are not, we will feel like we have failed them as well as ourselves. We may feel it is our duty to make people happy, but we have to remind ourselves that only they have that power. For example, if we meet someone who is underweight, weak, and in need of nourishment, what would we do to help him? We can provide him with everything he needs, such as lovingly prepared healthy meals, taking care of him, and encouraging him to eat, but he can only become strong and well if *he* eats the healthy food we provide. No matter how much we care, we can't eat the food for him so he will regain his strength. The same goes for love and happiness – we can lead a horse to water, but we can't make it drink; we can show people how to be fit and well, but we can't do it for them; we can love people and care for them, but we can't make them happy or make them feel loved. That is up to *them*. We can give them all that they need, but unless *they* feed and nourish their own souls, learning to love and care for their inner selves, they will never be truly happy and at peace from within.

It sounds harsh, but we can never fill that emptiness in another being, and they cannot fill it in us. We can never complete them, and they cannot do the same for us. We each have to take this journey for ourselves, going deep within to find that inner peace, love, and joy. The sooner we do this work for ourselves, the better all of our relationships will be.

Family

How many of you feel responsible for the happiness of your family? As a parent, grandparent, sibling, or child, we all wish for our family members to be happier and healthier. It's natural for us to want what is best for those we love, but accepting that we have to let go isn't always easy. We fight with our families the most because we want what is best for them, so we find it hard to back off and back down.

I was a full-time mother for 12 years, so my whole world and life revolved around my children and keeping my home in tip-top condition. In the beginning, I was thrilled, as I was in full control of every aspect of my kids' lives, what they ate, what they wore, what they watched on TV, and so on. They did what I asked, and they played the games and activities I had planned out for them. Because I had complete control and authority over all areas of their lives, I also felt in control of my life, but as they grew more independent and naturally wanted to do their own thing, I had a tough time letting go. I resented the feeling of not being in control anymore, and I desperately wanted to keep a tight hold on them. They were my children, and I believed that their happiness was my responsibility. I can now see that I was treating my children as if they belonged to me as if they were an extension of me, but by trying to control every part of their lives, I was limiting their growth and stunting their ability to make their own choices, good and bad. It got to the point where they couldn't get dressed in the morning without checking with me if it was okay, worried they might make a mistake. Writing this now makes me sound like a nutcase and control freak, but that is how I behaved. Why? Because I defined myself as a good mother who was fully present in the lives of my children, but I admittedly went overboard. I was using my children and my role as a mother to fill the empty space within myself.

My point is that I was giving them every single ounce of myself, thinking it was a good thing, but I was holding them so tightly they began to feel restricted and fought back. I can't speak for other mothers and/or parents, but I can imagine that we all have some instinct to overprotect our offspring far longer than needed and hold on a little tighter than is necessary. Some of us become so attached to our roles as parents that when our children grow and want to live their own lives outside of the family home, we sometimes find ourselves lost and feeling empty within. We instinctively know that it is a natural part of progression and growth, but it can still hurt when we are no longer needed or wanted for every aspect of their lives.

As a full-time mother, my children were my life, and when they stopped needing me for every little thing, I felt lost, worthless, and despondent.

My children were growing up and growing away from me, and I took it personally. I could not see it when I was in the midst of it, but looking back now, I can see that I unfairly put my happiness in the hands of my children when it was not their responsibility; it was mine.

Not long ago, I had a client who came to me with a bucket load of complaints about all of the people and things that were to blame for her unhappiness, but the majority of her complaints were about her sister: "She says this, she says that, she thinks this, she doesn't care, she is bossy, she wants to control everyone..." She was fixated on being the victim and blamed her sister for everything, including her unhappiness. I simply asked, "Do you really give your sister so much power over you and your life that she is fully responsible for your happiness?" As she looked at me, I saw the shift in her face as the penny dropped, but she didn't answer as that one question had given her all the answers she needed. How many of us do the same with our own lives? Who do we constantly complain about or blame? Who have we given power over our lives to, with the ability to make us or break us?

The beauty of knowing that other people cannot make us happy is that we know they cannot equally make us unhappy. When we attach our problems to other people and use them as the reasons for our unhappiness, we essentially hand over our freedom and happiness. We put them in the driver's seats of our lives and relinquish the rights to our personal power. Only by taking full control of our actions can we be free. In some cases, relationships cannot be mended, especially with co-workers or bosses. In this case, we have to take control and ask ourselves if it is worth sacrificing our emotional and physical wellbeing for the sake of our work. We can decide to speak up and express our qualms and try to smooth out any difficulties, we can put up, shut up, and let it go, or we can leave – whatever we choose, we are taking full control of our lives by taking action. We have the keys to our personal and emotional freedoms, but until we use them to free ourselves, we will stay imprisoned by our own limiting beliefs and lack of personal power.

DEALING WITH ANGER

Anger is another spanner in the works of healthy relationships, and learning how to deal with it when it enters our homes is essential for all parties concerned. I am not talking about anger in the form of physical abuse, but general hot tempers and the daily stresses of family life. In the family home, with growing children and ever-changing hormones, anger can be somewhat challenging. None of us is perfect, and we all lose our tempers from time to time, so if we cannot prevent anger, we must learn to extinguish it promptly before it spreads like wildfire and burns down the whole structure.

Once we know we cannot fight fires by throwing more fuel onto them, but instead, we must work on managing and extinguishing them, there will be minimal damage done. If we continue to try to fight fires with fire, then there is the chance there will be irreparable damage. Again, we cannot control what others say and do, but we can control how we react.

Personally, when I am on the receiving end of other people's anger...

1. I take a few deep belly breaths and remind myself that this is not about me, and my attacker is unable to control his/her emotions at the time. I try not to react in any way, knowing that anything I say or do will add fuel to the fire.
2. I steer clear of the fire if possible, subtly removing myself from the situation to give him/her space to vent.
3. I go somewhere to tap into my soul self and perhaps listen to calming music and repeat out loud or to myself things like...
   - 'I will not let anything or anyone ruin this day for me.'
   - 'I choose peace and harmony over anger and conflict.'

- 'This is not a reflection of who I am – it is a cry for help or to gain attention.'
- 'I live a life of love, balance and harmony. I am in full control of my emotions.'
- 'I choose how I feel. Nobody can hurt me unless I allow them to.'

I am one of the happiest people I know, but I am not a robot, so at these times, I still need to remind myself that I have full control over how I react to other's behaviours. That being said, there are also times I need to keep my anger at bay.

When I feel anger within myself I...

1. Stop and breathe.
2. Walk away to remove myself from the situation, get out into the fresh air, and go for a walk or run if possible. If not possible, I put on my headphones and listen to music or an uplifting podcast to change my train of thought and calm me down.
3. Remind myself that what I am feeling is an imbalance of my emotions due to being out of alignment with my soul self and acknowledge that I am allowing my ego to take control.
4. Check-in with myself and accept my imperfections. I remind myself that feeling out of balance is my body's natural response and a way of letting me know that I need to take time to realign.

These tips may seem simplistic, but they are worth putting into practice. Fires can destroy miles of beautiful land if not controlled, and anger can decimate relationships and families if not managed. Think of this as a planned escape route in case of a fire to ensure that no one gets hurt.

If you presently feel unhappy in any of your relationships, or perhaps, feel undervalued, unloved, underappreciated, uncared for, or unattractive, or if you feel trapped, imprisoned, mistreated, misunderstood, or even invisible, WORK ON YOURSELF. Do the inner work in this book to fill yourself with love. By all means, express your feelings openly and lovingly in your relationships if you feel the need, but don't hold your breath and expect that by some miracle, their behaviours will change overnight. If we sit around and wait for people to change for our relationships to improve, we are giving others the keys to our happiness, which they may or may not use, so stop waiting for them to make the changes and stop making demands of them. Step back to see the bigger picture, and take 100% responsibility for your happiness and your life. The happier you are within yourself, the better all of your relationships will be.

GROWING WITHIN

We can talk as much as we want about improving our lives, but nothing will change until we change ourselves. Any small step forward is a step closer to your desired outcome. The more steps you take, the more you will realise the power you have over how you feel, which will inspire you to keep going and keep growing, but before you get into the flow, you first have to make a conscious effort to keep moving forward until you build some momentum.

Most of us know how it feels to get on a bike and start pedalling. At first, you need to put in quite a bit of effort to get yourself moving, but once you get a rhythm going and some momentum built up, you can pedal happily away with minimal effort. The same goes for anything worthwhile in life. Whether it be improving your mindset, building a business, losing those extra pounds you are carrying, or getting fit and healthy, we need to put in a little extra effort to get started. We also have to step out of our comfort zones and leave our unpleasant habits behind.

I never said this work would be easy, but if you get on that bike and put some effort in right now, you will begin to see that your life will flow with more ease.

To create happier lives, we have to face the truth and acknowledge what isn't working and improve on it to make it better, not just for our benefits, but for the people around us whose lives we touch. Who is in the driver's seat of your life at the moment: your lazy husband, your nagging wife, your children, your controlling sister, your annoying brother, your interfering mother-in-law, your parents, your difficult neighbour, your jealous co-worker, your demanding boss, or YOU? We can sit back and complain and blame others for the problems in our lives, or we can take our lives into our own hands, play the game of life, and win with outstanding credit.

So, where do we start? Right here, right now, by answering the following questions:

- *Who do you want or need to improve your relationship with at this moment to bring more love and peace into your life and heart?*

_____

_____

_____

_____

- *Why is it important to make things better between you to make peace? How will your life look and feel if you make peace with him/her?*

_____

_____

_____

_____

_____

- *Take some time to stop and think about this person as a soul being as we talked about in the last chapter. Put yourselves into his/her shoes and try to imagine how you would behave if you had experienced his/her life's struggles. Do you believe she/he deliberately set out to cause you distress, or could he/she be dealing with some deeper issues? Explain.*

_____

_____

_____

_____

_____

- *What might be their reason for his/her current behaviour, something that has nothing whatsoever to do with you?*

_____

_____

_____

_____

_____

_____

- *What are his/her three best qualities? (If you can't think of any good qualities, note down any external characteristics they may have, such as great style or a nice smile.)*

1. _____

2. _____

3. _____

COUNTING MY BLESSINGS

All to often, we fail to see what we have until we make a conscious effort to find it, similar to the colour awareness exercise we did in Door #1. To open our eyes, we must focus on what we have, what is going well in our lives instead of what is not. In this section, I recommend two exercises to bring more awareness and clarity to your life experience.

- *In the table below, list everyone for whom you are grateful in your life, those who care about you. They do not have to be people who are in your life daily, but those who, if you called, would come to your rescue when you need them.*

People who care about me

_____

_____

_____

_____

_____

_____

_____

We may feel lonely at times in life, but the truth is that we are all surrounded by people who love and care for us, whether family, friends, neighbours, community members, and even strangers. We don't like to ask to spend time with people or intrude on other people's lives, and we tell ourselves stories such as, 'They are too busy to spend time with me,' or 'They've probably got better things to do.' The tales we make up are limitless, but we use these false truths to stop us from connecting with others. We fear rejection, so we use these untruths to tell ourselves we are alone and nobody cares.

If someone in your family, your circle of friends, neighbourhood, or community came to you to ask for help, support, or a listening ear, would you think less of him for it, or would you be delighted that someone felt he could ask you?

When I began my search for why we are here on Earth by studying scriptures, the question, 'Are you easy to be entreated?' kept coming up. I had no idea what it meant, so I looked it up and discovered that it asked if I was the kind of person who people felt comfortable going to for support or help?

When I learnt what this meant, I knew it was the kind of person I wanted to be, and it became one of my guiding principles and moral guidelines. It is who I am as a soul being, but I had to open up myself and realign my actions and behaviours to be more. I continually strive to be the person who people feel comfortable coming to when they are in need, and I work on keeping an open mind and heart. When I meet new people, they often open up to me, which I love, and the older I get, the more friends I seem to make, and the richer my life becomes.

All of my life, I have heard that after a certain age, it is hard to build deep friendships, but in fact, I have found the complete opposite to be true. I believe this to be true because I am open, and I wear my heart on my sleeve, just like children do. They do not fear what others think of them, and neither do I. I love people – it's that simple. My mum was the same. I remember cringing when, as a teenager, I went out with my mum, and she struck up conversations with strangers. I was embarrassed because she would instantly open up to people, but now, I realise what a gift her good influence was.

I see my children rolling their eyes just like I did at their age, but it just makes me smile. My sisters and I have inherited this attribute from our mum. Even though my mum was taken advantage of on occasion due to opening her heart and home to many people, she never closed her big, beautiful heart. She continued to shine her beautiful light and presence in the world by giving and sharing all she had and all she was.

Both of my parents were kind and generous souls, and even though they lived humble lives, people remember them for their kindness, generosity, and big, loving hearts. What a legacy!

Write a card, note, or short letter of appreciation to three people, telling them why you are grateful for having them in your life.

It could be to a parent or friend who is always there for you. It could be a teacher or mentor, a kind neighbour that helps you out when in need, a distant relative that never forgets your birthday, or anyone else that reminds you that you are blessed.

Post these letters or cards using regular snail mail if you can't give them by hand – a hand-written card is so much more personal than a text or email.

We all need to know that we are loved and valued, and this is a sure way to maintain love in your life and spread that love. We reap what we sow, so when we plant seeds of love, appreciation, and kindness, that is what we will reap.

Daily Regular Practice

While writing in your gratitude journal, always include the people who are closest to you, writing at least one thing you love about them, even more so if you need to improve your relationship with them. Some examples are: I am grateful for my wife, and I love her smile and the way she makes others smile; I am thankful for my husband,

and I love how he willingly massages my feet for me when I ask; I am grateful for my mum, and I love that she cares about my health, safety, and wellbeing. You can even take it a step further and tell them how you feel or write a little note for them. Not only will this practice be a reminder of how much these people mean to you, but it will also provide opportunities for them to feel loved and valued, which is often all it takes. It isn't about you trying to make others change to become more like you want them to be, but about deciding to be a loving spouse, partner, or family member. It's about opening your heart and soul to them and consciously focusing your loving energy into these relationships regardless of the reactions you receive from doing so.

All we can do is love them unconditionally, demonstrate that love, and let go of the outcome with the knowledge that we have shown up for them as our true soul selves.

To conclude this chapter, I can only remind you *again* that we are each responsible for our lives, our happiness, and the quality of our relationships. If we want to improve our relationships, *we* have to do the work to make changes within ourselves – not our spouses, not our parents, not our children, not our friends, but *us!*

If we wait around for things to get better, we may be disappointed, so get into that driver's seat, strap yourself in, and be prepared to take the high road to a happier you.

Unpack the blame, the excuses, and the past and move forward with your life with you at the wheel. I promise you that the high road has the best views. No one said it would be an easy road, but it is worth going the extra mile.

BE YOUR OWN BEST FRIEND

HAPPINESS FLOWS AS SELF-LOVE GROWS

Opening Door #4 and showering ourselves in its truth is of paramount importance when creating happiness in our lives. I believe that if we were all our own best friends and loved ourselves more, the world would be a happier place for everyone. There would be more love and peace surrounding us because we would no longer compete or compare ourselves with others, and our need to be recognised or acknowledged for our looks, work, or talents would, therefore, diminish. We would cease seeking value in society and stop striving to attain worldly treasures to feel a sense of worth. Most of all, we would be happier in our relationships because we would no longer expect or demand others to love us *for* us. Instead of looking to *be* loved, we would focus on *being* love.

If you were to apply only one lesson in this entire book, this is the one I would recommend, not because it is the most important, but because with this lesson firmly in place in your heart, mind, and soul, everything else you learn will fall naturally into place. I know this because, for me, this was the last piece of the puzzle I needed to complete myself. When we do not feel whole, life becomes about a search for something to fill the emptiness within. Some may turn to drugs, alcohol, sex, gambling, or other addictive behaviours to give them a temporary fix, but when the high wears off, they come back down with a thump, and they are left with an even greater sense of emptiness. They can become trapped on a rollercoaster of highs and lows, feeling both euphoric and worthless as they desperately seek that sense of wholeness. The truth is that the only thing to fill that void is pure unconditional love, but not from an external source. I'm talking about love from within.

We make the mistake of wanting others to love us, continually searching and striving but never quite achieving it when we leave our happiness in the hands of others. However, the only way to create *sustainable* joy and love within ourselves is to build it. The only love we truly *need* with which to strongly connect is that of our soul and the source of that love.

We are '*The Ones*' for whom we spend our lives searching, and no other person – be it our spouses, partners, or children – can make us complete.

Earlier in the book, we started this journey towards knowing who we are, and now it is time to learn to love that beautiful soul being and become our own best friends, but before we begin, ask yourself these questions:

- If your best friend were feeling down, would you tell her that others disliked her, that she was ugly, fat, useless, or not good or worthy enough, or would you lift her up and remind her of all her excellent qualities?

- If your best friend were feeling unwell, weak, and in need of some loving care, would you bring her unhealthy, processed foods you know will make her feel worse, or would you make her fresh and naturally healthy foods to help her feel better, stronger, and that will give her more energy?

- If she needed to feel some love and kindness in her life, would you put her down, ignore her, and carry on as if nothing was wrong, or would you take some time to listen to her and understand what she needed from you?

- If she were tired and needed some rest, would you tell her to keep busy, work harder, and guilt her into feeling bad for resting, or would you encourage her to rest to regain her strength?

- If she were fearful and needed moral support, would you put more doubt into her mind by telling her all the things that could go wrong, or would you talk her through it with love and kindness and remind her that she is worthy and capable?

The question is: are you your own best friend? If you pride yourself on being a good, kind, and loving human being, do you extend that courtesy to yourself?

Imagine living with someone who continually complained about you and put you down every chance she had, criticising your every move and telling you that you weren't good enough, not attractive enough, and/or not smart enough – how would that make you feel? Would you believe there was truth in what she said? Would you try to escape from such a relationship, or would you tolerate the constant abuse? I wish I could say that I would absolutely not accept it, but I did. I put up with the abuse for 40 years before I decided to make friends with my abuser and find out what was going on beneath the surface. Once I got to know who she was as a person and opened up to her, I realised that she was a hurt little girl desperately in need of some love. As I began to listen to her, support her, nurture her, and love her, she began to blossom into a kind, happy, open-hearted being, full of the purest love. She had been in pain, and I had shut her out, but all she needed was me and my love.

When I found the real her, I held on tight, and she has become my strength, my fuel, and my very best friend. She is an expression of divine love, and she deserves blessings of love, peace, and joy in her life; that 'she' was me.

I was my own worst enemy and my own abuser, but once I made peace with myself and asked for forgiveness, I was able to turn my life around. If I was the cause of my inner-torment, I was also the cure. I was my own bully, of sorts, and you are yours.

I know, with complete surety and all my soul, that self-love is the way to happiness, good health and all good things for the mind, body, and soul. Most of our day to day problems boil down to how we love and value ourselves, no matter who we are.

If we loved ourselves, we would...

- feed our bodies clean, natural foods that allowed us to be healthy. To give ourselves energy, strength, and vitality instead of filling them with harmful substances that hurt us or cause us any manner of pain.

- exercise our bodies to maintain good health and keep our joints and organs running smoothly and freely instead of subjecting our health to neglect and abuse.

- feed our minds with nourishing thoughts and truths through learning and personal growth. Try to bring ourselves clarity and peace of mind and heart instead of filling them with superficial mind junk that distracts us and leads us away from the precious things in life such as loving relationships, self-care, and mind-nourishing activities.

- feed our souls with all good things in the company of good people who lift and support our life's purposes instead of filling our lives with ego-led thoughts such as comparing, blaming, and complaining that drain and mask the essence of who we are.

Self-Talk

The very first habit we have to change to learn to love ourselves more are the words we use when we talk to ourselves and about ourselves. We are the creators of our own lives, and we become what we say we will become, so if all we do is focus on our negative qualities, that is the energy we will receive from ourselves. Alternatively, when we use kind and loving words, we feel nourished and loved.

Self-love is more about developing a deep love and connection with our soul selves and less about our external bodies, even though accepting our bodies and treating them with the respect that they deserve is an act of self-love. Each of us has only one body, so we have to do all we can to sustain, support, and care for it, ensuring ourselves the best quality of life. Those of us who have received the gift of fully functioning bodies must fulfil the responsibility of taking care of it, as everyone has not been given this blessing in life.

Most of us grew up believing that loving yourself is a bad thing, as in, "Who does she think she is?" but that is the key. Who *does* she *think* she is? Whatever we think of ourselves, good or bad, we *become*. We fulfil our prophecies as our ego selves go to great lengths to prove themselves right.

Proverbs 23:7 says, 'As he thinks in his heart, so is he,' meaning that we live up to who we believe we are. Therefore, we have to be careful about what we think of ourselves. For example, if we say we are intelligent, we will take actions to back it up by gaining the knowledge we need. If we say we are beautiful, we will put effort into the way we look. If we say we are stupid, when we do something stupid (let's face it we all do silly things from time to time), we will say, 'See? I told you that you were stupid.' If we say we are unloved or unlovable, we seek out ways to prove ourselves right, and we will always find that which we seek, even if it is a lie. As the saying goes, '[We] are what [we] eat,' but I would also add, "We are what we think," so if we think love, kindness, compassion, and light, that is what we will become.

One of my favourite quotes that keep me going during tough times is by the late great Henry Ford: 'Whether you think you can or you think you can't, you are right.'

We need to have faith in ourselves as human beings *and* in what we do. Without faith, we would never *do* anything. Would we get married if we thought it would all go horribly wrong? We imagine loving and happy relationships that will last a lifetime, and we do all we can to make it happen. Granted, things don't always work out the way we planned, but when we begin with positive outcomes in mind in whatever we do, we are more likely to succeed.

Opening up our awareness of who we truly are and the power we have over our lives is the path of joy. Happiness is not a destination but a journey of growth and love. Because we reap what we sow, if we put ourselves down, tell ourselves false truths about ourselves, and plant negative, self-defeating seeds, that is what we will grow. If we continue to nourish these seeds by feeding them consistently negative thoughts, they will become deeply rooted in our minds. The longer we leave them, the more work it will take to uproot them. The negative thoughts we hold onto are like tough weeds that wrap themselves around us, strangling all the goodness and life out of us.

As soon as we become aware of these weeds, we have to pluck them out to give ourselves the best chance of thriving. Ridding ourselves of these negative, self-defeating thoughts and unkind words and behaviour towards ourselves must start now!

If, like me, you have spoken meanly to yourself over the years, telling yourself that you are not attractive enough, not smart enough, and/or not capable enough, it's time to open your eyes and ears and become the guardian of your soul. Stand by the door of your heart, mind, and soul and refuse to let anything other than love inside.

If you have a deep desire to have more joy in your life and free yourself from inner-torment and self-abuse, begin by loving yourself first; the first step is to be your own best friend.

When we talk to our best friends, we don't tell them what we don't like about them, and we certainly don't point it out every time we talk to them, so don't do it to yourself. Make a commitment to yourself: from this point on, whenever you speak to yourself, you will do so with love and kindness in your heart and your words. An effective way to do this is to imagine you are talking to your child-self. If you could come face to face with your teenage self, what would you say? Would you say things such as...

- you're not good enough to get the job you want.
- don't ask them – they'll say no because you are not attractive enough.
- you are not smart enough to start your own business.
- don't follow your dream of becoming a singer because there are better singers than you out there.
- you are too young/old to try that.
- don't look for love because you'll probably get your heart broken.
- you were born fat, and there is nothing you can do to change that.
- don't try that because, with your luck, you will fail.

The list is endless, but we all talk down to ourselves, don't we? Even if, like me, you have learned to love yourself, there are times when self-doubt creeps its way back in to whisper these old, limiting beliefs in your ear.

Whatever we tell ourselves becomes our reality, and we become who we say we will be, so instead of saying, 'You're not good enough,' start telling yourself, 'You can do whatever you put your mind to.' Instead of thinking, 'With my luck, I won't get the job,' think 'With my newfound mindset and positive thoughts, everything that is meant for me will come to me.'

It is not rocket science, but it does take effort on our parts to become consciously aware of our thoughts and how we speak to ourselves as well as making commitments to change. Most of us have been telling ourselves the same old lies for years, if not decades, so it can take a bit of effort to break this old habit. Start today, and in time, you will notice a difference.

I made a commitment to myself to stop calling myself ugly a few years ago, which was a tough habit to break. In fact, until I had become fully aware of this habit, I hadn't realised how often I told myself I was ugly. Every time I caught sight of my reflection, I would hear myself use the 'U' word, but with my newfound awareness and commitment, I would promptly respond by saying out loud, 'Stop it, Nadia. You are not ugly. You are beautiful.' Admittedly, it felt uncomfortable to start, and I did feel a bit stupid talking to myself, but day by day, it became a part of my consciousness, and in time, I broke free of the habit. Even now, I catch myself using the 'U' word from time to time when I slip back into my old habits, but I remind myself that I am beautiful and move on.

I wanted to be treated with love and kindness by my family, but if they heard me putting myself down, what message was I sending them? I was setting the bar for how I thought I deserved others should treat me. I know this first-hand because I heard my mum saying the very same thing when I was growing up. She would call herself ugly all the time, and she hated having her photo taken. I actually believed she was ugly, too, because I heard her say it so often. In fact, I thought I was ugly *because* she was so ugly.

Because people used to comment on how alike we were, in my child-mind, I, too, was ugly, so be aware of your words and thoughts as not only do they shape your mind, but they also send negative messages to those who look up to you.

We influence others through our behaviours, words, and actions whether we want to or not, so we have to decide whether to be a positive influence or a negative one. The energy we put out comes back to us, whether it is loving, kind, and positive, or hateful, unkind, and negative. We can control how we think, so we can also control how we feel and how we act. We are the decision-makers of our minds, so we can choose whether or not to love who we are and live a life of joy and inner peace.

If I were to ask you if you presently love yourself, what would your answer be? If you had asked me the same question only five years ago, I would have said that I did not love myself, but I also did not think it was a problem. I grew up believing that people who loved themselves were egotistical and self-centred, so I was happy that I did not love myself. Little did I know, without self-love and self-worth, I would never be fully at peace with myself. Of course, we can get by without loving ourselves. We can still be kind to people and be considered gracious people by serving others. However, if we don't love ourselves, we are unable to emit our loving energy to others unconditionally, we will continue to seek validation from outside sources to fill ourselves up or feel good about ourselves.

Many people spend their whole lives looking for true love. Looking for 'The One' to complete them, as I talked about in the last chapter, but we are all whole, *every single one of us*! We may not be perfect in our physical forms according to society's standards, but we are in spirit, underneath the layers that mask who we are. We come from a perfect source of love, and the closer we stay to that source, the happier we will be. The only way for us to feel fully complete is for us to love ourselves completely.

Accepting this fact may have been the trickiest challenge for me on my journey to becoming a happier version of myself. After years of self-defeating behaviour, self-loathing, a lack of self-worth, and self-abuse, I finally made peace with myself and began to love the soul being deep beneath my skin, but it had to start with me. I had to change the way I saw myself, and I had to begin by being my own best friend and treating myself as well as I treated others. That does not mean I had to treat myself as if I were better than anybody else, but I had to love myself first, which was tough. As a mother and wife, I was always last on my list of priorities, and I was the one least deserving of my love, not because I felt I was a terrible person but because I did not see the value in myself. I put my family first and gave myself no thought whatsoever, just like so many other parents do.

When we start families, we take responsibility for them, but we forget that we are also a part of our family units. That we, too, need the same love and attention. We wouldn't dream of ignoring one family member's needs or neglecting him, yet we do it continually to ourselves. Every day, I hear of mothers who lose themselves, their self-confidence, and their sense of identity when they take on the role of motherhood. They don't even notice it happening at the time as they are so busy juggling life, work, children, and home, but eventually, they find themselves totally lost, despondent and disconnected from the growing world. When these beautiful little humans come as blessings into our lives, we happily take on the responsibility of loving and caring for them. Equally, we have to take responsibility for our own wellbeing to fulfil our role as parents. How can we be good role models for our children if we are not happy, healthy, and peaceful beings? Is that not what we want for our children when they grow up? If so, it is our moral obligation to be the people we want our children to become. They do as we do, not as we say.

When we travel by air, the safety instructions always state that when travelling with young children, we must first put on our oxygen masks before helping them with theirs. Why? Because if we do not take care of ourselves, how can we help them? How would our children deal with the crisis if we passed out due to lack of oxygen? The same goes for life. As selfish as it may sound, *we have to love ourselves first!* Not necessarily the most, but first.

When we are happy, healthy, fulfilled, and enjoying life, we teach our children by example. They, too, have to learn self-love and self-reliance, so we have to *be* examples. When we take responsibility for our own happiness, they will, too. We cannot only hope that our children grow up to be happy and healthy adults; we need to show them how.

I learned this lesson the hard way, which is why I am telling you the story. You may or may not be a parent, but there are people around you who look up to you or are influenced by you somehow. Either way, the only way to help others, be they family, friends, co-workers, or clients, for example, is to take care of yourself first.

In my case, instead of being my own best friend, I was my own worst critic, my own worst enemy, and I was the destroyer of my own happiness and my own dream life. At the time, I had no idea that I was the enemy I desperately tried to escape. Once I understood this, I realised that I could no longer keep running away from the truth – it was time to look within myself and face my demons. It was time to make changes and learn to love myself first. I took the necessary action and courageously faced my enemy, determined to rebuild my life.

So, how did I start to love myself? Firstly, by simply being kind to myself, eliminating hurtful words from my self-talk, and treating myself in the manner in which I expect to be treated by others, the way I deserved to be treated.

Previously, I had no idea of the power of my mind or how I had been the culprit sabotaging my wellbeing and my life because I was focused on what I didn't have, and I could see others who were happy in life (or so I thought). I dug myself into a deep mental pit, and allowed myself to shrink into an insignificant and useless human being. I was not as good, smart, beautiful, slim, successful, or happy as others, and I reminded myself of this often. So, the first step was to stop looking around me, start looking inward, and begin the journey of discovering who I was to tap back into my soul.

Selfish or Selfless?

The words selfish and selfless in the *Collins English Dictionary* mean...

- Selfish: 1. caring too much about oneself and not enough about others. 2. (of behaviour and attitude) motivated by self-interest
- Selfless: having little concern for one's own interests

We generally think of selfishness as being a negative trait and selflessness as a positive one. I have spent time contemplating this and concluded that a healthy balance between the two is so much better than living a selfless life. Let me explain. If we all took responsibility for ourselves – minding our own businesses and focusing our energies inward – we could work on *being* kind and loving human beings. We would all be so much happier by becoming self-reliant emotionally, physically, and spiritually. That does not, however, mean that we should not lift and support others and hold their hands when they are in need, but if we all "minded our own business" a little more and become self-reliant first, we would be more openly willing and able to help others in need. Being selfless means having little concern for ourselves, but how does that help anyone? What kind of examples are we setting for those who look up to us? I know people who spend their lives selflessly putting the needs and wants of others first, believing they are doing well, but in reality, they are run-down physically and emotionally and ultimately have no thoughts for themselves or their wellbeing. We all know that we cannot lift ourselves up by putting others down, so equally, we cannot put ourselves down to lift others up. We have to remember that we are all equal, ourselves included. We are all equally deserving of life's true treasures, so we need to be neither selfish nor selfless, but to find a healthy balance of both and be loving, kind, and compassionate towards ourselves and others, always.

Others called me selfish when I was a little girl because I often put myself first (another label). Truthfully, I was selfish when it came to sharing my toys and clothes with my sisters, but they also called me selfish because I used to do what I wanted instead of doing what others wanted or what they expected. I always thought of it as a negative trait, but with age, wisdom, through taking this journey of self-growth, and much contemplation, I have concluded that if we were all a little more selfish and did what made us happy, the whole world would be more fulfilled. Imagine a world where we are all brave enough to follow our dreams and be and do what we love. The collective loving energy would skyrocket, and we would be a kinder and happier human race.

Now, you may disagree with me here, but think about it: if every single one of us took care of our own physical, emotional, and mental health and lived according to the guidance of our souls, we would become physically and emotionally independent. Therefore, we would be able to deal with life's challenges without relying on others to come to our rescues. By doing this work of knowing who we are, taking care of ourselves first, and pursuing our dreams instead of living life to please others, we'd be able to live with a greater sense of freedom.

Perhaps I have been selfish over the past few years as I put my personal growth and wellbeing above all, but thanks to that, I am no longer a burden and have become self-reliant. When I stopped worrying about what others thought of me and trying to make other people happy, I was able to be my true self and follow my dreams, which freed my soul. In doing so, I became happier, and everyone around me in my daily life became happier, too. It didn't happen overnight, but because I was taking my happiness into my own hands, my family was free from responsibility.

Now, I am not saying that we do not have to consider the needs of others, but if we take responsibility for ourselves, our happiness, and whatever we want in life, then we will stop trying to change others to conform to our ways.

We seem to live in a world where we frequently compete and strive to be better than others, but if we were a little more selfish and worked on becoming self-reliant, kind, loving, thoughtful, healthy, compassionate beings, we would stop looking at what others are doing and concentrate more on being and doing what makes us happy. We would focus on developing ourselves to give more, not to be better than others. It's in our nature as human beings to desire significance in the world in some way, and the best way to do this is to be true to ourselves and share our wisdom and experiences with everyone within our reach. In the Bible, Jesus says, 'Love thy neighbour as thyself,' He does not say love thy neighbour more than thyself or put others before thyself, does he? Of course, we still have to be humble and remember that we are all equal, but imagine a world where we do not compare ourselves to others, and we do not try to rule over, command, or dictate how other people live their lives. The conflict begins when one party wants to dominate and control the other, be it a state, population, race, or one another. Alternatively, if we all focused on bettering and growing ourselves, striving to be the best we can to create our own best lives (essentially minding our own businesses), then conflict and the desire to control others would not enter into our minds.

If we all focused solely on being better today than we were yesterday instead of trying to be better than any other human being, we would all live in peace with one another. Imagine a world where we treat others how we want them to treat us, a world where, if we needed help, people would come to support us and help us in our endeavours, a world where, if others needed our support, we would willingly and open-heartedly do all we could to help them.

Call me naive, but this is a world I envision for the future, which is why I do the work I do. I cannot change the world, but I can change myself, and I can inspire others and show them how to create more love, inner peace and joy for themselves, so they, too, can inspire others to do the same. In time, and through opening the awareness and the hearts of others, I believe the world can change for the better, one person at a time, one step at a time, but we each have to start by working on ourselves.

A new nursing mother is responsible for taking care of her body first by eating clean, wholesome foods to nourish her newborn in the best possible way with good quality mother's milk. How she takes care of herself determines how she shows up for her newborn, and the same goes for us in life. How we nourish our minds, bodies, and souls determines how we show up in the lives of others.

If we were a little more selfish and worked on becoming self-reliant and emotionally independent, our relationships would improve. By making ourselves happy instead of fighting for love and attention from our partners, we would be more content, filled with more love, and show up as better partners or spouses. We would no longer need our partners' love and attention to *make* us feel loved and wanted. Instead of feeling the pressure of being a good spouse or feeling responsible for our spouses' happiness, we will simply be free to love and be loved.

Are you Feeding Your Soul or Your Ego?

There is often a stigma attached to self-love, as I mentioned earlier, as we often confuse it with narcissism, but let me clarify this for you again: self-love is about loving your soul self and not about loving the physical aspect of yourself. I don't mean that we cannot value our bodies and the lives we create, but it all comes down to which part we feed. Whatever we feed grows; whatever we don't will die. It doesn't get simpler than that. We have already talked about the ego in previous chapters and the labels we use to define ourselves, but when we focus our life's goals on attaining these labels and accolades, we are essentially feeding our egos instead of our souls. That does not mean we cannot achieve great things in our lifetimes, but when we focus our attention on *giving* value instead of attaining labels, we will ultimately gain a sustainable sense of self-worth. When we 'succeed' in our worldly endeavours (win an award, reach a financial goal, secure a prestigious position, etc.), we may initially feel a sense of achievement, which feels like a high, but we can confuse this false sense of worthiness with self-love. When we achieve what we want or reach our goals, we falsely believe that we have made it somehow, but as soon as the high wears off or we stop getting that rush, we are faced with that emptiness once again. Our lives become rollercoasters of ups and downs, but our souls are left unnourished and neglected.

It is not unlike someone who goes from relationship to relationship, hoping each of them is 'The One', but once she gets deeper into her relationships, she realises that the high doesn't last, and her search for that sense of wholeness resumes.

Falling in love is magical, and for a time, we need nothing more than that love – the attraction, the excitement, the newness of it all – to feel whole and complete. The racing heartbeat, getting to know each other, and the chemistry can be incredible, but as each relationship progresses, it naturally evolves. Once all of the excitement wears off, and the high begins to fade, if we do not love ourselves, the emptiness within will start revealing itself again, and a renewed search for something to fill that space and elevate our egos so we can feel that high once more will begin. We long to be loved by that one special person, but the only love we truly need to fill that space is our own. Without feeding our souls and learning to love ourselves, the ego will take charge, which will lead us further and further away from inner peace and away from the pure and perfect love within.

The egos is the part of us that desires to be significant, and it will go to great lengths to lift us above others or shut us down if we are at risk of failing. It's the part that wants us to look good and be recognised for our greatness, beauty, or accomplishments to make us feel whole, but just like falling in love, this wholeness cannot be found anywhere but the depths of the soul. I don't like to think of the ego as being the enemy – I think of it as more of an insecure child who craves love and attention and who will go to great lengths to get it.

The ego lives in and acts from a place of fear and the soul from a place of love, which makes it easy for us to recognise our own thoughts and behaviours to keep our egos in check. When we feel fear of any kind, we know it is the ego dominating our thoughts, but when we have loving thoughts, they come from our true soul selves. The soul only knows love, so there can be no mistaking the source. In the today's world, with all the distractions and comparisons in life, we are led easily down a dark and dangerous path as the ego seeks to dominate our lives and shut out our souls because once we connect with them, we no longer feed the egos. When we chase accolades and recognition to feed our egos, we can lose sight of who we truly are, neglect listening to ourselves as soul beings, and eventually, somewhere down the line, we find ourselves lost in the fog of life.

We spend so much of our time, money, and energy grooming our bodies and very little on feeding and strengthening our souls. We spend time and money filling our minds and bodies with things that do not support them and then wonder why we suffer unnecessarily physically. Ask yourself how much time and energy you spend on nourishing your ego by grooming your body, collecting possessions, or gathering prestigious labels and achievements compared to how much you spend on fuelling your soul.

Even though our bodies are not who we are, they are still vessels of great value housing our souls, and we must take care of them. We give the outsides far more attention than we do the insides, including our souls, which are eternal and everlasting. We decorate the glove, so to speak, without working on keeping the hand in good working order.

I like to think of it as spending hours and hours decorating a cake. Yes, it can be beautiful and creative, and we can enjoy making this creation, but its end purpose is to eat it. If the cake is delicious, nutritious, and full of goodness inside, then it is worth taking the time to make it beautiful on the outside, but if we spend time and energy decorating a disgusting cake with a nasty flavour and texture, what is the point of decorating it?

I once went to an 18th birthday party, and in the corner of the room, there stood a cake, a spectacular, three-tiered masterpiece, beautifully decorated with icing sugar and flowers. I had never seen anything quite like it. We all took photos of it and admired it greatly, but when the time came to cut the cake, the birthday girl was presented with a different one. The guests had been excited and curious to taste the beautiful cake that stood proudly in the corner, but we were served the very ordinary-looking – albeit delicious – cake. Intrigued, I asked why and discovered the stunning, beautifully decorated cake with icing sugar and flowers was inedible as it was made of polystyrene and was only for show.

The reason I tell you this story is that we *can* sometimes be that polystyrene cake, beautifully decorated on the outside, yet inedible, unhappy, unfulfilled, and unloved on the inside. We put on façades to mask the darkness within and hope nobody ever notices. We spend so much time decorating the outsides, but in comparison, we put little into creating the insides, ensuring they are full of goodness, flavour, and love.

A Personal Promise

In life, we make contracts and promises for a lot of things. We sign agreements to say we are committed and willing to bind ourselves to the terms. It may, perhaps, be a business, work, mortgage, or even marriage contract. When we sign a marriage contract, we commit to spending our lives with another human being. We spend our lives caring for each other, vowing to love each other for richer, for poorer, in sickness and in health, until death do us part, but how many of us make such a contract with ourselves? We willingly and openly vow to love, value, and cherish our life partners in front of a roomful of people and happily dedicate our lives to them, but have we made that same promise to ourselves? Don't *you* deserve the same level of love and commitment from yourself?

I believe that before taking even one more step on this journey, we first need to make personal promises of love to the people staring back at us in the mirror every morning. It is now time to make your own vows and make this promise to yourself, to love yourself, care for yourself, permit yourself to be happy, grow, receive abundance in this life, and demand to be treated with love and kindness by everyone, including yourself.

How do You Want to be Treated by Someone You Love?

- Do you want to be spoken to kindly?
- Do you want them to speak to you using only kind and loving words?

- Do you want them to treat you with love, even in your darkest moments?
- Do you want them to treat you with patience and understanding?
- Do you want everyone to be forgiving towards you?
- Do you want them to love you when you lose your looks, when your body gets old, and life is not so carefree?
- Do you want them to support you no matter what life throws at you and be there to pick you up if you fall?
- Do you want them to laugh with you and help you see the brighter side of life?
- Do you want them to support you when you need to get your health in order, exercise, and improve your diet and lifestyle?
- Do you want them to aid you in living your dream life?
- Do you want them to tell you that you are beautiful and remind you that you are loved?
- Do you want to be respected and treated with appreciation?
- Do you want them to thank you for all your hard work and effort?
- Do you want to be pampered from time to time, encouraged to put your feet up, and take time for you?
- Do you want the freedom to go where you want and live the life you want, knowing you are still loved and not being judged?
- Do you often want to be reminded how valuable you are to those whose lives you touch?

We all deserve to be treated the way we choose to, but it has to start here, with you!

GROWING WITHIN

For us to love ourselves, we first have to know ourselves. Once we know who we truly are, we have to accept the things we cannot change and start working on the things we can to help us to grow. Personal growth never ends – it will forever be a work in progress – but it's making progress that brings us a sense of satisfaction and helps us to feel complete and whole.

We have so much more power over our lives and happiness than we think, but we use excuses to stop us from trying in fear of failing. Is it better to try and fail, or is it better to spend our lives in a state of powerlessness and fear, never growing, never progressing?

One of my biggest fears was coming to the end of my life and wishing I had done more with the time I had, the fear of reaching infirmity in old age and being filled with regrets, not of what I did, but what I didn't do. I live my life with this question in my mind and heart: 'If I were to die tomorrow, would I be happy that I have lived my life the way I have chosen?'

Living this way does not mean I am fearless. It means that I feel the fear and do it anyway. I would sooner try and fail than never try at all. In fact, for me, the only real failure in life is never trying.

I have failed at many things, but if I never tried, I would never have known that each of those paths was not for me. For example, I worked in network marketing briefly a few years ago, but no matter how much work I put into building my business, I kept coming up short. I believed in what I was doing, but it wasn't for me. I had invested a few thousand pounds into building my business, but I still failed. I gave it my all, but now I know it was not the path for me. Still, I am incredibly grateful for the experience.

During my time in network marketing, I learned about business, marketing, branding, and networking, and it opened my eyes and mind to many more opportunities in life. It introduced me to some incredible people who have greatly enriched my life, and I learned so much about my capabilities and myself as a person. So, even though my business failed, I still won because I gained life-changing experience. The money I invested was worth every penny in the end as it led me to where I am today. Because of that time in my life, I discovered a love for coaching, which led to me training to become a certified life coach, which, in turn, led me to start writing and become a published author.

If I had been too scared to try something new, or if I had listened to what others thought I should do, I would not be where I am today.

So, failure does not need to be feared – it is merely a lesson and a nudge in an alternative direction, like giving our lives an audit to get us back on the right road again. Failure is, essentially, a slap in the face, a wake-up call, a kick up the backside to shake us up and remind us that we have to keep growing and learning to fulfil our life's purposes.

Today is a new day, and the past is behind us, so learn from it and move forward with more knowledge and experience. Look for the good in yourself and want the best for yourself, just as you would your best friend. If your best friend was not living up to her potential, would you remind her of how much she has to offer, or tell her not to go after her dreams?

- *Describe a time when you felt as if you failed in life – be it a relationship, work, or personal situation – that taught you a valuable lesson, a time that helped you grow into the person you are today, someone you would not have been had you succeeded.*

_____

_____

_____

_____

For example, I neglected my health, ended up with chronic asthma, and nearly died. I failed to take care of myself, and because of that, I turned my life around, transforming my life and health. If not for my near-death experience, I would not have learned that I have full control of my life and the quality of my health, and I would not have been able to teach others that they, too, have the power to change their lives and health.

- *Imagine you had the opportunity to send a letter back in time to your 13-year-old self to give her some encouragement without giving away any details of the future. What would you say to her? Begin writing a letter to your child self below to help her make a happy life for herself. Mine, for example, would look something like this:*

Dear Nadia,

You are a strong and beautiful soul, full of love, light, and joy, and I truly value you. It may take you some time to truly understand who you are, but always know that you are truly loved. My advice to you is to never stop being the love you are. You are meant to be here, and you are more valuable than you think. You can do and be whatever you decide in life; we all can. All it takes is for you to learn to love and believe in yourself. You have a beautiful soul, so don't ever let others tell you otherwise. You have the strength and power within you, not only to transform into a beautiful butterfly but also to help others do the same.

Everything that happens in your life, good and not so good, teaches you something that will lead you to the path of greatness, so don't ever let anything or anyone hold you back. Keep listening to your heart, keep growing, and you will receive everything that is meant for you. You may not always have everything and everyone in your life that you want, but know that you are loved, and the life you make for yourself is the right one. Happiness comes from within, and it will not happen by chance – you have to create it, so keep working on yourself by seeking wisdom, light, and truth and by following your soul.

Make your own money and become self-reliant. Be your own best friend, always. No matter how many times you have your heart broken, never stop loving; it's what makes you. Do what you love, and don't ever settle for less than whatever makes your soul smile. Smile always and share the love you have within. If others do not value you, it doesn't mean you are not of worth; it means they cannot see your worth.

Treat others as you want to be treated. We reap what we sow, so be kind, forgive quickly, and spend your life lifting others, as this is your life's purpose, and it will bring you great joy. We get out of life what we put in, so if you want love, peace, goodness, and joy in life, spread love, goodness, peace, and joy. It's that simple.

You won't always get what you want, but hang in there because something even better is on its way; be patient.

Finally, remember that love has to be shared. The more you give away, the more you will receive. You have a well of love within your soul, so share liberally.

And always be true to yourself.

If you choose what is right and listen to your inner soul, you will have a wonderful life of love, peace, and joy ahead of you. Always follow your soul instead of the world because that is where true happiness lies.

Thank you for being the beautiful human that you are...I love you!

Nadia

- **Now, it's your turn:**

Dear...

_____

_____

_____

_____

_____

_____

_____

_____

_____

_____

_____

_____

_____

_____

_____

_____

COUNTING MY BLESSINGS

It is essential that we change our habits and the way we talk to ourselves to turn those negative thoughts and words around. Seeing ourselves as blessings in this world will encourage us to take better care of ourselves and remind us that we deserve to be treated with love and kindness. Our habits shape our lives, whether good or bad.

The way we talk to ourselves reflects the way we want to feel and the energy we direct at ourselves.

When I called myself ugly, I was harming myself and inviting bad energy inside instead of love. It's no wonder I felt so bad about myself, but don't we all do this subconsciously with various aspects of our lives?

For example, we may be overweight but call ourselves fat and disgusting – imagine how we might feel if someone else said that to us. Would it hurt? You bet it would. Why is it different coming from you?

As kids, we were often told, 'If you've nothing kind to say, say nothing at all!" In this section, we extend this wisdom and kindness to ourselves.

To break unhelpful habits, we need to become aware of and acknowledge the self-sabotage and internal bullying that goes on and put a stop to it.

- *What three unkind, negative phrases do you consistently use when talking to yourself or about yourself that invite negative energy into your soul and prevent self-love and acceptance? What alternative words can you use to change this habit?*

  For example, instead of saying, 'I'm so ugly,' one could say, 'I am working on seeing myself as the beautiful person I am,' or 'My beauty shines out through my soul.'

  Instead of saying, 'I'm too old,' say, 'The benefit of being older is that I have experienced more; therefore, I have more knowledge and wisdom.'

Phrase 1: _____

Change to: _____

Phrase 2: _____

Change to: _____

Phrase 3: _____

Change to: _____

- *To look at yourself through kind eyes and focus on what you like about yourself, use the list below as a guide to come up with the top ten attributes that make you a valuable human being and a worthy soul.*

1. _____

2. _____

3. _____

4. _____

5. _____

6. _____

7. _____

8. _____

9. _____

10. _____

- *Describe the top ten attributes you would want to have in a best friend.*

1. _____

2. _____

3. _____

4. _____

5. _____

6. _____

7. _____

8. _____

9. _____

10. _____

- Brave
- Caring
- Cheerful
- Compassionate
- Courageous
- Devoted
- Easy going
- Energetic
- Enthusiastic
- Exciting
- Forgiving
- Friendly

- Generous
- Genuine
- Good listener Helpful
- Happy
- Honest
- Interesting
- Kind
- Loving
- Open Minded Outgoing
- Passionate
- Patient
- Powerful
- Sense of Humour Sensitive
- Sincere
- Strong
- Thoughtful
- Trustworthy
- Understanding
- Warm
- Wise

- *How can you be a better best friend to yourself? What habits do you need to change for you to feel more loved by yourself?*

_____

_____

_____

_____

_____

DAILY REGULAR PRACTICE

Rewrite the list of your attributes and display it somewhere you will see it daily. Check in regularly to see if you are being treated the way you deserve to be treated by the person looking back at you in the mirror.

Commit to using only kind words and actions and be aware of your inner- and outer-dialogue.

Meaningful change will not happen overnight, but with consistent action, you will leave the self-bullying behind you. Every time you hear negative self-talk, apologise and rephrase the words you use. Remind yourself that you embody and deserve love by acknowledging that it all starts with you. With consistent awareness, the habit will be broken – or shaken, at least – and you will invite more love and kindness into your life, heart, and soul.

Simply put: be your own best friend!

SELFISH SERVICE

THE JOY OF LIVING COMES THROUGH GIVING.

Yes, you read the title right. And 'selfish service' is not a typing error; it's a fact of life. Those of us that serve do so not only because we want to share our time and love with others but because it makes us feel amazing.

Everything any of us does in life is for one of two reasons: to gain pleasure or avoid pain. Serving others gives us tremendous pleasure. No one goes in search of pain and heartache – why not increase our levels of joy through helping and serving others? This way, everybody wins.

The more we give in life, the happier we are, and it all comes down to our intentions. When we serve, we feel good about ourselves, not because we desire to receive praise and thanks but because it helps us to know that we are of real value *and* we are significant in the world.

It nourishes our soul. When our intentions are pure, we find joy in the giving regardless of whether the receiver values us or not. These seemingly selfless acts are actually acts of selfish service due to the feeling of enjoyment we get from giving.

In giving a part of ourselves through service, we receive so much more in return. We are gifted with joyful hearts by seeing the joy in others.

How Can I Serve?

We somehow get caught up in a life of collecting – be it qualifications, titles, awards, friends, or possessions – to give us a sense of worth, but we gain far more from giving rather than gathering. What do we have to give? We can donate our time and love in the service of others. Often, the most valuable service is expressed through simple, everyday acts of kindness, so we must open our eyes and look for opportunities to serve others. When we consciously seek out ways to help people, we will find them. No matter who we are, we are all able to serve, which means we all have the opportunity to create more joy in the world.

Genna, one of my closest friends, is a wonderful example of the power of giving, and her influence has taught me so much. We were two girls from the UK who ended up in the same small village here, in the north of Italy, who literally bumped into each other on the street. Genna heard me speak English to my little boy as she walked past, pushing a buggy, and she sparked up a conversation with me to invite us to her house for a play date. We hit it off right away, and because our children were the same age, we spent most of our time together. Genna turned out to be one of the kindest, most thoughtful people I have ever met, and I grew so much from being around her. I used to think of myself as being a kind and giving person because my mum had taught me by example, but Genna's kindness went far beyond the norm, even for me. She didn't just help others in need – she had the gift of seeing everything going on around her and anticipating the needs of others before I was even aware of them. With my children around me, I could barely focus on anything other than them – we all know how full-on it can be to deal with small children and their needs – but Genna always looked outwards, seeking ways to be of service to others. She inspired me to be a better person, and my eyes and heart began opening to other's needs. I realised that I had been living my life with blinders on. I did help others when they were in need, but I did not *purposefully* go looking for people to serve. Once I did look, I was able to see all the good I could do, just by being myself. The more I helped others, the happier I became as I experienced the joy of giving.

As the years went by, our families grew. I had another child, and she had another four, but she never stopped serving others around her. To give you an example of how generous she was, I remember one of her neighbours having a ton of topsoil for his garden delivered and dumped in his driveway. Genna, her husband, and her small children each took a shovel or spade and spent an entire evening moving the soil from the driveway to the garden. If we were to be completely honest with ourselves, how many of us would do the same? I'm sure if our neighbours asked, the majority of us would help out if we could, but would we go out of our way with five kids in tow? We would most likely justify it by convincing ourselves that we didn't have the time because we had so much to do already (what with having so many children to take care of), but, Genna being Genna, she used this opportunity to let her children experience that sense of joy and self-worth through serving. This was her idea of family time, and her kids loved it.

When she left Italy to move back to the UK while carrying child number six, I felt a great sense of loss, but her example of how to live as a kind and beautiful human being continues to inspire me. With her seventh child now on the way, she is still an example of love and service in the world and continues to teach her children the same. She spreads love wherever she goes, and I am so grateful that I have her as one of my greatest teachers.

Now, we don't all have to have Genna's superhero level of giving, but we all have something to share, no matter how small, and we can all make a difference in the lives of others through simple, everyday acts of kindness. Even a quick visit to see an elderly relative or neighbour or checking in on them with a five-minute phone call is enough to brighten their days, reminding them they are valued. It doesn't take much on our parts, but it can mean the world to them.

The late Maya Angelou said, 'I've learned that people will forget what you said, people will forget what you did, but people will never forget how you made them feel.'

We all need to know that we are not alone in life and that someone out there cares. It's those moments of kindness from others that restore our love and faith in humanity, and we all have to play our parts. Often, all people need in life is a friend and to be heard. I know, first-hand, the benefits of having someone to listen when the storms of life come. We can cry on the inside, but no one in our immediate circles seems to hear our cries. Just being a friend to someone is all it takes to make a difference. We don't need to have special skills and abilities to serve; all we need are willing and openly loving hearts.

We all have times when we allow life to get us down. We can all become consumed by day to day life and get sucked into negative thought patterns. We ask ourselves, 'Is this it?' wondering if this is as good as life gets, but deep down, we know there must be more to life even though it feels impossible for us to attain.

It's at times like this that we need to break the pattern by turning our focus away from what is wrong and what we can't control and focus on what we *can* control. We choose what we think about, so if we decide to focus on gratitude and giving, that is where our thoughts will go. Once we start focusing on what we already have and are and what we have to give, we can recognise how blessed we are. There is always someone worse off than us that needs our love and support.

No matter who we are, our age, how much time we have or don't have, or how able-bodied we are, we can all serve in some way. Whether you take five minutes, two hours, or the entire day serving another human being, I promise you a great sense of joy when you realise your life is of worth. The giver *and* receiver of service are both blessed; there are no losers in service.

To heal our bodies and minds, we need to look inwards and do the work on ourselves, but to heal the pain and nourish our souls, we also have to look outwards, seeking ways to serve others. It's through actively helping others that we remind ourselves how much value we have to give and what we have to offer the world.

In my lifetime, I have been, fortunately, surrounded by people who desire to serve, so it feels natural to me, but deep down, I believe we all have a natural tendency to watch out for our fellow human beings. We are all soul beings, with naturally loving and caring souls, but sometimes, life gets in the way, and we become distracted by our sense of responsibility towards others.

We just have to look at small children to see how they empathise naturally with their peers, comforting them when they are in need of comfort. They don't stop to ask themselves whether they should go over to talk to the person crying in the corner; they walk straight up to him and put an arm around him without thought. We are instinctively good, kind, and compassionate soul beings, as we talked about in Door #2, *Know your soul,* but as we grow, we are tainted and conditioned by the world. We forget who we truly are, and we often fear how others will react to us. Sadly, some people are dealt a challenging hand in life and become so trapped in their misery that they can no longer see what is going on in the world around them. They become so shrouded in darkness, they become despondent, and they feel as if there is no escape, but serving others provides a possible door, leading to their freedom from darkness.

Most of us are willing to give of ourselves and serve when needed, but are we quite as willing to allow others to serve *us?* We can all be guilty of trying to get by on our own without turning to others for help. Our egos do not like to be served, as they see it as a sign of vulnerability or weakness. However, if we do not allow others to help us, we are doing them an injustice by preventing them from having the opportunity to feel the joy of giving.

I know so many caring and inspiring people who would do anything to help others, but these same people do not like others to serve them. For instance, my mum was an excellent example of a good, kind, selfless human being. She would do anything for another person, even taking the coat off her back to warm someone in need, but she would rarely accept help from anyone else, even when she desperately needed it. And she certainly never would have asked for help. All too often, we think of receiving help from others as a weakness, or perhaps, an admission that we don't have our lives in order, but we all need help from time to time in life. It does not make us weak; it makes us human. We are all a part of the human family, and we were all born into the same world, here to help, support, and lift each other. Denying our need for help is like setting ourselves apart from everyone else. When others offer us the gifts of their time and service, we owe it to ourselves, and to them, to accept. In receiving help and allowing others to serve us, we pass on opportunities for them to recognise their own worth and experience the joy of serving, essentially contributing to their joy. If we do not accept this gift and offering of love, we are doing these people a great disservice.

In the Bible, it says, 'Let no man seek his own, but every man another's wealth,' which to me means that instead of going through life, looking to enrich your own life, seek to do that very thing for others. That is where life's true treasures lay. We feel joy when we give, we are rich if we share, and we feel more love when we give it away.

Again, we reap what we sow.

Looking outside of ourselves through serving may sound contradictory to what I have said up until now, but we also have to work on filling our hearts and souls with love through giving and serving. Like I said earlier, we can only give away that which we have inside, and now is the time to fill the well of love within you so you will have an abundant supply to give away.

I do what I do here, sharing my experience and knowledge to serve you.

As I write, I have no idea how you will receive my work and words, but I know my intentions are pure. I am here to serve you in the best way I possibly can with the knowledge and resources I have. I spend hours at my desk every day, spilling my soul onto paper, in the hope of lifting you and guiding you to know your soul's worth here, upon the Earth.

I cannot *not* serve you. It is like a burning desire within me that bursts out of me to share with you. It is not about me or how the world receives my words and books – it's about sharing all of the love and wisdom that has taught me so much.

An old Chinese proverb says, 'When someone shares something of value, and you benefit from it, you have a moral obligation to share it with others,' and that is what I am doing here. All I have learnt in my lifetime that has improved my life in some way, I openly and lovingly share with you, not because I have to, but because I choose to do all I can to help make your life better. Because it brings me tremendous joy, ultimately, I am serving you selfishly.

We all have something valuable to offer the world, and when we have that burning desire to do what we can to help others, we have to follow that calling from the soul.

My mum, for example, had a burning desire to serve, but she did so in her own way. If anyone popped in for a visit unexpectedly around mealtime, she always insisted they eat with us. She made everyone feel so welcome, and whatever food she had, she shared, even if it meant she had to do without. Being an Italian Mamma, food was her way of showing love. Therefore, anyone that ever came to visit always left with a full belly and a heart full of love. She was famous for it. Growing up in a small picturesque town in Scotland, we did not often encounter homeless people, but I remember there being a young man with very little who lived in our town. Because we had a family restaurant, this young man came to ask if we had any leftovers we could share with him, so my parents gave him what they had. He was grateful, but from then on, he kept coming back for more. Every day for months, this young man came to the door, and mum gave him a takeaway meal. When there were no leftovers, mum asked my dad to rustle up a quick meal for him.

Just like Genna, my mum never grew tired of serving others. That young man needed her help, and she did what she could for him. As the months went on, she found odd jobs for him to do in the garden so she could pay him a few pounds, and he would feel a sense of worth

138

again instead of begging for food. She never questioned his lifestyle or judged him; she only ever helped him. Some people thought she was crazy to continue helping the man, but it was not in her nature to sit back and do nothing. She had a burning desire to help others, and that was how she served one of the many people crossing her path. The young man eventually moved away from our town, and I hope he used my mum's example and generosity to improve his life. My parents worked so hard to make a living, and they didn't have much, but whatever they had, they shared.

When it comes to serving, we have to make an effort to dedicate time and energy to others. Some of you may tell yourselves you just don't have the time or the energy to spend, but I ask you this: can you afford *not* to invest time and energy into serving others?

You may already live a life in the regular service of others and feel fulfilment and joy in your life, but if you currently feel of no worth or wonder why you are even here, it's time to remind yourself of your value in the world.

I can talk from experience about this subject because when I was at my lowest, and I had lost all of my confidence, I asked myself what the point of life was.

I had become so consumed with family life at one point that I lived without joy from day to day. I survived, but I did not thrive. I endured life and told myself I was lucky, but I didn't feel much gratitude. I talk about this openly because I believe so many of us feel the same way, but we just don't admit it. We know we should be grateful because we have nothing to truly complain about, but we feel empty at times. Those of us who have fully functioning bodies, a home, a family, friends, food on the table, and so on, know we should be grateful, and perhaps we tell others we are, but we don't always feel it, do we? How dare we think such negative thoughts? How ungrateful is that? Shame on us! This mindset was my reality for a time. Since then, I have realised that so many of us have had these feelings of darkness or fog at one or more times in our lives. I believe it is important to share my feelings so those of you who have experienced that shame, too, can know you are not alone. We may reason with our heads and know how fortunate we are, but our hearts don't always coincide. Not only do we feel lost in the fog, but we also carry the guilt and shame around with us for having all that we need and still feel unhappiness.

When I felt that way, acts of service saved me. I lived day to day, but at times, I felt invisible and unappreciated by my growing family. Even though I served my family, I felt unfulfilled and – to be quite honest – I felt like a slave to the monotony of day to day life. All of that changed when I met Licia. You may already know my story about Licia – I share it in all of my books because she played such a significant role in my life's journey. My experience was a turning point in how I valued myself as a human being.

Licia and her husband were an elderly couple that lived across the road from me, but they kept to themselves, and quite frankly, Licia used to scare me a little. To give you an idea of what she was like, she wasn't the sweet, little old lady type but more like the kind of lady we would have called a witch when we were kids. I used to say a polite hello when I passed them, but it was very clear they were not interested in any interaction, so I never tried. When I found out her husband had died, I made a conscious effort to check on her. It was the right thing to do, so I put my fears aside and knocked on her door to see if she needed anything. She politely declined, but she seemed grateful for the concern.

A few days later, I saw her at the supermarket, five kilometres away from where we lived, piling a heavy shopping load into the basket of her three-wheeler bike, so I insisted I take it in my car for her. She handed me her bags reluctantly, but I could see the doubt on her face as she wondered if I was going to run away with her shopping. When she arrived home to find me standing at her gate with her shopping in hand, a grateful smile spread across her face. It was a joy to have made a difference in her day, and ultimately, her life. From then on, both of our lives changed forever. One simple act of kindness had brought two lonely people together.

I began taking Licia shopping every few days and visiting her often, and a deep, loving friendship grew between us. She was 90, and I was in my 40s, but we developed a strong bond as we spent time getting to know each other. I was like the daughter she never had, and being with her filled an emptiness in me that remained after losing both of my parents. We simply needed each other. Every Sunday morning, my children and I would go to play cards with Licia, and I loved watching them have so much fun serving her. They grew to love her as much as I did, and she became a part of our family in just a few short weeks. She only had one friend but no family that lived close by, so she was grateful to have us in her life.

Sadly, her health deteriorated within a few months, but I was there by her side, every step of the way. I began taking her meals every day and spent time listening to her stories, not because I felt a duty to, but because I genuinely wanted to be there for her.

In her last days, she expressed how grateful she was to have known me, and that in all of her 90 years on Earth, she had never experienced a friendship like ours. She said that she had never known there could be that level of love in a friendship, and she wished she had known me for longer. My heart grew ten times bigger that day, and I knew, without a doubt, that I was of value, and I mattered.

It was not about what I had done for her – it was about the love and time we had shared that had made the difference in her life.

Losing her was really hard on me, but I am truly grateful I was able to be there to share the last part of her life with her. I originally made an effort to be there for her as a good neighbour because I wanted to do some good in the world, and it was the right thing to do, but what I had not prepared myself for was the love that filled my heart from knowing, serving, and loving Licia. She gave me far more than I could ever have given her: she gave my life meaning and purpose. Helping her and seeing the gratitude on her face allowed me to see myself through her eyes. She taught me that by just being me, I am not only enough, but I am of great worth.

From that moment on, it was clear to me that we are all here to love, and we each have the power to touch the hearts of our fellow human beings to bring joy to their lives. Through service, I realised that I, too, was valuable, and my life and love mattered. I learned that love and service are not only *my* reason for being – they are everyone's.

I cannot stress enough that we all have something truly valuable to offer the world, no matter who we are or our gifts and talents. Just opening our hearts and being shoulders to cry on, hands to hold, or smiling faces to brighten someone's day is all it takes. Deep down, we all know how to best serve the world by using our innate gifts and talents, but we are often too scared to jump in, in case we fail or others judge us.

Each of us has a sacred mission for life with unique gifts we can use to share with others to make a difference in their lives, but we need to ignite the lights within and allow our souls to shine outward. Hiding away serves no one. It only suppresses our souls. If our love for people or our life's purpose is not shared, these burning desires can eat away at us and leave us feeling trapped and unfulfilled. We risk coming to the end of our lives filled with regret by not listening to the longings of our souls.

When we do what we love in the service of others, not only does it make a difference in the lives of those we serve, but it also makes a difference in our own lives. Whether we desire or have the talent to sing, dance, make people laugh, compose music, cook delicious food, write, or even just be our open and loving selves, we can all use these gifts to serve the world in some small way. For example, if a person loves to sing, she could start by singing in service for those who need to be lifted or for the elderly in a nursing home or community centre. In doing so, she will feed her own soul by sharing her gift. She may have to step out of her comfort zone to do it, but nothing beats the feeling of seeing those we serve smile. The more we yield to our souls' desires in the service of others, the more we shine from within. It's a win-win.

Victim or Hero?

We have to understand that we have much more choice over the quality of the lives we live than we believe, and *we* get to decide the direction we take. We cannot always control what comes our way, but we can choose how to face it and how to react to it. We can spend our time moaning and complaining about what is wrong, or we can do what we can to make our lives better despite the difficulties that come our way. We can play the heroes in the movie of our lives, or we can play the victims. We are the casting directors, so we are in charge of the parts we play.

When we play the victims in life, we allow life to happen to us. We surrender our power and accept the consequences, but when we play the heroes, we take charge of our life's circumstances and use our personal power to transform our lives and manage our emotions to give us the best possible outcomes. We choose the roles we play, no matter which side of fortune we are on. One thing I know for sure is that we all have challenging times. Granted, some people seem to have more than their fair share of emotional or physical turmoil, but not one of us has a carefree or problem-free life. The sooner we understand this reality, the better life will be for all of us. It may sound harsh, but I believe that some people subconsciously stay in that victim mode because, quite frankly, it is so much easier than actually having to *do* something to enact change. Playing the victim is like an acceptance of being powerless, and we use this as an excuse for not being happy with the quality of our lives. We may also receive sympathy and attention as victims that we wouldn't otherwise get, so playing this role is the easy option. Without a doubt, being unhappy attracts more sympathy than holding yourself together with a smile, even if a person is dying on the inside.

I have a dear friend who lost her husband in a boating accident when she was only 25, and her third child was only a few weeks old. She struggled to bring up and support three children on her own as a single parent. Not only did she have to deal with financial difficulties, but she also had to deal with the emotional trauma of losing her husband and help her children deal with the loss of their father.

The trauma in her life did not end there; it was only the beginning. Once her children had grown, one of her sons sadly took his life, and then, just a few short years later, her only daughter took her life as well. It was far too much for one person to endure in a lifetime, but she survived. And to top it all off, she had a car accident, which left her with a brain injury, and more recently, she has overcome her battle with breast cancer.

I can't even begin to understand the anguish my poor friend has had to endure in her life. She has had the pain of many lifetimes all rolled into this one, but it has not broken her. When I first met her a few years after she had lost her daughter, she was in the midst of her grief, but on the surface, she always looked immaculate and had a smile on her face. Only when I got to know her did I discover the pain she carried around inside her every day. That pain was nowhere to be seen on the outside, but as soon as I scratched the surface, the flow of pain came flooding through her every pore. At 67 years old, she is a stunningly beautiful woman; she looks confident and happy; she does her best to be a light for others; and she stands as a survivor. Even though she has every right to play the victim, she faces the world bravely. Sadness and loss are her daily companions, but she refuses to be a victim to circumstance, making the most of the life she has. I admire her courage, strength, and resilience as she continues to keep living and smiling.

Nobody can deny that life has been unkind to her, but despite her suffering, she finds gratitude in the simple things in life and makes the most of what she has. Her pain of loss will never leave her, but she wears it as a badge of strength instead of carrying it around like a ball and chain. She understands that nothing she can say or do can change the past or bring her family back. Her survival depends on her ability to face forward and play her part in being a friend to others, essentially choosing to play the hero even though she has every right to play the victim.

My point is that we cannot look at others and know what is going on inside, and we certainly cannot judge whether they deserve our time, love, or attention. We have to give of ourselves, openly and to everyone, regardless of who we think they are or how they act on the outside. Who are we to judge what others say or do or how they live their lives? We all do the best we can with the cards life has dealt us, so we have to treat all the people we meet with the same energy and love, whether they are rich and famous, homeless and lonely, cheerful and bubbly, grief-stricken or angry, or seem as if they have everything in life, we cannot make assumptions. Every single one of them could need a friend at any given moment. Some may look happy and together on the outside but are battling crippling pain within. Some may have made some bad choices and taken a few wrong turns in life, but we cannot choose whether they deserve our love and service. We have to open our arms and hearts to all, without judgement and with plenty of love to give.

When I reached out to my neighbour, Licia, because it was the right thing to do, I had no idea that she would touch my heart in the way she did. Through serving her, I saw the value of my life, which enabled me to know my worth as a human being and recognise that my life mattered. If I had not reached out to her that day, I never would have known the treasures that laid ahead that would bring both of our lives so much joy, and I would not be sitting here, telling a tale with the message that the joy of living comes through giving.

When we treat others as we want to be treated, we cannot go wrong.

The Power of a Smile

The one thing we all crave is love and happiness. Some spend their lives waiting for them to appear magically by themselves. They hope, dream, and pray for these blessings in life, but what they most likely don't know is that love and happiness have to be cultivated and grown. Ultimately, it's all down to the seeds we plant – if we plant seeds of love, kindness, and service in our daily lives and continue to nurture them, we will grow the most delicious fruits from our labours.

In this book, we are learning how to create joy, inner peace, and love, understanding that the more we have inside, the more we can give, but smiling is different.

> *By smiling freely and openly, magic happens, even if we lack happiness inside. Smiling is the external button to which we all have access, enabling us to flick on the light switch within. If you don't believe me, try it now. Wherever you are, try putting on the widest, cheesiest smile you can muster and stay smiling for no less than five seconds.*

Go on – do it!

Notice what you are doing now: smiling naturally, right?

Well, that is the power you have to brighten your day, but the best part is that you can also use that mood-lifting smile to make someone else's day brighter.

When we are around smiley, cheerful people, *we* become more cheerful; it's a simple fact. The energy of the people surrounding us affects us, regardless of whether the energy is light and bright or heavy and dark. Not only do we have to surround ourselves with positive people to live bright and cheerful lives, we, too, have to be bright and cheerful, to *be* lights in the lives of others. It is that simple, and it starts with a smile. If you want to see unhappy faces in your day to day lives, then, by all means, wear your scowl, but if you want to feel bright and cheerful, then don't leave your house without turning on your inner light, your smile.

GROWING WITHIN

Through applying service to my life, I learned so much about who I am and the difference I can make in the world, and now, if you have a willing heart, it is your turn. You could decide to skip this section and tell yourself that you do not need to help others to bring more joy to your life or that you don't have the time to serve, but if you genuinely want to make your life count and not let this gift go to waste, I urge you to do this work on yourself, too.

Living a life of balance and harmony through living peacefully means we have to spread our energies through all essential areas of our lives, and service is one of them. If you serve in your career, then this may overlap, but we still have to show up as the best version of ourselves every single day, not just for those we serve, but for ourselves and our families as well. Even making an effort to smile throughout your day can make a difference in the lives of others. Smiling is an act of service on its own.

Taking the time to complete this section will give you more insight into who you are and help you learn to love yourself and others.

WHY AM I HERE?

We all have a divine purpose for being, and we all have something valuable to offer the world, no matter how small or insignificant it may seem. We have already discussed the power of a simple smile – imagine the difference we can make in the lives of others by sharing our gifts and talents. I believe that, deep down, if we are honest with ourselves, we know what our greater purposes are as they will feel like deep longings, but we allow our egos to suppress the visions in our hearts and the voices of doubt and fear banish them from our minds' eye.

148

If we feel like we have nothing to offer the world or have nothing of value to give, it's because we haven't yet taken the time to know and understand who we are as soul beings. The question, then, is not *if* we have something valuable to share; it is *what*. As we come to know who we are and allow ourselves the freedom to be ourselves through doing this inner work, our lives' callings will reveal themselves in time.

- *What are your gifts, talents, and passions? What do you love to do that makes you feel good about yourself and makes you want to share your abilities with others?*

  For example, you could have a great passion for football, singing, or playing a musical instrument, or it could be making people laugh, smile, or feel comfortable enough to open up to you.

_____

_____

_____

_____

_____

_____

_____

_____

- *What can you do to serve, others using your gifts, talents, or passions?*
  List below.

  For example, if you love football, you could:

  1. *Organise a weekly game with other football lovers to have fun and to keep you all fit and active.*
  2. *Offer your time coaching football to kids or other groups of people that would help to improve their games.*
  3. *Get together with others to start a team that would bring your community together.*
  4. *Fund and/or sponsor a local team if you have the resources.*
  5. *Offer to take your kids and their friends to the local park and organise friendly matches.*
  6. *Invite friends round to your house to watch the match on your big screen TV and provide food for them.*

_____

_____

_____

_____

_____

_____

- *Name five people you know that would benefit from spending time with you or who would be over the moon to hear from you regularly. What can you do to lift each of them?*

For example, I have an elderly auntie I call every couple of weeks to catch up. She loves to hear from me, and I love to hear how she is.

1. _____

2. _____

3. _____

4. _____

5. _____

- *If you had unlimited resources and power, how would you change the world for the better?*

_____

_____

_____

_____

_____

_____

- *How can you play even a tiny role in making this change happen today, to make this world better in some way?*

_____

_____

_____

- *What subject do you love talking about that lights a fire within your soul? What is it that makes you so passionate about this subject?*

_____

_____

_____

_____

- *If it were obligatory to write a book about something you know would help others in some way – perhaps about your good or difficult experiences – what would that book be about, and with what would it help them?*

_____

_____

_____

_____

- *What do people compliment you about the most when it comes to your character or personality, and why do you think this is?*

_____

_____

_____

- *Deep down, we all know our strengths and weaknesses, even if we don't like to admit them. What are your greatest strengths, and how can you use them to make a difference in the lives of others in some way?*

_____

_____

_____

- *If you had a daily, 30-second window on every TV channel, radio station, and media coverage platform, what positive message would you broadcast that could potentially change people's lives for the better?*

_____

_____

_____

COUNTING MY BLESSINGS

I have shared my experiences with you and how engaging in acts of service has played a vital role in helping me know my worth, but now it is time for you to share yours. Doing this task will remind you of the benefits service has on the giver and the receiver.

- *Recount a time when you served someone who appreciated your love, time, and effort – how did it affect him? How did it make you feel to know you made a difference?*

_____

_____

_____

_____

- *In the past, how have others served you or your family to give you hope, enabling you to restore your faith in the kindness of other human beings?*

_____

_____

_____

_____

- *What are your intentions for your life? In other words, what do you hope to do with the rest of your life, and what impact would you like to make in the lives of others?*

_____

_____

_____

_____

_____

DAILY REGULAR PRACTICE

Keep your eyes and hearts open at all times.

> *When you are out and about, look around you and seek those who need your help. We find what we seek, so seek out those who are in need.*

It may be a parent struggling to get into a shop with a pram or struggling to keep a young child to stay amused in a long queue. It may be someone who is looking for change to put into the parking meter or who has dropped her keys with bags full of groceries.

It doesn't take much to serve, and we don't need to spend hours helping others if time is an issue, but being open to service and seeking out opportunities to serve will bring more joy and meaning to our lives.

155

Now, this may also seem obvious, but if we do not look for opportunities to serve we will not see them (refer back to the colour awareness experiment in Door #1, *Gratitude*). We can get so caught dealing with the stress and fast pace of our lives or become distracted by the confusion of what is going on in the world through social media and the like that we are no longer aware of what is going on around us. As human beings, we become desensitised to others' needs and are no longer aware of those who are struggling and in need of our love and support. So, becoming quiet and focusing on our intentions in life will keep us on track to living with more joy. Just as I said at the beginning of this chapter, the joy of living comes through giving.

Note; If people do not respond to your kindness, do not take it personally. It's the love and good energy we put out that matters, our intentions and not how they are received. We reap what we sow, but it may take time to show!

CREATING THAT DREAM FEELING

HAPPINESS IS NOT A GOAL – IT'S A MANIFESTATION OF
LOVE FROM THE HEART, MIND, AND SOUL!

If I were to ask what you truly wanted from life, what would your answer be? I can only speculate here, but I imagine that happiness would be right at the top of your list, and not just for you, but for everybody. Do you agree? You are probably reading this book because you are curious to find out what insights it holds to enable you to live a happier life.

So many of us sit back and wait for happiness to come to us. We hope and pray life will bring us all that we desire and need, but in reality, to get what we want, we have to step forward to claim it for ourselves.

Every single thing we want to manifest in our lives takes action. Even having a baby takes action on our parts – we can't just pray that we get pregnant without putting in the work, so to speak. Okay, I could have used a better example, but you get my point.

If you desire love, joy, success, good health, wealth, or anything else in life, you must take action and do something practical to attain it. The fact you are here tells me you already know this; otherwise, you'd be sitting in front of the TV or scrolling through your social media newsfeed instead of reading this. You are taking charge and doing something constructive towards creating the life you desire, which demonstrates that you are an action taker and ready to thrive, but just because you are here does not mean that you will instantly feel happiness. Through understanding who you are and what you truly desire in life with clarity of heart and mind, you will know exactly what you have to *do* to achieve what you want in life.

I cannot tell you who you are – nobody can, no matter how well you think they know you. I also cannot give you the answers that you seek, but I can point you in the right direction and ask you the right questions to guide you towards understanding who you are and what you desire to do and be in your life. You and you alone are responsible for revealing who you are, your deepest desires, and most importantly, how you want to feel.

I originally named this door "Creating Your Dream Life", but after some deep reflection, I felt inspired to focus more on the *feeling* you want to attain by creating your dream life. Whatever we do in life we do because of how we *think* it will make us feel, not necessarily because we want what we think we want. For example, we may want to get married to feel secure, loved, worthy, distinguished, or even to experience a wedding day or publicly declare our commitment to someone, but ultimately, we get married because we want to feel happy. If we did not think it would bring us happiness, would we rush in, excited to tie the knot?

I can show you how to create a dream *life* because I have been there, done that, and got the t-shirt, so to speak, but in my personal experience, creating a dream life wasn't the most demanding part – *maintaining* happiness within myself was the real challenge.

Each time I had attained my personal goals and felt content as if I were living my dream, I made the major mistake of thinking I had made it, that I had reached my destination, and my journey was complete. Oh, boy, I was so wrong. I had not accounted for the fact that everything was subject to change. As humans, we grow and evolve by design, but I was oblivious when living in my perfect little bubble. I overlooked that I would outgrow it at some point, and my bubble would burst.

As a result, each time I achieved what I desired, I began to feel unhappy again after a time, as if my world was closing in on me as I grew. I became trapped, living in an old dream because I failed to focus on my evolution. I had attached my happiness to a vision of the goals I wanted to achieve but failed to focus on the 'feeling' I was chasing.

Let me explain...

I had this romantic picture in my heart and mind when I was a teenager, living and working as a super-successful hairdresser, being recognised for my success and talent, and enjoying doing what I loved most in the world. My dream didn't turn out exactly as expected, but I didn't begin with a clear plan, so it was close enough.

When I started my own business with one of my best friends at only 21, I was on cloud nine. I used to leap out of bed every morning and spend every day laughing and having fun with my bestie, making plenty of money at the same time. I couldn't have been happier. It was my idea of a dream life. I was getting paid to do what I loved, even though I would have done it for free. I was having so much fun that the money was a bonus. I never once doubted I was on the right path because I lived each day with excitement and joy. Being in a partnership with my best friend meant that each of us was free to take as many holidays as we wanted, so I ran off to the sun every chance. It was a perfect life in my eyes.

Even though I called it work, it didn't feel like work at all. It was how I chose to spend my days, living my life on my terms.

However, after a few years of living this life and my health going downhill, I stopped leaping out of bed with excitement to go to work. Instead, I woke up in floods of tears and dragging myself to work, wishing I was somewhere else all the while, wishing I was lying on a beach somewhere with blue skies, the sun shining, feeling the warmth of its rays on my skin. I had developed a taste for a warmer climate from the holidays to which I had treated myself over the years (which I missed in Scotland), and I found myself dreaming of a better life for the future. I fell out of love with hairdressing, but it was the only thing I knew, so what then? At 21, I had been over the moon with the life I was living, but the same lifestyle at 29 was no longer enough to fuel me. In addition to the added health problems from working in that environment, I no longer felt happy. I had outgrown my bubble, so I went in search of a new dream with which to start my life over.

One thing I always had as a young woman that I have again now is an intolerance for an unhappy life. I'm not one for accepting difficult circumstances and making do. I am a soldier that fights for the freedom of my soul, and I will do whatever it takes to free myself from the chains that hold me down.

What did I do when I stopped loving my successful business? I kept dreaming, envisioning a newer, brighter future, and I started to plan my next move. In a matter of months, I had sold my half of the business and my flat and moved to Italy with a plan and enough money to live frugally for the next five years. I looked at the risks and decided that the worst that could happen if I failed was that I would end up back in Scotland, living with my parents and returning to hairdressing, but for the next five years, I would enjoy life in Italy, even if it meant using all my savings. My life and happiness were a worthy investment and a risk worth taking. I started with nothing, so I was positive I could do it again if I had to.

My motto has always been that I would rather live a life of failure than a life of regret, so I once again went in pursuit of my dream life, and for a second time, I succeeded. It wasn't always easy, and it didn't happen overnight, but in time, I was living life on my terms again. I had stepped out of my comfort zone and taken a risk by giving up my old, unhappy yet safe life, but there I was, years later, happier and healthier than I had ever been, married, with two beautiful children, 15 minutes from the sea and loving my life, living with joy once more.

Motherhood was amazing when my children were small. It was hard work but truly rewarding, given the showers of love that flowed into my life every day. I studied every parenting book on which I could get my hands, determined to be the best I could be for them, and I was over the moon with my work as a mummy. I was living my dream life, yet again, this time in my mummy bubble, but a few years down the line, I hit a wall...*again.*

I had been so distracted being the best mummy I could be for my children's happiness and wellbeing by taking care of them that I neglected to take care of myself. As they grew and needed me less and less, I came to realise that I had lost my identity. I hadn't prepared myself for change as my role as a mother evolved. I began feeling despondent, lost, and fearful. I had lost both of my parents during those years, and I suddenly found myself amidst darkness, surrounded by self-doubt, feeling invisible, wondering why I was there; why any of us were there. I had given all of my energy and nourishment to my family, but I had failed to nourish myself.

I had escaped my unhappy existence once before to create my dream life in Italy, but would I be able to do it again in my 40s? I had lost all of my confidence and closed myself in. I was no longer the spunky teenager or enthusiastic girl who had ventured abroad all those years ago. I wondered if I was too old to start again and thought I had to accept that life would be all downhill from then on. I had been lucky enough to live my dream life for so many years, and as the saying goes, all good things must come to an end. As the months went by, I became increasingly pessimistic and slipped into a deep depression. My surroundings had not changed, and I still had all of which I had once dreamed, but my dream life had become my nightmare, and I couldn't seem to find a way out. My bubble was about to burst again, and I didn't know what to do.

The picture of the life in Italy of my dreams that I had created in my external world had not changed, but I had, and my outlook on life had, too. Instead of seeing blue skies and feeling the joy of the warm sun on my skin, all I saw was fog, and all I felt was emptiness.

What I learned from those dark moments in my life is that whatever we create on the outside, no matter how perfect it may seem at the time, it will not sustain our happiness on the inside. Just look at all the celebrities who have what most of us believe to be everything: fame, fortune, success, respect, and all the benefits that come with that lifestyle. Many of them struggle with addiction and depression just as we mere humans do. The truth is that happiness comes from within, regardless of what is or is not happening in our lives. We may strive to attain the lives we think will make us happy, but as I said right at the beginning of this chapter, happiness is not a goal – it's a manifestation of love from the heart, mind, and soul. It's a continual path of growth and progress.

Happiness comes from connecting to the source of love within ourselves, knowing and growing our souls, and cultivating a happy *inner* world, and not from anything we create in our external, material worlds.

I could look back at that time of my life as a failure, but I am truly grateful for experiencing the darkness that surrounded me because I learned so much about myself I would have never known otherwise. It forced me to look deeper within myself, to make the journey towards rediscovering who I am. If not for the darkness and misery, I would not be here writing this book. It was all a part of the divine plan for me, and I had to go through it first to experience it and enable me to empathise with others. I think of that time in my life as one of my most valuable gifts because I am now living life with the greatest joy I have ever experienced. I still face challenges, but I see the world differently now, and I trust that everything is just how it should be.

Whatever journey you are on right now, no matter how you feel, this is where you are supposed to be, right here, reading this very book. We may not always recognise it at the time, but everything we experience, good or bad, leads us on paths to connect us to better futures, even if we feel it makes no sense now.

I share the details of my life and open my heart to you in my books, not because I necessarily want to talk about myself or convince you that my way is the only way, but to remind you that no matter who you are, we all face emotional hardship at times. We all have periods of darkness and powerlessness. It is a part of life and how we experience growth as people. Obviously, I don't talk about all of the private, intimate moments within my soul, but I do open up to a certain degree to encourage you to do the same. If we were a little more open about our deepest, darkest fears and thoughts (not to be confused with complaining), we would soon realise that we are not alone in the ways we feel. Fear, doubt, a lack of self-worth and self-love, depression, insecurity, jealousy, guilt, anger, and so on are emotions we all feel at certain times in life. Society leads us to believe that we *should be* happy all the time, but we are human and here to experience all aspects of life. After all, we would not be able to experience joy if we had no pain, just as we would not know what hot felt like without feeling cold. We all experience highs and lows in life, no matter who we are. The only difference between us is that some people hold tightly on to negative thoughts and feelings while others work on letting them go. *We* choose whether to feed these peace-stealing thoughts to keep them alive or let them starve.

By fostering negative thought patterns, we give them energy and feed them fuel, allowing them to grow. When we focus on gratitude, as we discussed in Door #1, and focus on what we do want, the negativity naturally leaves.

I am here to guide you through ways of managing negative mind chatter and emotions, reminding you, in the process, that we all have more control over our feelings than we like to believe. These toxic thoughts sabotage our peace of mind, body, and soul, but it's important to remember that we are in charge of them.

Life itself can't make us unhappy – it unfolds organically – but our negative thoughts can. The silver lining is that *we* have the power to eradicate them.

We are here to love and support each other through life using our personal experiences and what we have learned from them to lift, support, and carry each other throughout this journey. When we open up to others, revealing pieces of our souls to them through sharing our feelings, we develop connections instead of feeling alone, separate, or different. Inside, we are all the same as we all originate from the same source: LOVE.

HOW DO YOU WANT TO FEEL?

Getting back on track to creating that dream feeling, ask yourself: What does happiness look like and how does it *feel* to me?

I managed to create my dream life, but because I had attached happiness to something outside of myself and my control, I could not maintain that feeling. I had put my joy and emotional state in the hands of my circumstance and my family, essentially relinquishing my power by allowing something other than myself to be in charge. *I* had to put myself back in the driver's seat of my own life, emotions, and happiness.

So, you want to be happy, but what does happiness look like to you? How does it feel? Think about this next question carefully: do you believe it is possible to make your vision a reality if you don't know what your dreams are or understand why you want them? We can stumble upon something and discover that we love it, but I don't believe we can create something we truly desire unless we put our minds to it.

For example, if we desire ice cream, all we have to do is go out, choose which one we want, and buy it. However, if we want a new house, we wouldn't just nip out to the estate agent's and buy one within the hour as if it were ice cream, would we?

There is a thought process in which we design a picture of what we truly want and need in our minds, starting with questions like: why do you want a new house – to have more space? To be closer to work?

Whatever the reason, you would give it a lot of thought.

When you decide that buying a house is the right thing for you, you will think more about what you really want in a property to suit your needs. Once you have an idea of that for which you are looking, you'd start looking for houses that ticked some – if not all – of the boxes, otherwise, there would be no point, would there? Why on Earth would someone buy a property they didn't like or fit their list of criteria?

In the end, you'd make your decision based on what you want from the house and how you want to feel when you live there.

For it to be the right house, it would have to:

- be in the right area,
- be within your price range,
- be the right size for your needs,
- be the style of house you like, and
- feel like home.

You would also take many other things into consideration because it is one of the largest investments most of us will make in our lifetimes. Before buying, you would view the house in person to know whether it is right for you by the way it makes you feel. You could either see yourself living there or not, and you would make your final decision by listening to your gut instinct, aka your soul.

We have established that we consider so many factors when making an investment like buying a family home, but I ask you:

- Do we put as much time, energy, and thought into shaping our lives and happiness?
- Do we give ourselves and our lives the same levels of care and consideration?
- Do we value our happiness as much as our financial investments?

I don't believe we do because if we did, most of us would be living life on our own terms, yet so many of us are chasing lives we don't have yet. We invest our time and energy freely into living lives that don't feel right, so why continue living that way? Our time is limited, but we endure lives we don't love because we think there is nothing more to it. We may have been conditioned by listening to the opinions of others who also felt powerless over their lives, hearing things such as: 'It's a hard life! It's a cruel world! Life sucks! Bad things happen to good people! Nobody cares! We are born alone, and we'll die alone!' The list goes on and on, but life is what *we* make it. Our lives will only change when we do. We get out of life what we expect to get; it's that simple. The Bible says, 'Ask, and it shall be given; seek, and ye shall find; knock, and it shall be opened unto you,' which, to me, means that the Universe will give us that for which we ask of it, but what I am trying to say is that we have to ask wisely and have clear internal pictures, not only of what a dream life *looks* like to us, but more importantly, how it would *feel*.

If we expect life to suck, our egos will seek ways to confirm we are right. Equally, if we expect life to give us what we desire, we will actively seek those things, no matter what they are. Whatever we put our thoughts and energy into will manifest in our lives in some capacity, regardless of whether they are things we want or don't want. If you expect to find struggle and heartache, you will, but if you seek love and abundance, you will find that, too.

Do you plan your life according to the desires of your soul, or do you follow the well-worn path travelled by others before you because you believe it is the safest way? Has the route you have taken up to now brought you a life of joy, or have you come to a dead-end? I have mostly taken the untravelled path that led me to where I believed I wanted to go; however, because I failed to focus my energy on creating *lasting* happiness and growth as a part of my plan, I did not receive it. I had manifested the physical world I wanted but not the emotional one; I needed to envision a dream feeling.

I have learned my lesson, and I am now walking the continuous path of growth, living my dream feeling without a fixed physical destination, but with clear intentions of love, connection, inner peace, balance, and harmony while loving and serving my fellow beings. I make plans with good intentions and follow through. If they lead me to financial success, I am happy, and if they don't, I am still content. My happiness is not dependent on my financial success; it's dependent on how I *feel* as I live my life each and every day, as I serve as a mother, author, life coach, and teacher of life's true treasures.

Imagine if I were writing this book, with the fixed dream of being determined to sell 10,000,000, and it only sold 5,000,000 – would I feel a failure? And if I sold under 5,000 copies, would I be a total loser? I can't lose because I am sharing love, independent of success, and if my book does become an international bestseller, then who is to say if I would be happy or unhappy?

I write this book intending to serve and touch the lives of as many people as possible, feeling the joy of helping you each day as I write with infinite love in my soul. That is my dream feeling, and I live it every day.

I surrender and trust that whatever good thing I put out into the world will come back to me if it is my destiny to receive it. I don't do what I do to receive – I give in selfish service because of how it makes me *feel* today. Anything I gain in the process is a bonus. With my dream feeling clear in my mind, I believe, with all of my soul, that all will be well, no matter what happens.

Why do so many people leave life to chance? I believe it's because of two main things:

1. they don't have a complete understanding that *they* have the power to change their lives, and
2. they don't have a clear enough picture of what they want, so, by default, they settle for less than they desire.

They make do with what life gives them because they don't truly value who they are, perhaps considering that life is predetermined and their circumstances are the unfortunate result. They dare not dream of lives they feel are out of their reach, seeing it as a waste of time.

Maybe, to some people, it would be like spending time researching the features they would add to their brand new, top of the range Ferrari sports car, even if they didn't own one, but we all have the means to have brand new, top of the range *lives*, so start deciding the detailed features you want for your life, focusing on how they will make you *feel*.

We all desire things, health, wealth, success, great bodies, life partners, and so on, but we first have to understand *why* we want these things and how we hope to feel when we obtain them. To explain what I mean, let me break it down:

If, for example, you are unhealthy and overweight and you decide to work on getting the weight off to get your health back on track, what would you expect to gain by attaining your goal from a physical aspect?

- Longevity?
- Vitality?
- Strength?
- Energy?
- Agility?
- Being pain-free?
- Enabling better sleep?
- Increased mobility?
- Increased stamina?
- Attractiveness?
- All of the above?

Whatever you hope to attain from achieving your health goals, it ultimately boils down to how you want to feel. Would you be content achieving the body of your dreams if you still felt unhappy and lacked confidence? Probably not. So instead, let's focus on what emotions you would expect to feel...

- care-freeness,
- lightness,
- confidence,
- happiness,
- accomplishment,
- power,
- strength,
- control,
- peacefulness, and/or
- contentedness.

The mistake I previously made in my life was that I was so focused on the life I wanted, and I failed to focus on how it would make me feel. Even before I became a mother, I had a fixed, clear vision of becoming a full-time mum and what it would look like to me. I made a promise to myself that I would give my kids every ounce of love and attention I felt I didn't have, and I did precisely that.

I was the obsessive mother that tried – and mostly succeeded – to control every aspect of my children's lives. As they grew up healthy, happy, and loved, I felt whole, as if I had found my place in the world. I believed that being a mum was my reason for being because my children completed me.

As they became more independent and no longer needed my constant attention, I stopped being the centre of their universes. It left me feeling empty, both physically and emotionally, and suffering from depression. Again, I had attached an external, fixed goal to my vision of motherhood, and I hadn't left any room for flexibility or growth. I hadn't prepared myself emotionally for the development of my children, and as a result, my dream crumbled along with my happiness; my bubble burst. I had an unmovable goal in my mind and was too rigid when picturing my outcomes. Instead, I should have connected to my *reason* for being to help focus my energy on the perpetual growth of my soul.

The reason for telling you this is that it is paramount to be crystal clear about what we want to *feel* when we envision and make plans for our lives. If I had conceived a way of feeling, I would have adjusted the sail and taken an alternative route to where I was headed, keeping on track consistently, regardless of the weather outside. The storms of life will always come, but when we are willing to make adjustments on our journeys, we know we are still piloting the boats rather than being dragged through life with no control over our fates.

To be happy in life, we must perpetually grow and evolve. Without the constant flow of energy, we fail to progress, which results in the stagnation of the natural flow of life. Emotional and physical blocks begin to form to hold us back. These blocks compromise our growth and happiness, so the best way to keep moving is to keep our souls open and stay in alignment with our flows by focusing on how we feel instead of having fixed ideas of what we want to achieve or attain. Essentially, we have to keep open minds, hearts, and souls.

You'd think we would all say yes to wealth, health, and happiness, but sometimes, old self-defeating habits get in the way to stop us from opening ourselves up to these blessings. We may not even know we are the ones blocking the flow, unwittingly sabotaging our own successes due to the limiting belief systems we may carry with us through life. Again, using myself as an example, I will try to explain.

As a full-time mum, I had a negative mindset concerning wealth. I had made up a whole story in my head that earning money meant consciously disconnecting myself from my children. I had blocked any form of income from entering my life due to old thought patterns I had formed over the years: working mothers equate to unhappy mothers and unhappy children. I uncovered this mind block while working with Steve, my coach at the time. I had no idea that I had any sort of block concerning wealth because when I had my business years earlier, wealth flowed freely into my life.

I told myself I wanted to gain financial independence, but my feelings of anxiety around money wouldn't shift. I was upset I was not earning, but at the same time, I'd run from any opportunity that came my way. Once I recognised that my mind blocks were old conditioning, I could work on releasing them.

Looking back, I can see that *I* had put a spanner in the works of my life. I wanted to get back to work after my kids started school, but because of my mental block and unwavering determination to be a *good* mother, my fixed mindset stopped me from doing so. It prevented me from stepping out, reclaiming my life, and reclaiming some independence.

After working through the limiting mind blocks, I saw that I had, subconsciously, thought my children would be unhappy if I went to work, but what I hadn't taken into consideration was *my* happiness. Parents often put their children's needs before their own, but we must remember that we are responsible for *showing* them what satisfaction looks like, not just telling them. I was their role model, and I hadn't been a very good one. I stopped being an example of a *happy* mother raising happy children and had become an unhappy mother who was struggling to get through my days. Because I had pre-set the coordinates on my boat to the specific end goal of being a good mother without considering my own happiness, I had rendered myself powerless, unable to steer myself onto a better and happier path.

My point is that when we make rigid plans without allowing room for us to *feel* our way around them, they can become stagnant, and the flow of life stops running through them. Because I hadn't yet understood the concept of happiness being a path and a way of living, I had unwittingly made 'happy' a final destination. I had trapped myself into a dark corner with no view of the road ahead.

Due to my steadfast determination to succeed and lack of flexibility concerning my emotions throughout my life, every time I achieved an outcome, I came to another dead end. I was so focused on my goal that I could no longer hear my soul.

Although this is my story, I do not doubt that when you look within, you will uncover your own story when you realise that you are the one who has been sabotaging your own happiness, wealth, health, or even love. Once we recognise that *we* are the saboteurs, we feel more in control – if we are responsible, we also have the power to change it.

I have friends who sabotage their chances of meeting significant others because of their stubborn mind blocks that prevent them from opening themselves up to change. They say they want to be in relationships, but they use past experiences and fears to shape their futures. They may say things such as: If I met someone...

- I'd have to give up my independence;
- I'd have to answer to someone other than myself;
- she might break my heart; and/or
- it might not work out.

In effect, they have convinced themselves of false truths by talking themselves out of stepping beyond their comfort zones due to fear, protecting themselves from future disappointments. These fears and untruths are just stories for which they have pre-decided the endings. When we live life this way, we do not focus on what we want or what could go right – we sabotage our futures, using excuses not to try at the risk that our choices may not work out the way we have planned, but is that the way any of us truly want to live: in fear? My only real concern is coming to the end of my life, wishing I had lived and loved more fully, so I often step out of my comfort zone. Courage is not the absence of fear but feeling fear and going ahead anyway, taking a leap of faith.

By living with hope and believing we can be happy, we may risk subjecting ourselves to hurt, but it's a risk worth taking. Ultimately, we can only be hurt if we allow ourselves to feel and love, so we should focus on how we want to feel and stay in alignment with our soul selves. If you don't feel good on your journey, adjust the sail and take an alternative route to where you want to be.

YOUR "WHY"

In the world of entrepreneurship, the focus is almost always on *why* we do what we do by understanding and strongly connecting to what fuels our desires to succeed. By having a strong why and using it as a focus, we won't give up at the first hurdle, helping us to keep going when we feel like giving up. In my brief stint in network marketing, our mentors asked us to find our why. An example of some of the answers shared included:

- My children, so I can give them all they want in life.
- Financial freedom.
- To make a difference to the world.
- To let my parents retire.

This list is endless and personal, according to the individual. However, the one constant in the exercise was that we were asked to find a why connection so powerful it would make us tear up. Now, I am not saying this isn't a helpful practice, but what I believe now is that our why has to go far beyond how we want to transform our lives and the lives of others. It has to bypass our external worlds and connect to our souls.

When we feel good, we are living the moment in alignment with our true soul selves; when we do not feel good, it is because we are not – it is that simple. Our souls are our guides, and we instinctively know if we are on the right or wrong paths by the way we feel. Now, we should not compare this to feeling fear. Fear is ego-based and tries to protect us, but when we know something is right, even if it feels scary, it most likely is. To make life decisions, we first have to stop, look within ourselves, and listen carefully.

The majority of our desires in life are not what we truly desire but what we *think* will make us happy. As I talked about earlier, we are conditioned by the world around us, and we start to believe what we see, but is that a true reflection of ourselves? Are they really what we want, or are they ego-led desires? Do we look at others, wishing we had their lives without knowing if they live full and happy existences?

- If you want to be famous, why?
- If you want to be a millionaire, why?
- If you want to be a successful business owner, why?
- If you want to be a doctor, fireman, actor, singer, teacher, or author, why?
- If you want a top of the range sports car, why?
- If you want to be married, why?
- If you want to be single, why?
- If you want to travel the world, why?
- If you want to win awards, why?
- If you want to have your version of a perfect body, why?
- If you want to be attractive, why?
- If you want to be healthy, why?

You may think you know why, but do you truthfully? Have you broken it down to how it will ultimately make you feel? It's too easy to get caught up in other people's ideas about what happiness is, and we often veer off course, believing we want the same things, which leads us to places we did not intend to be.

Let's get crystal clear about how *we* want to feel and why. If the answers to our why are not strong enough, we must question whether we are trying to force ourselves into a box too restrictive to fulfil our true desires.

I liken this to trying to squeeze ourselves into clothes that do not fit. Imagine how you would feel if you wore something that was the wrong size, something too small, in particular – uncomfortable, annoyed, frustrated, fat, restricted, like you can't breathe? Would you squeeze into it anyway? I do not wear uncomfortable clothes or shoes for extended periods because all I can think about is freeing myself from them. I cannot be at peace or feel good when I squeeze myself into items that are not a good fit for me, and I cannot live my life that way either. I need to feel free, have space to move, and feel content and happy with what I am wearing, or I feel as if I am being smothered and have no air.

What about you? Do you wear hand-me-downs that never really fit well but you make do? Do you wear the latest trends and labels to win others' approval? Or are you wearing a life you designed to fit the way you want that allows you to feel amazing despite what everyone else is wearing?

SETTING YOUR INTENTION

My reason for being, my intention for doing what I do – apart from being an example for my children – is not to gain worldly success or leave my mark on the Earth; it's to be at peace within myself as I listen to and follow the calling of my soul. In doing so, I live from my true soul space, being my best self for my family and the world. When each of us resolves to live at peace with ourselves, our lives flow easier.

I have spent most of my life consciously seeking answers to life's challenges, questioning everything and everyone and becoming a lifelong student. I do not mean the kind of student who has been awarded accolades and certificates, but one who has delved deeply into understanding why we are here. In return, I have gained knowledge and wisdom of life's true treasures. I could sit back and be proud of myself for receiving so much even though I know I still have so much to learn in my lifetime and beyond, but gaining life's treasures alone do not bring peace and joy to my soul – sharing them does.

I feel like a millionaire as I have all I need to live the rest of my life in comfort, but how can I really sit here, stuffing my face with this great feast of knowledge and understanding while watching the people of the world go hungry? I don't know about you (as I can only speak for myself), but I want to share with others all that I have and all that I am.

I live my life to serve, lift, and give as much as I can of myself, not just for the benefit of my family and myself, but for every other person who needs knowledge of life's true treasures. Sharing this wisdom and love is what a peaceful soul feels like to me, and that is my WHY!

By setting an intention for the day – and on a larger scale, my life – I can push through when self-doubt starts to creep into my mind and heart. I am human, so I am not immune to negativity, but by setting an intention every day as soon as I wake up, I am reminded of my mission and calling in life, to serve the world with love, peace, and joy in my soul. I also affirm to myself every morning and many times throughout the day: I live a life of love, balance, and harmony. Reaffirming this statement ensures I do not let anything or anyone interfere with my intentions for the day. I do not always succeed, but I keep reminding myself that I have chosen love, peace, and joy.

The same goes for life. My why is my intention for life, and because I have a clear vision of why I am here and how I desire to feel each and every day, nothing can stop me. I have made a personal promise to be a force of love in the world, and nothing and no one can stop me from trying. With a clear why and intention set, I cannot fail. I may not accomplish that for which I hope, but as long as I live each day with a clear purpose and joy in my heart, I am playing my part and sharing my soul.

My vision for the world goes beyond even my lifetime, and I hope and pray that others will carry it through when I am no longer here in form. I dream of a world full of love, connection, and peace within every soul. I look around at the world and see too much sadness and a lack of self-love and worth. I see people who have disconnected from their soul selves and who are so lost they don't even know who they are anymore. They feel powerless over their lives and have no idea they hold the keys to their futures and happiness. I know this because, for a time, I was that person.

More and more, people turn to drugs and alcohol to escape their emptiness and detachment from themselves.

We feel good when we align with our true soul selves, but in the world today, we couldn't be further away. I believe that if we all take responsibility for our happiness, by looking within, we can ignite the lights within our souls and be lights to others as we live our lives with joy. Call me naïve, but this is my vision for the world and who I am. When I am my true self, I feel at one with God and all life, and my soul is aligned.

THE POWER OF LIVING IN THE PRESENT

Even though it is essential to set clear, soul-felt intentions for life, so we know which paths to take, it is also vital to take each day as it comes, to live in the 'Now' instead of living for some future event or success. The past is behind us, and we cannot change it, so we have to accept and learn from it. The future is yet to unfold, so don't waste time worrying about the possible outcomes. The only thing that matters right now is now. Open your eyes and heart at this moment and share the love within. Each day we are alive is an achievement and success in itself, so enjoy every single one of them. In the same vein, none of us can guarantee tomorrow, so let's make today matter. Most of us know the famous phrase about the past being history, the future a mystery, and today being a gift, which is why it is called the present, but do we treat today as the gift it is? When we live each day with good intentions and love in our hearts, we live the true gift of life.

GROWING WITHIN

How Do I Choose to Feel?

I *now* know who I am and how I desire to feel. Like most of us, I have been through a spectrum of feelings including sadness, depression, and worthlessness. The benefit of experiencing these emotions is that I can now identify and reject them from being a part of my life or my being; knowing exactly how I *don't* want to feel has helped clarify how I *do* want to feel. Feeling contentment every day is at the very top of my list. It would be unrealistic to expect to feel joyful 100% of the time, but feeling contentment is an attainable goal, which I work to maintain every day. What does contentment mean to me personally? It is feeling...

- peacefulness,
- gratefulness,
- freedom,
- satisfaction,
- happiness,
- light-heartedness, and
- wholeness.

How do *you* want to feel on a daily basis? Think of a time when you felt amazing, and you wished you could live that feeling every day, not thinking about how others made you feel, but rather, how *you* felt – what emotions did you experience?

Once I knew how I wanted to feel, I decided I would never settle with less than that in the long term. When I don't feel content, I know I am out of alignment with my soul, and I have to realign myself to feel good again. By becoming still, quieting my mind, reminding myself of who I am, how I desire to feel, and why I am here, I can get back to a freer and more peaceful state of heart and mind. I remind myself I have the power and don't have to wait for another person or situation to change for me to feel good. I know this because not only do I understand all of the lessons I learned on my journey, but I also apply and practise them. You may think that this is too much work, but every small step forward is a step towards gaining more power over your life and happiness. This work is not a competition or a race, and there is no time limit. You have the key right there, in your hands, for when you are ready to open your life to a happier existence. This is *your* choice, *your* key, and *your* life.

How do you choose to feel?

Take some time to be still and meditate on how you want to feel instead of dwelling on your current state of heart and mind or circumstances. For example, focus on feeling love instead of not feeling loved, and focus on loving instead of being loved. This is because only you can control how you respond to your emotions; you certainly cannot control how others feel about you. If you tell yourself that all you want is for someone to love you, you may get what you want, but would you be happy being loved by someone if you did not love him/her back in the same way?

I experienced a time when I was loved and felt loved, but I did not reciprocate the sentiment. It was a horrible feeling. No matter how much I tried to feel romantic love for that person, I could not force it. It might have happened in time, but it also might not have. When I was young, I remember saying to myself that I just wanted to be loved, but that was an untruth – I wanted to be in love with someone who loved me back equally, and treated me the way I wanted them to.

This also applies the other way around. Have you ever loved another person who did not reciprocate your feelings? Perhaps the love of your life, for whatever reason, decided s/he no longer loved you, even after declaring his/her love for you? It's not only heartbreaking, but it can also be soul-destroying, as your whole life feels broken open. So, be specific about how you want to feel in all of your relationships.

Understanding what you truly desire will take some deep contemplation on your part – as it did on mine – but once we truly understand and know the desires of our souls, instead of what we think success looks like in the world, we can stop chasing false dreams and let peace inside. To help you to open your mind and soul, answer these questions as lovingly, openly, and honestly as you can. Keep in mind that we will find that for which we are looking, so if you focus on the negative, that is all you will see.

Answering the questions openly and honestly will help you understand your deeper soul self. If you find it difficult to articulate how you feel, you can use the "Feeling" table at the end of this chapter as a guide.

- *Imagine coming to the end of a perfect day, and everything went exactly as you had hoped. As you lay in your bed, you have a giant smile on your face. Describe how you feel.*

For example, I feel joy in my soul, and I feel loved beyond measure. My soul is at peace, and my belly hurts just a little from all the laughter. I feel light and joyful.

_____

_____

_____

- **Give three examples of what, rather than who, makes you smile and why.**

  Examples: 1. Walking in nature because... 2. Playing golf because... 3. Seeing other people happy because it lifts my soul to see others living a full and happy life.

1. _____

2. _____

3. _____

- **Describe what a perfect day in life and work would look and feel like.**

  For example, mine would be:

  Life: Being at the beach with my family, floating in the cool seawater, listening to the muffled sounds of my children laughing and playing nearby. The sun is beaming down on my smiling face, and I feel at perfect peace.

Work: Sitting at my desk like I am right now with a smile on my face, feeling joy as the words flow freely from my soul.

Life: _____

Work: _____

- **Describe how you would like to feel when you wake up each morning.**

_____

_____

_____

- **How do you presently feel when you wake up, and what can you do to improve that?**

_____

_____

_____

- **About what are you passionate? What energises you that you can talk about it for hours? What brings joy to your soul?**

_____

_____

- *Imagine that you can create a happy feeling within your existing relationship or manifest a new love into your life – how do you want to feel?*

  For example, I want to feel free being myself and live my life according to my soul's longings, to feel secure in my relationship and the knowledge that my partner will support me in all I do. I also desire to share feelings of mutual, unconditional love, trust, and understanding between us.

  _____

  _____

  _____

  _____

We are *all* guilty of blaming others for making us feel certain ways, even though we are the ones responsible for how we feel. No one can *make* us feel any emotions, but becoming aware of our thoughts and reactions is the first step towards gaining our power back. Therefore…

- *Who do you blame for the way you feel at times and why (see example below)?*
- *How can you change that train of thought?*

  *Example: I sometimes blame my children and find myself thinking or saying that they make me angry or upset due to the way they respond to me, and I take it personally. To change, I can keep reminding myself that I have no control over what **they** say or do, but I have 100% control over how I feel and how I react. I can then open an inspiring book, say a silent prayer, take a few deep breaths, or meditate for a few minutes or get some fresh air and space.*

_____

_____

_____

_____

_____

COUNTING MY BLESSINGS

Imagine this scenario: we find out that every type of cake will disappear from the face of the Earth, never to be seen or eaten again, but before we embark on a life without cake, each of us has one last chance to make and eat one final cake.

Would you make do with whatever ingredients you had in your cupboard and rustle up something quick, or would you plan to make your absolute favourite cake and enjoy every last crumb? If you want to make the most of this opportunity and make that cake magnificent, where would you start? First, you would have to stop to think about what kind of cake you wanted most – this will be your last ever cake, after all.

Would it be a sponge cake, fruitcake, cheesecake, chocolate cake, or one of the hundreds of other possible cakes? Once you decide exactly what you want, you can begin planning what you need to make it.

Hoping and praying for a magnificent cake without any plan to make it happen yourself won't guarantee you'll get the cake you want, or any cake at all, so what do you do? Would you...

- tell yourself it didn't matter and that you weren't that interested in cake anyway?
- get upset because the people around you are making delicious-looking cakes, but you don't know how?
- lash out, complain, and blame others that you cannot make or have any cake? or
- choose which cake you want, find out how to make it, and make the cake you want?

What is needed to make this delicious cake?

1. a desire
2. a good recipe
3. the right ingredients
4. the correct method
5. a willingness to do the work

...not to forget the main ingredient: love.

The only question that remains is...how much do you want that dream cake?

We often forget – or choose to block out – the fact that our time on Earth is limited and that we only have one chance. We accept lives we don't love, even though we have the opportunity to create magnificent lives for ourselves, whatever we perceive that to be. Whether we want to travel around the world in private yachts, be dance teachers, become ministers, coach kids football, or be full-time parents, our dreams are our own, and we do not need to justify them to anyone, but we do owe it to ourselves to follow them.

As we talked about in the first door we opened in this book, while we must actively seek our dream feelings, we must also be grateful for all we have. When we go through life with gratitude in our hearts and minds, we open ourselves to receiving greater things. Alternatively, when we focus on what's missing, we shut ourselves out from all of those dream feelings.

So, what is the recipe for life?

1. Dream and envision yourself living your dream feeling.
2. Write down exactly how you want to feel and what your dream life looks like, no matter how far-fetched it may seem right now.
3. Set intentions in life for your dream feeling, and commit to working on them.
4. Step out of your comfort zone and take action, no matter how small; any step in the right direction is progress.
5. Start living your dream feeling today. You are in control of your thoughts. Your thoughts determine your feelings. *You* – and only you – are in charge of how you feel each day.

The exercise below will open your awareness to the feelings you are experiencing at this moment in your life to decide if you want to continue on the path on which you are currently or change direction. The beauty of our feelings in life is that we can choose them. We are 100% responsible for the ways we feel, and we only have ourselves to which to answer.

- *Using the table of "Feelings" as a guide, in the space below, write down all the words that describe how you feel on a regular basis. Answering honestly will help you gauge how close or far you currently are to feeling your dream feelings.*

Presently, I feel...

_____

_____

_____

_____

_____

_____

_____

_____

_____

_____

_____

- *Again, using the table as a guide, write down your top ten dream feelings. How do you desire to feel and why?*

  For example: Joyful, because when I think of being joyful, I imagine myself being light on my feet, having a bounce in my step, and a smile on my face.

1. _____

2. _____

3. _____

4. _____

5. _____

6. _____

7. _____

8. _____

9. _____

10. _____

FEELINGS

FEEL-GOOD FEELINGS	NOT SO GOOD FEELINGS
Joy	Anger
Contentment	Sadness

Love	Depression
Peace	Powerlessness
Empowerment	Anxiety
Excitement	Envy
Passion	Frustration
Purpose	Doubt
Cheer	Fear
Hope	Loneliness
Gratitude	Shame
Confidence	Bitterness
Enthusiasm	Betrayal
Satisfaction	Guilt
Awe	Grief
Pride	Jealousy
Inspiration	Boredom
Amusement	Hurt
Fulfilment	Misunderstanding

DAILY PRACTICE

Changing our ways of thinking means we have to create new habits and daily practices. Some I have mentioned in this book will feel right to you; others, not so much, so do what feels right to you at this particular time. As we evolve and grow, we can adapt our daily practices to work for us. What once worked for you may no longer work, and what you felt was not right for you at one time may help now, so keep going back over the daily practices and use those that lift and inspire you.

In the moments you feel powerless, find yourself surrounded by fog, or need a good kick in the backside to step out of your comfort zone, remind yourself daily that...

- If you never ask, you'll never get!
- If you never step forward, you will always stay where you are!
- If you never fall, you'll never learn how to get up!
- If you never fail, you may never learn!
- If you never open your heart, you'll never know love!
- If you never serve, you'll never feel the joy of giving!
- If you never trust, you will always live in fear.
- If you never forgive, you will never feel true freedom.
- If you never love, you will never truly live.
- If you never try to get what you want, you will surely never get it!

Write this down and display it somewhere you can read it often to remind yourself that this life and your happiness is all up to you.

THE POWER OF FAITH

MIRACLES ARE CREATED THROUGH FAITH IN ONESELF AND
TRUST IN A HIGHER POWER.

What is faith, and why is it essential to unlocking joy within ourselves?

Some say that seeing is believing, but absolute faith is believing without seeing, and not only believing, but having a deep sense of *knowing* in the depths of your soul that all is as it should be, whatever the outcome. Developing a strong faith allows us to trust and let go of fear, worry, and anxiety. It enables us to live with more peace in our hearts, minds, and souls. Faith and fear cannot coexist; we decide which one we choose to shape our lives.

If we strive, push, compare and compete, we do not operate from places of peace but respond to the fear within. We fear not being good enough, loved, happy, wealthy, or attractive, but when we live with faith, we can surrender our souls to wisdom much greater than our own.

We are here on this Earth to grow and love. We *are* love, and all we have to *be* is our original, loving selves. As I talked about in Door #2, *Know Your Soul*, life is a journey back to who we once were, remembering our soul selves, and connecting back to the source of who we are: LOVE. We gain faith in accepting we are meant to exist, knowing we are the embodiments of love, and trusting that all we experience is exactly what we are supposed to undergo. When we seek evidence of that truth, we use our eyes to see, but faith sees and feels with our souls.

Life is full of beautiful truths we cannot see with the physical eye, including love, happiness, inner peace, and joy, and not one of us can deny their existence. We cannot explain why love exists or the power it has over us, but it is undeniably real and one of the greatest of all of life's true treasures. Even though we cannot touch, taste, see or contain it in any way, love is very much an essential part of us, as is faith.

Faith has many meanings:

- a belief in something beyond our control,
- a belief in a higher power without physical evidence of its truth, and/or
- complete trust in someone, something, or ourselves.

We all need faith of some kind to live peacefully, or we would never do anything. Even the simplest of everyday actions takes some level of belief:

- We go to bed at night with faith that we will wake up every morning, or we would panic every time we closed our eyes in fear of never waking up.

- When we eat, we have faith that the food we eat will nourish, sustain, and provide us with what we need to survive.

- When we get married, we have faith that we have found the right people to spend our entire lives with, who will love and support us through good times and bad. We trust that we will treat each other with loving kindness and respect.

- When we brush our teeth, we have faith that by cleaning them daily, we are protecting them with the hope they will last us a lifetime.

- When we take a trip in the car, we have faith in our ability to drive and faith in other drivers, and we trust that they will do their best to keep us all safe on the roads.

- When we read books – such as this one on personal growth – we have faith they will teach us something valuable to improve our lives in some way.

We all have some level of faith to enable us to function in life, regardless of our religious beliefs. If we had no faith, we would spend our lives in complete fear and anxiety, never growing, never moving, and never truly living.

Those who live with little faith in themselves, others, or God, rarely step out of their comfort zones, sadly losing out on life's wonderful experiences. They imprison themselves within walls of fear when all that it takes for us to escape the confines is a leap of faith.

My understanding is that we all need to experience the pain of failure and adversity to grow in strength and resilience. I like to think that challenges in life are like resistance weights for the body – one enables

195

us to build physical muscles and the other emotional and spiritual muscles. Without a doubt, both are physically challenging as we lift the extra weights, but faith is the knowledge that, in the end, we can stand as stronger and improved human beings.

All of our experiences become blessings, whether they feel like it or not at the time. We certainly do not ask for difficulties, but faith is also accepting that we have to experience certain things to learn the necessary lessons.

Think of a time you felt helpless and thought you would never get through it, but you managed to get back up on your feet. Whatever you had to go through made you stronger and enabled you to overcome difficulties. You may be going through some life trauma right now and wondering if you can get through it, so now would be an appropriate time to take that leap of faith and simply trust. Life happens *for* us, not *to* us, and challenges can teach us that:

- every fall is a wake-up call for us to redirect and reassess the directions of our lives;
- every failure is a test of our resilience and strength to remind us that we can use these experiences, not only to help others through their tough times but also for us to question whether we are on the right paths;
- every time we lose a loved one, we are reminded of the value of our lives here on Earth, helping us to recognise how precious our time is and reassess the meaning of our lives;
- every time we experience rejection, we are perhaps being protected from taking paths that were not right for us; and
- every time we have our hearts broken through damaged relationships, we discover that we are stronger than we thought

196

and that we need to learn to love ourselves more instead of expecting someone else to do it for us.

Most of all, these difficulties remind us of how we are all the same, that life refines each of us to reveal the true treasures within our souls. We all suffer, and we all experience pain, and because of that, we are reminded to be compassionate towards others because, without empathy and compassion, life would be cold and meaningless.

When we live with faith, we understand that all we experience, good and bad, is meant for us, and life shapes us into what we need to *be* to fulfil our purposes here on Earth. Faith is recognising that even though we do not know *why* we have to suffer at certain times, everything is as it should be.

Who is God?

God is nameless, yet there are many names we use, including Creator, Heavenly Father, The Universe, Divine Source, and Holy Spirit, to name just a few. A lot of us have images of God as a white male with long white hair and a beard. He's a personage that lives in the clouds and speaks with the voice of thunder, but how many of us truly know God? I am not here to tell you who God is – who am I to describe God – but I will share my thoughts and personal experiences.

When I had my salon many years ago, I imposed a rule that the two subjects we could not discuss with our clients were politics and religion. Why? Because my clients were separate people, and politics and religion tend to divide people into boxes when we are only one race: the human race. No matter what God means to us or whether we believe in Him, we are all equal, deserving, and worthy human beings. Discussing religion and politics can cause disharmony or conflict between good and honest people, but I wanted our salon to be a place of peace, harmony, and most of all, fun, to provide a safe space for clients to come and feel welcome, have a wonderful experience, and leave, feeling brighter and happier.

My intention for my work as a life coach and author are not dissimilar: to create a way for people to feel peace, harmony, love, and happiness. The nature of my work has changed completely, but the intention of my work is the same: to help people feel more content with themselves.

In this book, it is paramount that we talk about faith, as this is the predominant factor when living with joy. We are all so diverse, and each of us has our personal spiritual beliefs, which we are all absolutely entitled to hold. I am not here to sway your opinion or question your religion, only to help you awaken and strengthen your faith, deepening your relationship with your divine source of love within.

If you were to ask me who God is, I would say that God is the divine loving energy of our souls. Personally, my religion is LOVE. I believe that LOVE and GOD are one and the same. Every time we feel love within our souls, we feel God. He is the source of our being.

When I was small, I was told that God is everywhere and in everything, but it made no sense to me. How can God be in all places at all times? Even as an adult, I still could not understand who God was, but I put it to the back of my mind along with all of my other unanswered questions. Only now, after many years, can I truly understand what that phrase means. I now see God everywhere, and I wonder how I could have been blind to it for most of my life. Now, I know that God IS love, and I see love in all places and at all times when I seek it.

You know that feeling when you look at your child – or any child, for that matter – and a feeling of abounding love pours through your body? Well, that is you feeling God within you. It's the same kind of feeling you get out in nature when you look around, and your body feels elevated by the beauty surrounding you – that is God. When you take the time to really look at a flower and marvel in its complexity and beauty, that, too, is God. When you sit watching the sunset on the horizon, and you get that warm, fuzzy feeling, there God is. He is everywhere: in the clouds, the sea, the mountains, the sun, the trees, the food we eat, and every single soul that walks the Earth. When we do not see or feel God's love within another person, it doesn't mean it is not there. Rather, it means that either she, we, or both of us, are disconnected from love and out of alignment, or has lost our connection to our divine sources within, but God is everywhere at all times in all places, only a call away if and when we decide to reconnect. He is the pure energy of our souls, so he is within every single one of us. When we seek God, we find him. When we look for the infinite higher power of love within everything and everyone, we will see and feel God.

I do not follow one organised religion, yet I love to learn about all of them. I have close friends and family who are Catholic, Mormon, Jehovah's Witness, Buddhist, and atheist. I love them all equally. They are all amazing and loving human beings. We are all on this journey through life together, and I believe that, ultimately, all paths lead us to the same final destination, and we are free to choose which paths will take us there.

Although, among my friends and family, I have noticed that those who have a strong faith in God tend to go through life easier than non-believers. They live with hope in their hearts and believe that all things are possible, just as it says in many scriptures, which, alone, is a key to living with more joy. Belief in a higher power enables us to:

- believe in miracles,
- know we are never alone,
- see that life is happening for us and not to us,
- trust that whatever will be is for our greater good, and
- be willing to receive, grow, and learn from our experiences.

I am not saying we need faith in God to be happy – I am saying that without faith, it is hard for us to be free to experience abundant happiness. Faith is a foundation on which to build lasting happiness and an acceptance that some things are predetermined as we surrender to higher powers of wisdom. True faith means we know the universe has our backs, allowing us to let go of worry, fear, and anxiety to some extent. We cannot control all areas of our lives, so, at times, we have to surrender, sit back, and allow life to unfold.

Faith in God allows us to trust in the great sources of love from within.

As you work your way through this book, you will realise that I am a go-getter. When I set my heart and mind on something, I live it 100%. This is what I did when searching for answers concerning God. I'm not saying it is necessarily a good thing, but that is me, and I have accepted who I am. I used to describe myself as obsessive, but now that I am kinder to myself, I have rebranded my behaviour as intentional and on purpose. I have accepted that this is my path, and it may not be for everyone, but I am here, writing this book *because* of my quest for knowledge, so I trust.

My quest for answers began when my mum died suddenly, when my first child was only one year old, and my whole world fell apart, leaving me shocked and confused. In my eyes, she had disappeared from the face of the planet, and I couldn't understand where she had gone. My spiritual journey truly began because I was seeking the truth, so

I spent the next 15 years studying scripture of different kinds, five of them studying the Bible with great conviction, trying to get my head around who God really is and why we are here.

I grew up a faithful little Catholic girl, doing what I was supposed to but not really understanding who God was or even if I really believed. I went to church and said my prayers because I was told to. In fact, I feared God and worried that if I *didn't* pray or go to church, something horrible would happen to my family, so I followed the rules. There I was, in my thirties, ready to know God, desperate to know where my mum had gone. During my five years of study, I read the Bible from cover to cover, drinking in all the knowledge and writing about how I felt. This process answered many of my questions. I reached a high level of understanding to the point where reading from "The Book of Isaiah" was like reading beautiful poetry. When I read the words of Isaiah now, they don't make much sense to me, although, at the time, I felt elevated in spirit every time I read them. In fact, I felt so close to God at that time I actually thought I knew it all. I believed I completely understood the meaning of life, and I felt truly enlightened. However, as I reached that pinnacle point on my spiritual journey, my life became unstable. I became fearful, thinking to myself, "If I have *all* the answers already, is it time for me to die?" I felt as though I had completed my work concerning faith and fortifying my relationship with my divine source. I had reached the highest point, and I could see everything so clearly – I had made it!

Now, it makes me laugh when I think of how my mind worked then. Oh, how naïve I was. It was one thing to learn *about* God, but quite another to *know* God and live a divinely-led life. I thought I knew it all, and because I had faithfully studied the scriptures, I (my ego) somehow expected me to be protected. I foolishly thought that I would no longer have to experience difficulty, but I couldn't have been more wrong. It was then that my faith was tested – big time. Little did I know that, from that moment on, I would go through the most challenging years of my life. I was broken mentally, spiritually, and in the end, physically. I felt as though I had lost a piece of my soul that I never thought I would recover. I felt abandoned by God, and I questioned His very existence once again.

During my so-called enlightenment, I felt on top of the world, and my ego was having a ball, thinking I was somehow special.

I would compare how I felt to how I assume an obese person might feel after losing 30 or 40 pounds, as if I had worked diligently on getting my body down to my perfect weight and size with breathtaking muscle tone and felt incredibly healthy, strong, light, and free. I no longer carried the weight of my fears and doubts around. I felt elated, untouchable...and then complacency set in.

The problem with reaching places where we think we cannot improve is that we let go of the steering wheels that have directed us to where we wanted to be. We believe that by reaching our final destinations, it is safe to let go and relax. However, what we often fail to realise is the minute we do so is the moment we spin out of control and crash. When we lose 30 pounds and let go of what has led to our successes, we revert to our former ways of being, and the weight spins out of control again, leaving us, in some cases, in an even worse state than when we first embarked on our weight-loss journeys. This downward spiral is what I experienced on my path to finding God. Once I crashed, I realised I had learned nothing, and I was back to square one. I asked myself, 'Why me?' I had done everything I had learned in my studies, yet there I was, feeling worthless and alone. Was it because my faith was being tested? Was it because I didn't have enough faith? Was it because I just wasn't worthy of happiness? I couldn't understand why. Even though I still had faith in God, I had none in myself.

I prayed to God to help me. I expected something other than myself to come to my rescue to mend my broken soul, and nothing changed.

After I hit rock bottom and started a new journey towards self-discovery and self-love, my life experience gradually improved. I soon came to an understanding that 'God' doesn't *do* anything. God is love, and love does not *do* anything; it just *is*. God isn't something outside of us that is separate from us, commanding our lives. We co-create and build the lives we want with God, the divine loving source within, but we have to find our own ways. What does co-creating mean? It means we have to take God and our faiths by the hand and create the lives we want with divine guidance and love.

When we ask for help, it shows up in the form of this book, for example, in some wise words from a friend, or a kind act from a stranger, or maybe in illness, grief, or the loss of a job or relationship. We don't always get the answers for which we hope, but when we co-create with God, we receive guidance from the whisperings of our souls. We have a deep knowing when we are on track because of the way we feel within our souls. We cannot listen to fears of the ego – we must be *still*, and the answers will come.

It is said that prayer is us talking to God, and in my understanding, intuition is God answering back, but for us to hear the voice of our loving guiding source, we need to be still in prayer or meditation, open our souls, and tap into the energies that reside there, which is God. Whether we pray or not, God is ever-present in our lives. Every falter we make is a whisper from our source to remind us where we are going. Reminders to keep us on track can be as subtle as a little nudge, gut feeling, or being given this book. If we do not listen to the gentle voices, we may be reminded by what feels like a slap in the face, perhaps an injury, fall, or accident. We may even feel as if we have had wrecking balls to the sides of our heads – like how I felt – to wake us up and force us to take notice.

I am meant to be here now, writing this book, and the wrecking ball to the head made that happen. I am 100% sure that my semi-dormant life of just existing would not have led me to live my purpose. God did not abandon me; he was shaking me awake to expose my reason for being, pointing me in the right direction. Every desire, passion, gift, and talent with which we have been blessed is meant for us. We can ignore them, but we are each here for a reason. We can take God's hand and trust in Him by co-creating the lives we desire, or we can close our hearts and souls to our lives' purposes.

We have been blessed with free will, which means *we* choose. We choose what we do or don't do to improve our lives and circumstances, and we command the quality of our lives. God is the very source of our love, the energy that makes our hearts beat, the blood flow effortlessly through our veins, and every hair on our bodies grow, moment by moment. God is like electricity for our cell phones, and prayer is our opportunity to recharge. Electricity does not *do* anything – it is simply a source of power for us to plug into to provide us with energy. God is also there for us to tap into as a source of power and love. We are made from that same source of love, as we are all parts of God, and we need to be refuelled and nourished through that source. The scriptures say that we are His children, made in His image, which, to me, means we are designed and made with His energy of love. Our parents are not our creators – they are vessels into which we are born, coming through them and not from them. We are made in the image of love, and we can, undoubtedly, witness it in every child born on this Earth. Each one is pure love, divine.

Only when I started this journey, working simultaneously on my mind, body, and spirit, did everything fall into place. I had been running forward, looking obsessively outside of myself for answers, but it was only when I looked within myself that I found the Divine Spirit within my soul. The 'God' I had sought years earlier in my studies was separate from me and someone who wanted me to live by His rules, but I soon realised that is not who God is. I found 'God' in me, and I was able to see Him in every other living thing upon the Earth. Today, my faith is stronger than ever, but I do not chase a God with labels and rules to follow, keeping us separated – I listen to the voice of love within my soul.

I still have many questions, and of course, I do not have all the answers, but I accept that my journey of faith is an ongoing one that will continue beyond the grave. I trust in divine timing, that more wisdom and understanding will unfold as I journey through life and grow.

I like to describe our lives as if they are artichokes, growing up from the ground. God is the earth, and each of us grows from below it. When we separate ourselves from the ground, we wilt and die spiritually, but if we stay grounded and keep ourselves well-nourished, we can grow into sturdy plants whose primary roles in life are to nourish others. As we go through life, we grow tough, external layers to protect our soft and tender hearts, but the essences of who we are remain the same. As we peel back the layers and look inside, we see that each of us is made of – and is a source of – love. As I said earlier in this book, these layers are the labels we use to protect ourselves, but deep down, we are all loving, tender hearts, nourished by the Earth and God, independent of what we believe.

We all have different levels of faith for every aspect of our lives, but complete trust is what brings that inner peace we so desperately crave. We can manifest tremendous miracles by having tremendous faith. We have been blessed with the greatest spiritual teachers and exemplars who have taken this path before us. They have led the way to achieving our own greatness and finding God within. Jesus, Buddha, Lao Tzu, Mahatma Gandhi, Mother Teresa, and the Dalai Lama are just a few examples of teachers who have played a big part in informing how I live my life, and their colossal love and faith for humankind opened my heart to God.

LETTING GOD IN

Using my personal experience and the power of my faith, I share my thoughts and principles on how to create more joy within through welcoming God (Love) into your life. Whatever you believe, life is better with love in it.

- Pray.
- Love.
- Serve.
- Ask.
- Receive.

- Believe.
- Trust.
- Be humble.
- Be honest.
- Face mortality

PRAY

'Prayer is the gift of never having to feel alone.'

What is prayer, and why do we need it? The simplest way to explain prayer is to think of it as being plugged into your source of energy to be refuelled and keep your true self fully functioning, to nourish you and provide you with power.

God does not need us to pray to worship him, as he certainly does not *need* our love. GOD *IS* LOVE and not some ego-led being who thrives off idolisation. God is the Creator of the Universe, and He needs nothing from us except that we thrive.

Prayer is only for our benefits. It is a time for us to switch off from the world, tune into the spirit of who we are, and connect with our divine sources within. We are all spiritual beings living life as human beings, not the other way around. Prayer is that call home to release our fears, free our souls from troubles, and be nourished with unconditional love and light once again. It's a time to be thankful for all we already have, to express gratitude for our lives, health, families, and everything with which we are blessed to have. Prayer is what keeps us humble as we kneel and surrender to the forces of love within each of us. It is a moment of pure peace and connection within, to ground and centre ourselves and tap into our sources of divine love. Prayer is also an outlet for our hearts' desires, a way to open our souls to reveal our purposes in life. By connecting with our higher powers and asking for what we truly want, we invite a vision of our ideal lives into our minds, enabling us to manifest our greatest desires and open the doors to let all good things inside.

I believe that when we ask for something with pure hearts, we get it, but we must also trust that if we do not get it, it is not because we are not deserving but because that for which we ask will not take us where we need to be to fulfil our souls' purposes and hearts' desires. It may not show up in the forms for which we had hoped, but whatever does happen is for the benefit of our growth and progress. And sometimes, miracles happen!

LOVE

'Where there is love, there is God.'

To me, God IS love, but what does that mean for us? Because God and love are one entity, if we are made in His image, we can assume that we, too, are love. Fundamentally, we all know this truth. Every new baby or animal born into this world is pure love, and not one of us can deny it nor the miracle of life, but as we grow in life, we become tainted by the world. We learn to survive by mimicking those around us and often cut ourselves off from that love, but essentially, we are all pure love to the core. When we see and feel the love in others, it awakens within our souls as the beautiful, loving energy flows through us.

When we connect to our true spiritual selves, we feel that love, not only in ourselves but within everyone that crosses our paths. God does not discriminate, and when we truly connect to that divine source, neither do we.

Once we know that we embody love, we can recognise and see it in others, even if their lives' traumas mask it. It allows us to become more compassionate, forgiving, and tolerant of other people's untoward actions and behaviours as we begin to understand that others merely suffer from a disconnection from the sources of love within themselves.

I like to think of anger, heartache, unforgiveness, jealousy, bitterness, and the like as that tiny piece of plastic that slides in between the battery and the conductor in electronics that stops the energy from getting through. Only when we remove the piece of plastic by forgiving, giving, and loving openly will the loving energy flow back to resume full power. Once we remove all the blocks, love will naturally flow back into our souls, and we will fully function. When we were born, we did not know anger, bitterness, or hatred; we only knew love. As we grew, we allowed life to influence us and taint our life experiences, disconnecting us from our soul selves. As I emphasise throughout this book, life is simply about finding our ways back to our true selves, finding our ways back to love.

SERVE

In Door #5 of this book, *Selfish Service*, we talked about how serving others brings joy, but another advantage is that it strengthens our faith in humanity, as well as God. When we reach out to others, we spread the love that so many souls are in dire need of receiving. Because of life's trials, they may feel lost, alone, or broken. All they need is an outstretched hand to lift them and restore their faith in love.

We have all been there – no one is free from difficulty. Some of us face more challenges than others, but we cannot compare pain. All of our lives have been touched by death, illness, and broken relationships, and we all know how it feels to be in physical and emotional pain. However, when we are surrounded by loving, caring souls in our times of need, our faith is restored. Their support and love give us the strength and courage to pick ourselves up and keep moving. Even the tiniest steps forward help us to progress. Progress equals growth, which leads to more love, peace, happiness, and contentment.

When life gets us down, the magic pills we can take is 'giving'. Serving others with love reminds us – and reconnects us to – our loving sources within. Because we *are* love, as is God, serving others connects us to that source of love and our higher powers within. When we understand this truth, we realise the love and joy we feel and give is the cure-all.

ASK

The words 'Ask, and it shall be given you; seek, and you shall find; knock, and it shall be opened unto you' are probably among the best-known in the Bible, and they are the ones most widely used. Whether you are asking, seeking, or knocking, it is essential to take action when creating the life you want because if you don't ask, you don't get, if you don't look, you won't find, and if you don't knock, you will stand forever until someone opens the door. It doesn't get any simpler than that.

If you want something and ask, there is a 50% chance of the answer being yes. However, if you don't ask, you have a 100% chance of it being no. Again, we need faith. When we have faith, we accept that whatever answer we get is the right one and with less resistance. Without faith, we will not ask, and therefore, we will not get what we want.

As an example, imagine that a once in a lifetime job comes up for grabs, but you doubt if you are sufficiently experienced or qualified to get it. You either can apply for the job with enthusiasm and faith that whatever the outcome, you'll be happy you tried, or choose not to apply, thus, ensuring you will not get the job. Which would you choose? Self-doubt tries to talk us out of stepping outside of our comfort zones, but that is where faith steps in. One thing for sure is that if we don't ask, we don't get, leaving us with regret and self-hatred for not having the courage to ask in the first place. Is that better than rejection?

As I mentioned earlier in the book, I would rather live a life of failure than regret. For me, rejection is better than never trying. It would eat me up to get to the end of my life, wishing that I'd only tried when I had the chance. Being rejected could result in our egos taking a bashing, but our souls will be at peace with the knowledge that we were brave enough to try.

When we ask God in prayer, we release our true desires out into the universe and open our souls, but in doing so, we have to be willing to accept any possible answer. We may not get that for which we ask in the shape and form we expect, but answers will come, so it is essential that we also listen.

Here is a story demonstrating this truth:

The Faithful Man

There was once a man who always prayed and had unshakable faith.

Because he had complete faith in God, when torrential rain came and flooded the small village in which he lived, he fell to his knees in prayer.

As he prayed for his safety and that of the villagers, the man felt the presence of God, reassuring him that he would save them, and a wave of calm washed over him. As the storm continued, the villagers worked frantically to keep the rising water out of their homes but to no avail. Within a few hours, they had a plan to evacuate the village and retreat to safety.

When the other villagers came knocking on his door, ushering the faithful man to go with them, he refused, saying with surety in his heart, 'You go on without me; I have faith that God will keep me safe.' The villagers could not convince him to leave his home, so they reluctantly left, fearing for the lives of their families.

Hours went by, and the rain continued, and as the water began to reach the windows, the man moved upstairs, feeling safe and sure he would be protected.

Soon after, a rescue boat came by, beckoning the man to climb out the window into the boat. Again, he refused, waving them on, saying, 'Do not worry about me. I will be fine. God has reassured me that I will be safe.'

As the floods reached the second floor, the man was forced to climb up onto the roof of his house, but the waters continued to rise, and the man drowned.

When the man got to heaven, he stood before God and asked, 'Why did you abandon me? You said you would save me!'

God replied, 'I sent some villagers to help you escape and be safe, but you sent them away. Then, I sent a man with a rescue boat, and you also sent him away. I outstretched my hands to save you, but you did not take them!'

RECEIVE

We can ask, but we have to have our hearts, minds, and souls open to receive divine help. As I said before, life doesn't happen to us; it happens *for* us. Everyone that comes into our lives comes for a reason. They may come to be lifelong friends, life partners, or short-term teachers to relay particular lessons to help us to grow somehow. Some may even come to test our strength and faith, but they come into our lives for long term benefits.

I know what it feels like to have my heart broken into a million pieces, left wondering if I will ever be able to put it back together, wondering if I had the strength to keep moving or if I even wanted to, but I now know that my broken heart is what shaped me into the person I am today. I am strong *because* of my life challenges, not despite them. If I could go back to prevent my suffering, would I? Absolutely not. I've learned so much about life, myself, and my reason for being I would never have discovered otherwise.

The story about the faithful man is a reminder: we must keep our ears, eyes, hearts, and souls open to receive the answers to our prayers. God will not come to us and magically remove us from life's situations. The right people appear in our lives at just the right time to make us – or, perhaps, nearly break us – but we have to be willing to accept help when it comes. The faithful man had so much faith in God, he failed to help himself. He had the means, and so do each of us in our present circumstances. This book is one of those outstretched hands for you to grasp when you need someone to support you through your life's journey. Every word I write flows naturally through me from that divine source within my soul. I do not think about what sounds right or what I think you might want to hear. I allow the words to flow through me as if God were working through me. I know this may sound a little crazy to some (it sometimes even seems crazy to me), but I allow divine love into my heart, mind, and soul, and I surrender my will. I am no one special, yet I can allow divine love to flow through me, as can you. I am equal to every one of you, and my calling at this moment in time is to be here, right now, receiving and allowing life to happen for me.

Prayer is our way of communicating and talking to God, but intuition – that gut feeling of deep knowing – is God replying, but for us to hear, we need to be still. This book and the others I write are not necessarily planned – they are within me, and I feel inspired (in spirit) to write what flows through me. It feels like love divinely bursting out from within me.

Just as our children come through us, not for us, this book also comes through me, not for me. I have no idea how it will be received, but I believe that my inspiration is purposeful. I have my heart and soul open to receive divine input, and in doing so, I allow it to flow freely.

BELIEVE

One of my very favourite scriptures is 'All things are possible to him that believeth,' not just because I like the sound of the concept, but because I know it is true from personal experience. Even though I am a go-getter and I spent most of my life chasing happiness, deep down, I thought I wasn't good enough, beautiful enough, or clever enough, and my life was about proving myself wrong. I believed in happiness and kept finding it, but it always slipped back through my fingers because I did not believe I was truly worthy.

213

Only when the shift took place, and I looked within did I realise that I was as good, worthy, and capable of following my dreams and succeed in life as anyone, whatever I choose to do. When we truly believe, we take action and do what we need to do to achieve what we truly desire from life. It takes faith.

The fact that I write books takes a tremendous amount of faith. I write with the hope of touching souls to guide them to personal freedom and joy, but I do not know what the response will be to each one.

If I thought what I was writing could not help another soul, would I still write? I believe the words flowing through me are part of God's plan for me. If I desire to write, then that is what I need to do.

When we have great passion and love what we are doing, we align with our souls and divine love. When we follow the whisperings of our soul selves, we cannot go wrong. Worldly success is not indications of our worth – rather, it is about following our souls to bring light to our lives and shine that light on others, but for us to shine, we must first believe in ourselves, trust, and have faith.

TRUST

'Trust in the Lord with all of thine heart; and lean not unto thine own understanding.' Sometimes, we just have to trust, have faith, and know that all is exactly how it should be. It isn't always easy to accept what life throws at us, but we often have no other choice but to have faith and just trust. Imagine that you are a fruit tree. In the first few years of your life, your only job is to grow big and strong so that, one day, you can produce nutritious fruit to feed the hungry. This is your reason for being, your life's purpose.

Once you come of age, you begin producing delicious fruit, and each year, the gardener who tends to you comes along and cuts your lovely, long limbs off. You are left with little stumps, and you wonder what you did to deserve such brutal treatment. You ask yourself why the gardener needs to cut you back, wondering what his reason is for punishing you. You were doing a good job, living your purpose, and producing fruit, so why does life have to be so cruel?

The reality is that, for fruit trees to flourish and produce their very best fruit, they need constant pruning. They are not here to provide shade and grow as big as they can. They are here to make beautiful, edible fruit to feed and nourish the world. And we, as human beings, are the same.

In life, when we feel as if we are being pruned back, we have to trust that in doing so, we become stronger, healthier, and better quality human beings as we cut away the unnecessary extra branches that use up our energies.

Is it better to live barren lives with no meaning or be continually pruned and refined so we can live lives of meaning, live out our purposes, and produce beautiful fruit full of goodness? When we are refined, pruned, and shaped, it reveals our strength, resilience, and characters. We begin to flourish, radiating goodness, love, light, and truth. Only then are we ready to live our callings, feed the world, and nourish those who come to eat from our trees.

BE HUMBLE

What does being humble really mean? For me, being humble means truly knowing and understanding that every single one of us is equal, recognising that we are all on this journey together, and not a one of us is better than the other.

In the New Testament, we are taught that we are to be like children: willing to learn, understanding that life is neither a race nor a competition, but a journey that teaches us to care for one another, holding each other up when we become weak or need support or love. We all have times when we need to be carried, and there are also times when we have the strength to carry others, physically, emotionally, and spiritually.

Jesus, Gandhi, the Dalai Lama, and many other spiritual teachers have taught humility by example throughout the years. Jesus spent time among thieves and prostitutes and did not judge any of them. He didn't say, 'I AM THE SON OF GOD, STAY AWAY FROM ME.' Rather, He said, 'Come unto me, and you shall be forgiven, healed, and made new.'

Without humility, we would be judgemental, unforgiving, and without compassion and empathy towards others, but we all make mistakes because we are all human. When we recognise our own humanity and imperfections, we become more open and forgiving towards others, as well.

Humility and forgiveness aren't necessarily about accepting untoward behaviours from others to let them off the hook but about promoting an understanding that they may be in pain and reacting to their circumstances in the only ways they know. When we forgive others for their behaviours and actions, we free ourselves from resentment and anger. Resentment and anger destroy our peace, separate us from others, and the divine love within that maintains our wellbeing. When we are humble, we recognise that we are not perfect, and we all make mistakes. We forgive ourselves and others for the mistakes and bad choices we make and allow peace and love back into our lives and hearts.

Humility means surrendering our ego-selves and accepting oneness with God and reverence for all life. We are all here to fulfil our purposes, and we are all meant to be. Every tree, every flower, every creature, and every human being is of great value, and when we live with faith, prayer, love, service, asking, receiving, trusting, and humility, our true and beautiful selves will shine through, allowing us to be lights in the world around us. In effect, we simply have to *be*. We are human *beings*, after all.

BE HONEST

Being honest with yourself, as well as with others, is vital for our living joyful lives and being faithful to our higher selves. To align with God, we must quieten our egos and take good honest looks at who we are to decide if we are living our truths. If we desire inner peace and joy within, we must be faithful to ourselves in mind, body, and spirit.

Lying to ourselves serves no purpose. We may not like what we find, but by honestly looking at our lives, health, habits, relationships, faith, and of course, souls, we can see the truth of who we are. Fundamentally, we all *know*, but we all too often listen to our egos, making excuses and blaming others for our shortcomings instead of owning them and taking responsibility for our lives.

When it comes to health, we all know what to do – it's not rocket science: eat clean, fresh food, get sufficient exercise, rest, and fresh air, and drink plenty of water, while feeding our minds with good, nourishing thoughts. How many of us make excuses for our states of health?

It often takes extensive pruning – like the fruit tree – for us to honestly look at our lifestyles. It may take the form of an illness or a scare that awakens us to the ways we have mistreated our bodies.

People often need to be told they will die before they make the necessary changes, but I am here to say be honest with yourselves right now – don't wait. Small changes now can prevent catastrophic results.

No matter how strong your faith is, you are responsible for your health. When we pray for good health, we must also do our parts to take care of the gifts of our health and precious bodies. We received these vessels to house our souls for the duration of our time on Earth, and we all come in different forms, shapes, and sizes, but inside, we are all made of the same energy. When we honestly look, we realise that our bodies are beautifully designed, intricate engines with inexplicable forces, allowing them to heal and regenerate. We do not have the capacity to understand the complexity of that source of energy, but we have to trust our Creator and do our very best to take care of ourselves. Taking care of our physical bodies is an expression of gratitude for the gifts of life.

With tremendous faith, people have miraculously recovered from terminal diseases and even walked after being told they would never walk again. We, too, have the power of God within us to heal ourselves.

As in the story of the faithful man who prayed devoutly, faith alone is not enough. God provides us with knowledge and guidance to create healthy bodies, minds, and souls, and it is our responsibility to find our ways back, but ultimately, we have to be honest with ourselves and acknowledge the parts we play in preserving the condition of our wellbeing.

FACE MORTALITY

My near-death experiences in my twenties are among the greatest blessings in my life. They were the pivotal points that redirected my path and transformed my life, a divine wake up call. Death is a natural part of life – we should not fear it for those who pass but treat it as a lesson reserved for those they leave behind bereft and facing life with a great emptiness that had once been filled by their late loved ones.

On one particular occasion, I found myself gasping for air in the middle of yet another sudden asthma attack. All it took to trigger an attack was a bit of saliva catching the back of my throat. I was used to the regular attacks, but this one felt different. I tried desperately to use my inhalers, but there was zero air going in or out, so the medication had no open passage into my lungs. Amidst the panic, I felt a wave of serenity wash over me, and I accepted that my battle was over. I was powerless over my fate, and it was time to surrender. Time seemed to slow, and as I looked into my husband's eyes to say goodbye, I saw helplessness, fear, and desperation in his face. Even though he was panicking, all I could feel was an overwhelming sense of peace as I felt myself slipping away, with no fear, no pain, no distress, and no struggling for breath, just a still beautiful moment of pure love and light I will never forget. By some miracle, I started breathing again. It was not my time to go. I believe my brush with death was a gift, another chance at life, and I refuse to let that experience go to waste. Because of it, I turned my life and health around, and as you can tell, I am here to tell the tale. I needed this life lesson to remind me how precious my life was, and I was not about to waste it. This understanding was the blessing of my awakening and the first step on my journey towards truly living. From then on, I knew that death was not to be feared but a natural transition to more love and more light. That said, I also understood the fragility and beauty of living life and how our time here matters. This is our chance to embody love and spread love to grow our souls.

Having faith in a higher power and an understanding of who we are and the nature of God prepares us for every eventuality, even death, as we know that we are part of a plan in life and death. We are all gifted with power over our lives and destinies, but to claim them, we must have faith and trust in the unknown. Trust that all is exactly as it should be.

Whatever your spiritual or religious beliefs are – or the lack thereof – we all have our unique paths, none of which are right or wrong. Right and wrong are merely projected judgements. If we are being our naturally loving selves and living divinely realised lives, we accept that everyone has the right to choose their beliefs, just as we do.

When we hear stories of terrible acts performed by others in God's name, we need to ask ourselves if fighting is God's way. Is the separation and division of souls love? If we are judgemental or unkind, we are temporarily out of alignment with love, which, in turn, indicates a temporary separation from God. Think about it: when you say unkind words about another person, does it fill your soul with joy? All any of us truly want from life is to feel love, peace, and joy but when we judge another person for their beliefs, actions, or behaviour, are we embodying love? Does it make us feel love, peace, and joy within ourselves? Complaining, anger, judgement, unforgiveness, and bitterness do not come from the love within but from the ego. Being and feeling love at all times is a work in progress, but by becoming aware of who we are, how we behave and how we speak, we are taking a positive step towards making changes to be and feel more love and joy.

When we live in alignment with love, if we come into conflict with others, we are more tolerant and forgiving of their behaviours. We cannot change other people, but we can change and realign ourselves to face every situation with the source of our energies. When we do this, we feel more compassion and empathy towards our fellow beings as we acknowledge that they may be lost or misaligned within their souls.

Holding onto anger and resentment can only cause harm as hatred hurts the giver more than the receiver. It is the poison that will kill the joy within us.

GROWING WITHIN

Our Guiding Principles

What are our Guiding Principles? They are each person's set of golden rules, made up of our deep-rooted standards and values that, when set, guide us to where we truly desire to be and keep us en route. In essence, they are our very own commandments by which we live, reminding us what is right and wrong and preventing us from being lured away from our true selves. When we live life in accordance with our own Guiding Principles (GPs), we can experience inner peace, but if we make choices that go against them, we feel stressed and discontent.

The choices we make in life either take us towards inner peace or lead us away from it. When we use our GPs as personal satellite navigation systems, we radically improve our chances of arriving at our Dream Feeling destinations.

No matter what religion we are or how much faith we have, it is essential to our wellbeing that we follow our GPs and not someone else's because theirs will take us to destinations we were not expecting.

Having our own GPs means we can take the paths *we* choose and live in alignment with our higher selves. We inherently know what is right or wrong for ourselves, yet we still make poor life decisions as we listen to the world or our egos instead of our true soul selves. Writing your Guiding Principles will enable you to live by the standards you have pre-set to keep you on the right path, moving towards where *you* want to be, but if we follow society's standards instead of our own, we compromise our love, inner peace, and joy, essentially compromising our wellbeing.

When others enforce rules upon us, we often think of them as restrictions, but when we write the rules from a place of love within ourselves, we are in alignment with our truths and values. Your guiding principles will help you navigate yourself to your Dream Feeling and experience all of the treasures life has in store.

Here is a list of some of my Guiding Principles, reminding me who I am and how I choose to show up in my life. I am not perfect – no one is – but I do try to be my best self and live up to my core values.

My most valued Guiding Principle is to treat others as I wish to be treated by them, which I am always reminding myself to do. As I said before, life is a work in progress for every single one of us, but as long as we are consciously aware of how we treat ourselves and others, we are progressing, and progress equals happiness.

My Guiding Principles:

- To be a beacon of love and light in the world.
- To treat others as I wish to be treated.
- To treat everyone as my equal through practising humility.
- To be grateful for all I have and all I am.

- To be honest and trustworthy in all my relationships.
- To forgive, always.
- To be free from judgement.
- To be kind, loving, and thoughtful to all my fellow beings.
- To always use positive, clean language, being aware of the words I use.
- To treat my body with respect and feed it only nutritious foods.
- To be the kind of person people feel they can go to when in need.
- To treat others with kindness and respect and never talk down to them.
- To be bright, smiley, and cheerful, setting a good example for the world.
- To serve others to the best of my ability.
- To take responsibility for the wellbeing of others, as well as myself and my family.

Take some time to think seriously about who you are and who you want to be in the world. If you are not sure of your core values, pray or meditate on them and wait to receive the answers quietly. Prayer and meditation are powerful tools connecting us with the highest parts of ourselves: our souls. Remember: God is love and the source of your being; therefore, you, too, are love. As your GPs come to your heart and mind, write them in the table below, and use this as your Satellite Navigation System to keep you on track as you journey through life. When faced with life's decisions, ask yourself if they are in alignment with your higher self and your GPs before making your final decision.

- *My Guiding Principles:*

COUNTING MY BLESSINGS

Think of a time when you or your family received a blessing in some way. There may be one big blessing that comes to mind or many small occasions on which you felt God's hand in your life. Perhaps it was a moment of miraculous healing or a time when you had nothing but the universe miraculously provided for you and your family. Perhaps, when you gave up the hope of meeting a life partner or becoming a parent, the miracle appeared. Sometimes, we cannot explain why bad things happen, but it is equally challenging to explain the blessings and some things we initially perceive as challenges turn out to be the most precious gifts of all.

- *Recount one of the many blessings you have encountered in your life that has touched your soul and brought tremendous joy into your life.*

_____

_____

_____

- *Recount a difficult time that you thought would break you, but which you now recognise as a great blessing because it led you to something you would not have otherwise attained.*

_____

_____

_____

DAILY PRACTICE

Self-Belief

Faith in ourselves and our abilities, gifts, and talents is an essential part of living with more joy. Our God-given talents are within us for a reason: for us to share them and make a difference to the world. When we have the strong desire to do any good thing, we know these are our callings and reasons for being, but first, we must remove all of our limiting beliefs and replace them with a strong faith in ourselves, to trust in our abilities to make differences in the world, in any way we can. We can share our gifts with one person or a million – quantity is not the issue. It's whether we listen to the small voices within and follow the longings of our souls to live lives of meaning or whether we drag ourselves through life living only for ourselves. Imagine you are on a sinking ship, and you see a lifeboat with the capacity to hold every passenger aboard the sinking ship – do you get into the boat and row to safety, or do you go in search of other survivors? If we do not share our God-given gifts – even if that gift is being reliable friends – it is like rowing off to save your own skin without sharing your boat. It is not always easy to know how we make differences for other people and their lives, but we all matter, and we all have something valuable to give.

If we fear sharing our gifts – just like we fear losing our lives while rowing our empty boats to safety – we will come to the end of our lives with empty hearts and empty boats. This life is about what we can give and how we can lift those who walk beside us, no matter how insignificant we feel our gifts are. Even being a cheerful, smiley human being can brighten a room, but for us to do so, we must first take a leap of faith and be our true selves. This begins by having faith in ourselves.

Self-belief can be created by acknowledging and affirming that we are capable, gifted beings, each with our own unique talents but all equal in the eyes of God. Below, record all you are and all you want to be. We have to train our subconscious minds to have faith in our abilities and feel worthy of all good things. We are all embodiments of love, and we all possess the power to create happy lives for ourselves, but we have to affirm our faith in ourselves. By declaring, 'I am...' we acknowledgeing our worth. Loving ourselves and having faith in ourselves are expressions of gratitude for the gifts of our lives. By listing your positive beliefs about yourself – even if they are not a part of your current reality – and saying them each day, you will train your mind to develop faith in yourself.

For example, my list would look something like this:

- I am a happy and powerful divine being and co-creator of my reality.
- I am called upon to open my heart to the world, to share my knowledge and wisdom.
- I am on a spiritual path that lifts me to higher levels of awareness.
- I am rich in all of life's treasures.
- I am healthy in mind, body, and spirit.
- I am making a difference in the lives of others through my work.
- I am a good mother, shaping my children's lives to become reflections of their authentic selves.
- I am a beacon of love and light in the world.
- I am a good and kind human being.

The list can go on, but make yours personal for you. Faith in yourself is essential. Every good or bad thought about yourself, heard often enough, will come to pass, so choose your thoughts carefully. Trust in the source of love that created you. God does not make mistakes; all He creates is love.

I am...

_____

_____

_____

_____

_____

_____

_____

_____

Place this list where you will read it often to develop a deep faith in yourself, know your worth upon the Earth, and know that you matter!

BALANCE AND HARMONY

AS WE LEARN, SERVE, LOVE AND GROW,
BALANCE AND HARMONY WILL FREELY FLOW.

One of my morning mindset affirmations is 'I live a life of love, balance and harmony.' Second only to love, balance and harmony are absolute musts to live peacefully. In my view, happiness is living each day in peace, and I can only do that if I have the right flow of balance and harmony. Perhaps it is my age, but living a peaceful life sits pretty high up on my list of priorities. When we are in flow with life, we feel more relaxed and connected to the energy of our souls, living each day with purpose.

I do not feel as if I must strive for greatness in my life to be seen or valued by the world. However, I do feel the need to play my part as a force of love in the world. I know that for which I am here, and that I am doing that for which I was born, but for me to fulfil my purpose and calling, I need balance and harmony. When I tap into my inner peace, the flow of work and life comes with natural ease. I'm not saying that life is *always* easy, but I don't have to constantly push and strive to move forward. Balance and harmony keep life running smoothly, allowing me to live my life and do my work in peace.

When I explained the importance of balance and harmony to my children, I told them that, as a family, we all have to work together towards the same goal to run smoothly. I often tell them that our family is like a car, and each of us is a wheel. If one of the wheels does not move or play its part then the car can't run at its best; it will not run smoothly or with ease. The same goes for life. There must be some balance across all areas for it to flow with ease.

- When we are financially secure and have good relationships, but we are not healthy, do we run smoothly?
- If we are in good health and secure in our finances, but our marriages are falling apart, do our lives run smoothly?
- If we have healthy bodies and healthy relationships but struggle to pay the bills, can we live in peace and do our lives run smoothly?
- If we are fulfilling our life's purposes, but we are running on empty, do we have balance in life?

These are a few scenarios regarding how imbalance can affect our day to day lives. When we focus on one area too much and not enough on another, we disrupt the balance, become unstable, and risk break downs. The problem is that sometimes we get so sucked into a world of striving, competing, and comparing that we forget to stop to take the time to check. We often wait until we break down to bother looking under the hood to see what is going on and what needs attention. We willingly check our bank balances to ensure everything is running smoothly with our finances, but how often do we check up on the balance of our lives?

It is essential to implement regular life check-ups to reassess our responsibilities across all areas of our lives and look at whether we have them under control or if some areas control us.

It is said that with great power comes great responsibility, but life has taught me that the opposite is also true, that by taking full responsibility for our lives, we develop greater power. My observations of life may differ from yours, but looking back at my most challenging times, the thing that made me most unhappy was feeling powerless over how I felt. I felt trapped by my circumstances and like I had no control over the direction of my life. I was frustrated in feeling like I had no control over what was going on within myself or around me.

Despite my natural go-getter personality, when I lost all of my confidence in being a full-time mum, I lost all power over my life, or so I thought. I allowed myself to become a victim of my circumstances instead of being a hero, but once I took responsibility for my life, it changed profoundly, and I saved myself.

Stuff happens whether we are responsible for it or not; it is how we respond and react to situations that determine the outcome, not what happens. We have to take full responsibility for our lives, feelings, and actions. When we are in victim mode, we essentially hand the power to our abusers, be it other people, our circumstances, or our health.

What most of us cannot fully comprehend is the incredible power we each have within ourselves, but if we take 100% responsibility for ourselves, our lives, and our health, we regain that power. Playing the victim is like being passengers in our lives, having no control over where we are going, but if we play the heroes, we can climb back into the driver's seats of our lives. We may not be responsible for undesired circumstances or have the abilities to change them, but by acknowledging and accepting them as our own, we can take full responsibility. In doing so, we earn back our power, enabling us to continue advancing in the direction we choose. When we complain and blame outside factors or other people for the way we feel, we relinquish our powers. Believing that someone else is responsible for the states of our lives sends us the message that only they can make it right, but let's face it: when people hurt us so badly that we feel physical pain, what are the chances they'll walk back into our lives, fall at our feet, and beg forgiveness? Pain is pain, and it is only when we own it and take full responsibility that we change it into something that works for us instead of against us.

I do not deny that some people deal with tremendous physical and emotional difficulties that the majority of us can't even comprehend. I am saying that every single one of us can decide here and now to change the way we look at life, to enable us to bring more peace and joy into our hearts.

You may not be happy about where you presently are in your life, but remember that you are not a tree, and you do not have to stay where you are. We have far more power to change our lives than we think, but first, we must change our minds.

The late, great Wayne Dyer said, 'When you change the way you look at things, the things you look at change,' meaning that if we look at our lives and situations from different perspectives, the roads ahead will change.

Because God is everywhere and in everything, he is also in the hurdle we are currently tackling. When we look for love in every situation, we will find it, but equally, if we look for excuses and reasons to be resentful, we will find them also. We have to be consciously aware of that for which we are looking and acknowledging.

In Chinese philosophy, the concept of Yin and Yang is a widely known depiction of dualism. There is light in the dark and dark in the light – positive and negative principles exist in everything and everyone. One cannot exist without the other, so it's up to us to look at our lives differently and find the light in everything. It is not always easy, but when we focus on what we *do* have instead of what we *don't*, we open our eyes to all the blessings.

When we see what we can learn from difficult situations and how we can grow and become wiser, our lives can transform. We can use that wisdom to help others overcome the same difficulties because we have walked the path before them. The journeys we have taken on what might have been traumatic, treacherous paths qualify us to help others understand how to find easier ways. When we use our knowledge and experience to help others, we can turn life's traumas around to recognise them as blessings. We often hear stories of people using pain and loss to start charities to support the causes that, perhaps, have taken the lives of loved ones. They find ways to give back and make use of their pain and suffering to help others.

If we truly open our eyes, we will see the truth. Some people are born into this world with immense physical disabilities, yet they lead incredible lives, serving and inspiring others. They demonstrate that it's not what happens to us that affects us but how we respond to it.

No matter what we currently face – health problems, heartache, grief, financial difficulties, relationship issues, and so on – *we* have the power to change the way *we* look at things, and *we* can choose to see them as blessings instead of curses. When we change the way we look at things, the things we look at change.

RESPONSIBILITY

We each have the responsibility to create balance in our lives, not just for ourselves, but to keep the natural order of things. When we allow water to flow naturally, it is free to move and flow where it chooses. If we put up blocks and barriers, it puts on the pressure and has no choice but to be still, become stagnant, and place stress on whatever contains it. The nature of water is free-flowing, from ocean tides to rain cascading down the mountains into the rivers and streams. It is alive with nourishment and goodness to cleanse and nourish nature, bringing life to all. We, too, have a purpose to flow with pure, loving energy, nurturing those we touch as we go through life, but before we can do so, we have to remove the blocks to help us flow in harmony with who we are and take full responsibility for all areas of our lives, some of which are:

- personal fulfilment,
- personal relationships,
- family,
- work,
- health,
- finances, and
- 'Me' time.

PERSONAL FULFILMENT

No matter how successful, faithful, wealthy or healthy we are, balance is key to living in flow and harmony. Personal fulfilment is one of my top priorities, and that is not selfish. If I am to show up in life as the best version of myself for my family, I have to take care of me first. A lot of mothers, myself included, stop taking care of themselves when their children are born and end up so disconnected from themselves they get lost. Is that the example we want to set for our children in adult life?

Putting our lives, health, and personal fulfilment on the back burner shows those we love that our lives and happiness are not valued. How can we share our love and joy if we don't have any for ourselves?

When our cups are full of love and joy, lighting us up, the excess spills over and rains onto others around us. When we are satisfied, we radiate nourishment, love, and light, but when our cups are empty – or worse still, filled with resentment and darkness – either we have nothing to give or we shower negativity and resentment onto others.

Whatever we have within ourselves radiates to the people around us whether we intend it or not, so being on the path to personal fulfilment is paramount when creating balance and harmony within and around us.

People may question your reasons for seeking personal fulfilment, but if you know your intentions are pure and your actions come from a place of love, then what others say will not discourage you or hold you back in any way. When we listen to and use the passion within our souls, we express love for the gifts of our lives. When we listen to the whisperings of our souls and not our egos in our quests for personal fulfilment, we continually fill our cups, so they never run dry.

We were all born for specific reasons, and deep down, we all know what those reasons are. We feel it inside ourselves, but most of us push it deep down and quieten the yearnings of our souls. Our egos tell us we are not brave, virtuous, unique, or deserving enough in an attempt to protect ourselves from humiliation or failure, but we owe it to ourselves and those we love to be our true selves and live the lives we were born to live. To be the kind of person for which we were born and to love the way we are supposed to love.

If we keep pushing down the longings of our souls, our cups will run dry, and all of the passion and enthusiasm will fade away, leaving emptiness within.

As a mother to small children, I felt truly fulfilled, but as I said before, I had not considered my personal growth and progression. As my children grew, I felt like there was an imbalance within myself, but I brushed off the feeling and told myself it was common to feel redundant. The more time went on, the more insignificant I felt, but I continued to ignore the voice within. Instead of seeking a new path that would have kept me flowing smoothly, I kept quiet and pushed all of my sadness and insecurities inwards, losing myself in my negative thoughts until I became immobile. I stopped wanting to leave the house and refused to go shopping on my own. I reluctantly visited the shops in my local village to get food, but I was overwhelmed with anxiety and fear.

My relationship with my children was good because they were the only people I felt I could be my real self with, but to be honest, no one else knew what was going on inside of me. I could blame others and say nobody cared, but they were not mindreaders.

We are all so busy with our lives that we take everyone at face value and don't often try to build deep connections with others to know what is going on with them. So many people suffer in silence, allowing their doubts, fears, and sense of worthlessness to eat away at them.

When I hit rock bottom after life had thrown me a few slaps, punches, and finally, a wrecking ball, complete darkness fell. While my kids were at school all day, I'd spend hours just crying, sitting and eating my lunch with tears dripping into my food. I could see myself from an external perspective, but I felt powerless to do anything to change. I had completely lost my way and found myself wishing my life would fast forward to the end. Then, one day, I overheard one of my children say to himself, 'I want to die!'

Boom!

A second wrecking ball, but this one did the trick – I was finally awake!

Whatever you are going through at this moment in life, take responsibility for it. We cannot change the past or change what has happened, but we can take responsibility for how we want to feel and what we do from this moment forwards. Even if our lives run smoothly, we still have to maintain them and frequently assess what is going on within ourselves.

When we feel we play our parts in life, no matter how small, we nourish our souls and feel fulfilled, but we have to listen to the whisperings within, pay attention, and truly listen. We also have to regularly ask ourselves if we are living in peace, in our flow or being dragged along in the flow of someone else's life.

PERSONAL RELATIONSHIPS

This is an area to which we have to pay particular attention in our efforts to retain a life balance as it is often an area in which we become complacent. Perhaps because we feel safe and secure, we take our eyes off the ball, so to speak, or maybe it's due to the pace of the world in which we live. With all the distractions – technology is a huge one – even when we are in loving relationships and making time for each other, are we fully present? Do we communicate, truly giving each other our full and undivided attention? Are we so consumed with work or other daily activities that our minds are occupied by something else. even when we are together?

We can blame others and complain about the quality of our relationships, but it is down to us to improve them by taking full responsibility for them.

In Door #3, we talked about loving relationships, but in this section, let's look at how we can move forward when a relationship breaks down. This topic is challenging because it is hard not to take a broken relationship personally, particularly when you are the one left with a wounded heart. In my book for teens and young adults, *My Growing Heart,* I talk about my personal experiences with love. When I had to end a long-term relationship, it also broke my heart. As much as there is a lot of anger, resentment, and pain after a breakup, it's important to remember that in most cases, your ex will suffer to some extent, too. We may think those who break our hearts are heartless, but it must have taken great courage to speak up to reveal how unhappy they were. Perhaps they took the cowardly path and deceived you, but again, no amount of blaming and complaining can change the results. If you are holding anger and resentment inside of you, now is the time to let it go, no matter who was to blame. Blaming and reliving the pain and heartache over and over again in your mind will not turn the clock back, and the only one it harms is yourself. What's done is done, so take responsibility for yourself now and choose to take your life and happiness back into your own hands.

I am not saying that forgiveness is easy, but to restore your inner peace, you must let it go for *your* sake. Your life and happiness are *your* responsibilities and nobody else's. I know, from personal experience, what it feels like to be heartbroken. The feeling is that you will never recover from losing the love of your life, but the hard truth is that if s/he truly loved you, s/he would still be in your life, but s/he is not.

Getting over a broken heart was one of the hardest things I ever had to do in my life. When we do not love who we are as soul beings, when we do not know our worth, heartbreak can be devastating, which is why it is essential to love ourselves first. If not, heartbreak can feel like the death of a loved one, only somehow worse because of the rejection that comes with it. It's a double-whammy, so to speak, as we begin to question our worth. Why has he left me? Am I not loveable or attractive enough? What's wrong with me? What could I have done to make him stay? Was I too much? Should I have done more? Our insecurities come to the surface, but do we truly want to spend our lives with someone who doesn't love us for who we are?

Rejection from someone we love can feel personal, but we all owe it to ourselves to listen to our hearts and souls and not our egos. Perhaps, we, too, knew the relationship was going nowhere, but our egos hung tightly on in fear of being alone. It's also essential to ask ourselves whether we believe our loved ones deliberately intended to hurt us. They must have been in pain to some degree, too, because generally only *hurt* people hurt people.

Letting go and removing the pain of the past is essential to our well beings, but many people hang onto their broken hearts for years and sometimes even decades. Their past pain creates emotional blocks that affect all areas of their lives, preventing the flow of love that would reconcile the balance and harmony they crave. They allow the past and rejection to drive them in the present, but it gets them nowhere, and they wonder why they can't move on. It is when they take full responsibility for themselves and the ways they feel by starting to respond to life differently that they will be able to remove the blocks preventing the flow and regain some balance and harmony. There

239

may always be some love that remains, but by forgiving and letting go, joy can begin to flow back in, just as water flows.

Letting go doesn't necessarily mean we have to turn off our feelings. We cannot control whether we love another human being or not, so to move on, we have to change how we look at situations to change them. We can't switch off love because others no longer want us in their lives, but we can respond differently and adjust our ways of thinking. Let me explain my understanding.

When we experience breakups, we continually recount what went on in our minds. We either focus on the loving, once cherished feelings, replaying them over and over again, asking ourselves what went wrong, or we focus on all of the fighting and unkind words and deeds and replay them. Anger, resentment, or feelings of rejection can build up, causing us deeper levels of pain, but let's face it, none of this overthinking does anyone any good. I know – I have been there – and it got me nowhere, only making me feel worse. I found it hard to let go because I still had so much love for him, but holding onto my love was slowly killing me. There was no balance in my life at the time, and I concentrated all of my energy on how broken I felt. If only I knew then what I know now, I would not have had to suffer the way I did. So, I now share my personal understanding with you with the hope of helping you heal from your broken heart. Whether your broken heart is still fresh or you've been carrying it around for years, now is the time to let it go by using the power of your heart and mind.

Because love is not something we have but something we feel, we can't remove it. When we truly love someone, however, we love her unconditionally. If we fall out of love with someone, perhaps it wasn't unconditional love in the first place. True love is divine love and is, therefore, a part of us. If we truly love someone, we will set them free, as we want them to experience love and joy, whether that includes us or not. If we resent them or wish any form of unhappiness on them because they have hurt us, it's safe to say that our feelings were those of attachment or co-dependency, but not love.

You may still be carrying the pain of your ex's actions, but ask yourself whether it is your ego or your true self that is hurt. If your pain still runs deep, it is time to recognise that you are the one still holding on tightly to it, and you can choose whether to loosen your grip or let it completely go. The only way to restore balance and harmony in your life and your heart is for *you* to let go.

One way to free yourself from the pain of a lost love is to close your eyes and imagine you are a tree. You are tall and sturdy, growing out of the ground, nourished by the Earth from which the source of your love flows. That love is the very essence of who you are, and it, too, has to flow freely. Imagine that the love you have inside of you is being channelled back into the ground, towards the person who used to fill your heart. Release your love and light within, and imagine that person will receive your affection and be nourished by it. Let go of the pain and pressure that block the flow of loving energy within you and open the channel to release and receive love back into your soul, restoring the natural flow of love, balance, and harmony to your everyday life. All human beings share a connection through their souls. We are all made of the same divine energy and are connected in spirit, if not in body. We share love and divine energy in the same way we breathe the same air. When we fall in love, our souls connect, and we see beyond the surface. When the body disappears, the soul energy remains. After death, that energy returns to the ground, but we are all still connected.

When we lose loved ones through breakups, our souls are still connected, but instead of holding that love tightly to your chest, direct it through your souls and back into the ground to nourish your loved ones from afar. If you truly love them, their happiness is more important to you than having them in your life every day. Focus your mind on sending loving thoughts and light their way to bring joy to their lives.

I don't believe that people intend to hurt others or break their hearts – they are human, just as you and I, and they, too, are made of loving source energy. They are also divine beings, taking this journey through life, trying to navigate themselves back to their souls. We all make mistakes and bad choices, but ultimately, we are all love.

Restoring balance and harmony to your heart may not happen overnight, but by doing this practice, each step will bring you closer to freeing your soul.

FAMILY

Creating balance and harmony within our families takes consistent effort, not only because we have to live under the same roof most of the time but also because we tend to take out all of our frustrations on those we love the most. *Because* they are our family, we feel safe airing our thoughts and opinions, but are we showing up for them as our best selves, or are we or leaving them the dregs, that left-over sediment that remains at the bottom of the cup? Do we give the world the best parts and come home at the end of the day, empty or shaken up, ready to burst open as we walk through the door? Being there for our loved ones doesn't necessarily mean that we are there. What do I mean by this? Well, how often have you tried to speak to your partner, spouse, or kids when they are in the room with you, but nobody hears?

How often do you ask a question, and nobody acknowledges you even spoke? I can't speak to your experiences, but this often happens to me. With the world as it is today, we are all so busy and distracted by shiny objects that take our attention away, and we are not always fully present with our family and loved ones. If our relationships are not in flow, we become imbalanced, and we need to restore harmony.

Each member of our families has to take responsibility for his place and role. When we work together, we have a stronger sense of respect and love for each other. We all too often take our family members for granted. We may feel appreciation for them, but do we demonstrate or express it to them?

As a mother, it is my responsibility to teach my children to be self-reliant and not run around after them, serving their every need. Because my children are teenagers, I sometimes get, 'You are so cruel!' shouted at me. However, because I know it is my responsibility to teach them – and not their responsibility to love me – I continue to be 'cruel' by asking them to help out around the house. My children complain and say that their friends do not have to pull their weight at home, but I choose to believe that it is essential for their growth and development. If I spoil them and don't encourage them to work for what they want, how will they cope when they *do* have to work for a living?

When I was a teen, I thought my mum was a tyrant. Now, as I look back, I realise the value of my mum's parenting ideas. Apart from my first job as a teen, washing pots and pans in a hotel and hating it, I loved work. Sitting around doing nothing is, in fact, my worst pastime. I now meditate daily, but I must admit that it didn't come easily to me. Work, on the other hand, came naturally.

It's also *my* responsibility to teach my children how to eat well, protect themselves, be compassionate, serve, be kind, make the right choices, be polite, and teach them to take full responsibility for their lives.

It is also my responsibility to be the kind of person I would like my children to become – not only talk the talk – and *expect* them to grow into kind, compassionate adults; I must also walk the walk.

When it comes to our family members – such as our siblings, parents, and grandparents, regardless of age – we can all teach and learn from each other by setting good examples. I learn so much from my children. For example, my 13-year-old daughter came in excitedly from school the other day and said, 'I learnt something valuable today, Mummy. One of my friends wanted to speak to me in private, so I left my other friend for a few minutes to have a private conversation, but when I got back to my other friend, she was so angry, and she started shouting at me, saying that I was rude to leave her and it was unfair. So, instead of causing an argument, I just said to her, "You are right. I'm sorry." She didn't know what to say after that, and it all passed in a few seconds. Usually, she would have caused a big fuss, but knowing her, I thought I'd tell her she was right. It wasn't worth fighting over. So, I'm pleased with myself for working that out, and now, I have a secret weapon to dissolve arguments.'

I had to smile after she recounted her story. For a 13-year-old, she is very wise. I like to think that my influence has played a part, but I give her all the credit for her peace-making skills. She reminded me that I, too, could be more like her in certain family situations. My daughter taught me a few things that day, one of which was how essential it is to take responsibility for how we behave towards others.

We cannot change the way people respond to our actions or words, but we can change the way we react to theirs. When we take full responsibility for who *we* are and for the way *we* behave, we each fulfil our responsibilities as good and kind human beings.

WORK

Work and personal fulfilment go hand in hand for me. I sincerely believe that if we listen to our souls, acknowledge our passions, and follow our dreams to do what we love when it comes to what we do for a living, we never have to work a day in our lives so long as we choose to live harmoniously with our true desires. Work should be a joy – well, at least, the majority of the time. We spend around a third of our lives working, and it is our personal responsibility to spend our precious time doing something that brings us personal fulfilment. We all have our own unique gifts and talents for a reason. We have to value who we are and embrace the abilities and desires of our hearts. What one person loves to do might be another person's nightmare. Imagine how much happier we would be if everyone enjoyed their work.

We all know how it feels to be served by people who do not enjoy their work, don't we? We feel as if we are disturbing them or that we are an inconvenience. Even though we know that it's not about us, being faced with unenthusiastic personnel dampens our day with negative energy. We can decide not to take it personally, but it can still affect us in some way, especially if we are not having great days ourselves.

On the other hand, we also know how it feels to be served by someone with a smile. A smile has the power to make or break someone's day, and it costs absolutely nothing.

Whether you love your work or not, it is your responsibility to show up as your best self for those who surround you each day, from clients and customers to co-workers. By taking full responsibility for the way you show up, preferably with a smile, your days will be brighter, and that light will shine on everyone around you.

FINANCES

This is often an area for which a lot of us shun responsibility, but to gain balance and harmony in life, we must take full responsibility for our money matters. Money may not matter to us, but it is a governing fact of life, whoever we are, and the sooner we take responsibility for our finances, the sooner we can get control of our lives and attain balance.

Our number one responsibility when it comes to our finances is to live within our means. Thankfully, I have had this mentality ever since I was a little girl. I have two sisters, one was a spender, and the other was a saver, and I was a bit of both. The funny thing is that we have not changed. We have all led such different lives, but we have retained the same childhood habits when it comes to money. Our parents obviously taught us the same things, but it just goes to show how individual we are as beings.

The day I began earning money, I had to pay my parents for my keep. They took a portion of my wages to pay for my living costs every week. I thought it was unfair at the time as I didn't get much, to begin with, but they were secretly saving it up to give me later on when I needed it (oh, how I miss my amazing parents). I learned so much from their wise parenting as it taught me that we don't get anything for free in life.

Another major lesson I learnt from them was that I should only buy that for which I had the money upfront and not get into debt for things that were not essential.

This lesson seems too simple, but I had friends who built up thousands of pounds of debt on credit cards to buy things and do things for which they didn't have the money at the time. Why put an unnecessary burden on ourselves and our lives for the latest gadgets, handbags, or shoes, or to keep up with the Joneses, so to speak? We seek to fill the emptiness within ourselves and buy things to make us happy, but after the novelty wears off, the void consumes us once more.

When we connect with our love and inner peace, we no longer feel the need to fit in or feel as if we are missing out on life because of what we don't have. We no longer need to compare or feel the need to impress others using our possessions or social standing. Once on the journey of knowing and loving ourselves more and creating more inner joy, we no longer seek external validations for our worth.

We cannot find happiness in material items, but we continually buy and accumulate, trying to satisfy that emptiness within ourselves, but we can only fill that space with love for who we are and what we do every day.

I am by no means saying that we can no longer buy and appreciate beautiful things such as cars, shoes, or handbags, but I believe that we should only buy what we have the money to afford, and before we buy, we have to ask ourselves *why* we want them. Is it for us to enjoy, is it to impress someone, or to make ourselves look good in the eyes of others? We work hard for our money, so it is essential to spend it on what helps us enjoy our lives and not what we believe we should spend it on to fit in. I knew someone who used to get stressed out because of his wife's spending habits. He adored her and wanted her to have everything she wanted, but he desperately sought ways to earn more money so he would never have to say no to her. She was beautiful and a few years younger than him, so perhaps he feared she would leave him if he didn't provide the type of lifestyle she desired. However, between the weekly beauty treatments, hair appointments, and the latest trends, he started to fall into debt. I felt quite sorry for him, but they were both happy with the lives they had, so who was I to judge?

My point is that we have to look at how our finances affect our lives and wellbeing. If we get into debt over non-essential things, we need to step back to review the directions of our lives.

Are we spending to impress others to satisfy our egos, or are we living within our means and taking full responsibility? Are we working on improving our finances or just sitting around hoping for a pay raise or promotion? Are we actively doing something to get what we want from life, or are we merely buying lottery tickets and hoping for the best?

You may very well win the lottery, but I believe that you do not need to win the lottery because we each have the potential to gain financial freedom through making our own money doing what we love. I have faith.

HEALTH

Now, this is a biggie! If I am honest, I don't understand why this is such a big issue for so many, yet I would say that over 90% of the people I know experience issues in this area. I became a health coach at the beginning of my coaching journey because it brought me to tears to see so many people suffer, but after some time, I realised I was in the wrong business. I started my journey with so much passion, and I truly wanted to help people to turn their lives and health around, but the problem was that I desired it for others so much more than they did for themselves. That saddened me, but thankfully, I listened to the whispers of my soul, which led me to become a life coach.

I came to realise that the real reason people struggled wasn't necessarily to do with their love for food and alcohol, but their lack of love for themselves.

I felt for them and wanted to help, but I have learned from experience that we cannot help others unless they help themselves. In the same way that we cannot eat to nourish another person, it is impossible to do anything to aid someone to get his health in order unless *he* is determined to work for it himself.

My husband is a Chinese medicine practitioner, and I used to try to persuade people to use his services because I knew that he could help them. Despite my best intentions, he used to get annoyed with me and say, 'Nadia, if they want help from me, they have to ask me, and they have to decide for themselves.' I didn't quite understand it at the time, but what he was saying was that until they were ready to make changes to their lives and health, there was no point in wasting my time or theirs. He was the one who helped me all those years ago when I was suffering from chronic asthma. When we first met, he was working in a bar, but he always wanted to study oriental medicine. Because his love for me was so strong, my suffering was the push he needed to start doing what he knew he had inside him. If I had been well and had not nearly lost my life, perhaps he wouldn't be doing that for which he was born.

God works in mysterious ways. First, he whispers, and if we don't hear, he shouts, but often we need a vigorous shake before waking up completely, just as I said when we looked through Door #7, *The Power of Faith*.

As a side note: my husband also recognises that his work is a gift that comes through him, and his ability to heal runs so much deeper than his hard work, knowledge, and experience that there is a greater force,

249

a divine flow of energy, working through him that he cannot explain, but he listened to the callings of his soul and leant into his purpose and reason for being.

Most of us have a habit of making poor excuses in all areas of our lives that do not run smoothly, but we have to take *full* responsibility for them, especially our health and lifestyles. What excuses do you use? *I don't have enough time to cook fresh meals. Obesity runs in my family. I am big-boned. It is middle-age spread. Smoking keeps me calm. I've had three children. I'm too tired to exercise.*

We can no longer use the excuse that we don't know what to do because there is an overflow of information out there at our fingertips. Yes, it can be challenging to know who to listen to and which advice is best, but we all know that eating good quality food, drinking water, getting out into the fresh air, exercise, and rest is what we need. It's not rocket science, but do we give this area of our lives the time and energy it deserves? The time and energy that *we* deserve?

When you hear yourself make an excuse, remind yourself that these are only untruths you tell yourself. People have overcome many physical challenges despite others telling them there is no hope because of their faith, hard work, and lifestyle. I've had others inform me there is no cure for asthma, which may be true, but with a life and health overhaul I overcame all of my symptoms, and now I live a better quality of life. I am strong and healthy because I took my health into my own hands and turned my life around.

I spent years in awe, watching other people run and wishing I could run, too, but I had the limiting belief that I could not run due to asthma. Even though I was symptom-free, I still used asthma as an excuse for not trying, but why was I so scared? Perhaps I was afraid of not being able to breathe, failing, and being embarrassed – what if I made a fool of myself? Whatever excuse I made was an untruth. It was a story I had made up in my head that I had convinced myself was true. Once I began to run a few metres at a time while out walking, I got stronger, and within a few weeks of consistent practice, I was out and running for 20 plus minutes without having to stop. In 2018 alone, I ran the equivalent of over 11 marathons from running only a few kilometres every week. How awesome is that? This would never have happened if I had not changed my limiting belief and continued telling myself lies.

What stories do you tell yourself that stop you from taking full responsibility for your quality of health? There is no reason to lie to yourself. By neglecting your health, not only do you hurt yourself, but you also hurt those who love you, care for you, and who want to feel your presence on the Earth for as long as possible. Because we influence the people within our reach whether we choose to or not, if our children see us disregarding our health, they, too, will think theirs is of no value. Is that the example we want to set?

We also have to take an honest look at our lifestyles and identify what prevents us from moving forwards. We have to rid ourselves of excuses by owning up to the addictions and bad habits that destroy our chances at health and happiness. This begins by acknowledging where we need to change and forgiving ourselves for our pasts. We cannot change what we have done up to this point, but we can change what we do from this moment forwards. There is no shame involved in self-compassion.

The past is history; the future is a mystery, but for your own sake, make today the first step to victory. Every single one of us is of great worth, and we all deserve to be treated lovingly, especially by ourselves. We may have told ourselves how hard it is to give up our addictions, but is that because we don't want to let go? Is it because we don't value or love ourselves enough? Do we use that to distract us from what goes on within ourselves? Do we use them to bury the pain we cannot shake?

Whatever our reasons for hanging onto these life-damaging habits, we have to face up to our truths and take full responsibility for them; own them. No one else is to blame, but with self-compassion, love, and a lot of faith in loving source energy, we can overcome them, but before we change our habits, we need to change our minds and the ways we think.

In my late teens, I started smoking, and by my early twenties, I was smoking between 20 and 30 cigarettes a day (and wondering why I had developed asthma). I knew smoking wasn't helping me, but let's be honest here – I made asthma happen. I didn't ask for it, but it came as a result of not only neglecting my body, but abusing it. For as long as I can remember, I have had trouble breathing, and I could never run very far, even as a child, so asthma was inevitable when I began smoking. Both of my parents smoked, both of my sisters, and almost all of my friends, but it wasn't peer pressure that got me started – it was spite.

I have always had a mind of my own, so as much as I wanted to fit in, smoking wasn't for me. At 15, my friends used to smoke, but I'd sit happily next to them, sucking my beloved thumb. I only began smoking to spite my mum.

When I had been out with my friends, she smelled smoke on my clothes and accused me of smoking. Even after defending myself, she never believed me, so after the continued accusations, I thought that I might as well start because I was being punished for it anyway. Just think: that spiteful teenage streak nearly cost me my life.

I used to have my inhaler and cigarettes sitting next to each other so if I couldn't breathe and I wanted a cigarette, I could take a puff of my inhaler first. Looking back now, I think about how downright stupid I was, but there is always a price to pay, and I paid it.

Making the conscious choice to feed ourselves unhealthy things is like playing Russian roulette with our health, so why do we still play?

All I needed to stop my smoking habit was a fright. Not being able to breathe was somehow not scary enough for me, as I hadn't realised how ill I was making myself.

One evening, I went to a friend's clairvoyance party. The lady took one look at me and said, 'If you don't stop smoking, you are going to end up in hospital.' Whether she could see my future, or she saw me wheezing and smoking and thought it was my inevitable fate, I will never know, but I threw away my cigarettes then and there, and I have not smoked since. It took me a few years, time in hospital, and a few near-death scares before deciding to get my life back and take *full* responsibility for my health. Stopping smoking was only a small part of what needed to change.

I know it sounds crazy, but at the time, I honestly had no idea I had so much control over my health. I believed there was no cure for asthma, and I had no idea that what I was eating had such a profound effect on my body. Bearing in mind that this happened over 25 years ago before it was common knowledge that sugar, dairy, and refined foods are detrimental to our health and wellbeing.

Once I stopped smoking, I discovered how powerful it made me feel to overcome my addiction, and in doing so, I proved to myself that I could do anything if I put my mind to it. I then became addicted to knowledge-seeking, and I loved learning about the best ways to take care of my body. Stopping smoking empowered me to rid my body of the illness that had wormed its way into my life.

It was a slow journey back to good health, but within two years, my body was fighting fit, I was medication-free, and I had the evidence to prove that all things were possible if we believed and did everything we could to make them happen.

I always carry an inhaler with me, even now, but I have not used one in years. Having an inhaler on me at all times also reminds me not to take my health and life for granted.

The reason I share this story is to activate an awareness of your own health and wellbeing, to encourage you to check in with yourself and question your habits – do they contribute to your good health or pave the way to your demise? We can blame our DNA, our families, our ages, our lack of time and resources, but ultimately, most of us are in charge, and it is our actions that determine the quality of our health. Granted, life can present us with illness even when we have taken good care of ourselves, but we can still decide whether to allow our health challenges to break us or make us.

'ME' TIME

A few years ago, I did not understand the importance of 'Me time'. When my children were small, I didn't even know who 'Me' was, never mind make time for her. Due to the lack of attention I paid myself, I ended up tipping the balance, and my whole life came crashing down around me. When we neglect to nourish our souls, we become weak, and our energy dries up, just as plants dry up without water to sustain them.

Filling ourselves up first is essential, but most importantly, we must do so with pure, loving energy because love is the energy of our souls that give us life. Without it, we are merely empty shells living unfulfilling lives. When we make 'Me time' a common practice in life through taking time to be still, we allow ourselves to tap into those sources of love and recognise who we are and why we are here.

As I write this book, it reminds me how blessed I was to experience hard times in my life, as they broke me open and forced me to look inside where I discovered that deep down, I was full of love, light, and joy. I have shared only some of my challenges here with you in this book, but I, like many of you, have many other wounds that have scarred me deep to my core. Some past struggles we are open about while others stay locked away in our private, little vaults where we let them eat away at our wellbeing. My life's struggles may not run as deep compared to some, but we cannot compare adversities. We each have our demons to vanquish and our mountains to climb, but we must face them instead of brushing them aside and denying their importance, denying *our* importance.

Thankfully, after being broken open, I started putting myself and my wellbeing back on my list of priorities. I began making conscious efforts to get to know and understand who I was, but I could only do this by making time for myself. Once I started doing the inner work, which I have detailed in this book, it allowed me to alter my perspective and take deliberate action to improve my quality of life. Consequently, my life began to change.

Each of my difficult times provided the slap or punch in the face necessary to wake me up and get me back on track. There have also been times when life has thrown me a wrecking ball to the side of my head, forcing me to change the direction of my life.

I can say, hand on heart, that they were *all* blessings in disguise. I believe that every slap, punch, and wrecking ball happened *for* me as an experience from which to learn and grow. I always knew that I would write a book one day, but I had no idea what that book would be about, yet here I am, opening up my soul and sharing a part of myself to help others gain a clearer perspective in life.

I would never have reached this point if I had not experienced the dark side of my soul and taken the time to know myself and learn to love the divine soul that resides within me.

Keeping balance and harmony of mind, body and soul means continually feeding each one with fresh, nourishing fuel to keep it flowing with ease and grace in the face of adversity.

- Mind: feeding it positive, uplifting thoughts through gratitude and keeping an honest and accurate perspective.
- Body: feeding it sufficiently with clean, healthy food, exercising, fresh air, rest, and keeping it hydrated with water.
- Soul: feeding it with peaceful, quiet prayer or meditation, allowing love to flow through us and through kindness, service, and love for ourselves, as well as others.

I make a point every day to schedule in 'Me time' as I talked about previously. I wake up early to do my gratitude practice, nourish my mind and start my day with a full tank of gratitude, love, and peace before my children even get up. My morning ritual has become a part of me now. Some people say they cannot function in the morning without their coffee, and I feel the same way about my morning ritual. In the past, if I ever skipped a day, I felt unprepared and off-balance all day, so my gratitude practice is my 'coffee'.

No matter how busy I am, I also take time every day to get away from everything and everyone and go for a walk in nature, or during the summer, have a long swim *by myself.* We all need that time and space to stop and listen to our inner soul being. We all need our love and attention, too. When we put others first, we neglect our relationships with ourselves and with our Creator.

For me, my daily walk is equivalent to prayer and meditation in movement; I take in the beauty of the world in which we live and feel the elements on my skin, be it the Sun, wind, rain, or snow. I could easily make some good excuses not to go – too hot, too cold, too windy, too tired, too wet, no time – but taking time for me is the one thing that brings me back to myself, grounding me. Many people have a glass of wine or the like to unwind, but I recommend getting out into nature, as not only does it nourish our minds and bodies, but it replenishes our souls.

GROWING WITHIN

We all experience imbalance and disharmony at times, but when we keep regular checks on the running of our minds, bodies and souls, we are less likely to find ourselves stranded, broken, and alone. We regularly check up on our families, pets, gardens, homes, and cars, but what about ourselves? What happens when *we* do not run smoothly?

In this section, it is time for you to analyse the significant areas of your life to check for any blockages or an imbalance by giving your lives a Four-A check-up:

- acknowledge the challenge;
- accept responsibility;
- act; and
- aftermath.

By taking an honest look inwards and answering the questions below, you'll clarify which areas of your life could do with some work. In doing so, you take personal responsibility for change and acknowledge the actions you need to take. You will then be able to see that you have power over your quality of life. By looking ahead at the possible aftermath of *not* taking personal responsibility, you can make a more conscious decision about how you want to proceed in life. After all, your life will only get better when you take responsibility for it.

Personal Fulfilment

- *Acknowledge: What are your dreams and aspirations for life (no matter how far they are from your current reality) that you tell yourself are not available or attainable to you? What are your current beliefs about this?*

_____

_____

_____

- *Accept Responsibility: Who has the power to bring your dreams and aspirations to fruition? What steps do you need to take to realise your dreams and fulfil your potential to create happiness and personal fulfilment?*

_____

_____

_____

- *Act on It: What actions could you take to move you one, five, or 20 steps closer to feeling personal fulfilment in your life?*

_____

_____

_____

- *Aftermath: How will you feel in the future if you do nothing to change the direction of your life now?*

_____

_____

_____

Personal Relationships

- *Acknowledge: Does your love life light you up and bring you joy? What would an ideal relationship look and feel like to you? How do you feel about your current situation?*

_____

_____

_____

- *Accept Responsibility: Who is responsible for the way you feel in your current situation, and what can you do to invite more love, kindness, and fun into your life to deepen your relationship or point you in the right direction?*

_____

_____

_____

- *Act on It: What are you going to change to feel more joy and love in your life?*

_____

_____

_____

- *Aftermath: How will you feel in the future if you do nothing to change the quality of your personal relationships?*

_____

_____

_____

Family

- *Acknowledge: How much undivided attention, time, effort, energy, and love do you dedicate to nurturing your family relationships? Are you treating them the way you would like to be treated?*

_____

_____

_____

- *Accept Responsibility: How can you improve your relationship with your family? What changes do you need to make in yourself and in your life to make that happen?*

_____

_____

_____

- *Act on It: What steps are you going to take towards becoming a better version of yourself? How will you show up authentically and improve the quality of your family life?*

_____

_____

_____

- *Aftermath: How will you feel in the future if you do nothing to change the quality of your family relationships?*

_____

_____

_____

Work

- *Acknowledge: How can you use your natural gifts and talents to improve the world, whether you help people, animals, or the environment? If you could choose to spend your days doing what you love and getting paid for it, what would you do? What are you passionate about that sparks joy and enthusiasm within you?*

_____

_____

- *Accept Responsibility: What is holding you back from doing what you love? What adjustments do you have to make within your mindset and life to make your dream work (whether paid or unpaid) a reality? What new skills or qualifications do you need to gain to enable you to do what you love and get paid for it?*

_____

_____

- *Act on It: What can you do today to take you a step closer to spending your days doing what you love? What information do you need to gather to help you to understand where you can go from here?*

_____

_____

_____

- *Aftermath: How will you feel in the future if you do nothing to change the course of your life and continue living life as you do today?*

_____

_____

_____

Health

- *Acknowledge: How do you feel about the state of your health and the shape and size of your body? What current habits prevent you from living at optimum levels of strength and vitality? What needs to change?*

_____

_____

_____

- *Accept Responsibility: Who is responsible for the quality of your health, and what habits need your attention? What do you need to start doing to give yourself the best chance at creating a healthy body to make you look and feel energised?*

_____

_____

_____

- *Act on It: What three things are you going to implement, starting right now, that will take you closer to living a long and healthy life?*

_____

_____

_____

- *Aftermath: How will you feel and look in five, ten, or 20 years if you stay on this route and continue with your present habits?*

_____

_____

_____

Finances

- *Acknowledge: How secure do you feel about your finances at the moment? What amount of debt do you have, and who do you rely on to support you?*

_____

_____

_____

- *Accept Responsibility: What steps do you need to take to gain freedom from debt, enabling you to prepare a secure future with minimal financial worries?*

_____

_____

_____

- *Act on It: What changes do you need to make to take you a step closer to being financially secure?*

_____

_____

_____

- *Aftermath: How will your life look and feel in the future if you do nothing to change the current state of your finances?*

_____

_____

_____

'Me' Time

- *Acknowledge: How much time do you spend on yourself on a daily, weekly, or monthly basis, taking time out to learn, grow, nourish your soul by being in nature and spending time looking within, communing with and getting to know your soul self?*

_____

_____

_____

- *Accepting Responsibility: Who is responsible for the matters of your heart, mind, body, and soul, and what has to change to ensure your long-term wellbeing?*

_____

_____

_____

- *Act on It: To what daily or weekly practices are you willing to commit that will ensure your emotional wellbeing, be it prayer, meditation, walks in nature, reading books, or learning new practices? What can you start doing today to help you gain and maintain a sense of inner peace and infinite love?*

_____

_____

_____

- *Aftermath: What will your future look like if you neglect to make positive changes and make time to nourish your soul?*

_____

_____

_____

COUNTING MY BLESSINGS

Thus far, we have taken a profound journey within, facing the truth and taking an honest look at our lives to awaken us to the power we hold. By accepting responsibility in all areas of our lives, taking practical action, even in the smallest of ways, we can create more balance and harmony, and we can also count our blessings.

List three things or situations that bring love, peace, balance, and harmony to your present life. Some examples include sitting in your garden with a cup of tea on a beautiful day, listening to the birds;

cuddling up with your children, reading them bedtime stories; going for walks in nature; meditation or prayer; listening to the sound of the sea as you walk along the shore; and watching the sunset on a beautiful evening.

1. _____

2. _____

3. _____

DAILY REGULAR PRACTICE

Life MOT

Instead of daily practice, in this chapter, I introduce you to an exercise you can do weekly or monthly. It's a glance at the scales to check the balance and harmony in your life and keep you on track. When we track our progress in life, checking our compasses regularly to make sure we are going in the right directions, we are less likely to lose our ways.

To avoid finding ourselves lost and afraid, we can keep constant eyes on where we are and where we want to be. Without a compass, it is easy for us to steer off course. Even if we are only off by a couple of degrees, we can ultimately end up somewhere we don't intend to be.

Write a list of all the significant areas in your life, including those we have covered already, and ask yourself where they currently sit on a scale from one to ten, ten being an area that needs no improvement. Areas with a low score remind you that they need more attention to balance the scales and smooth out any bumps on the road of your life. Take a few minutes every week or month to give yourself an MOT (Measure of Tenacity) to keep you on track and prevent your life from breaking down.

MOT

Significant Area of Life	Rate of Satisfaction on a Scale From 1 to 10
Personal Fulfilment	
Personal Relationships	
Family	
Work	
Health	
Finances	
'Me' Time	
Friendships	
Other	

TRUST YOUR SOUL

TRUST IN THE ENERGY OF YOUR SOUL.

All of us, no matter who we are, how others see us, or how we see ourselves, are pure and perfect souls at our core. Because we were all born from the same loving source, we are all whole and complete soul beings. Our doubts and fears began to enter into our lives only when we lost sight of that truth, stopped trusting in our soul selves, and started placing that trust in the physical world. Imagine that God is the Sun, and we are its rays which shine light and warmth onto the Earth. We have tremendous powers to give and sustain life because of who we are at our cores. We bring life to the world through procreation, but due to the clouds, we cannot always see the sources of our power or understand who we are as soul beings. We go through life without knowing who we are or why we are even here, but regardless, we naturally and instinctively sustain human life. Some of us have come to learn this truth and know who we are. We know that when we cannot see the Sun, we can look inwards to feel that source of love within

271

our souls. Some become distracted or blinded by the ego-led world and forget who they are, but we are all rays of sunshine whether we recognise it or not. Our job here on Earth is to remember to shine and stay connected to the source of our love by trusting in the divine whisperings of our souls.

We have spent most of this book talking about how we have the power to create joy within ourselves and that we are co-creators of our lives, but we also need to put our trust in divine hands and know that all things, past and present, are just as they should be.

Every single thing that happens is meant to be and benefits us in some way. Practising gratitude and trusting God are the ultimate gifts we can give ourselves. We don't have all the answers, but surrendering and trusting in a greater power enables us to free ourselves from crippling fear by allowing our lives to unfold organically.

We may feel as if life has been unfair to us, that we have been singled out, but we have to trust that one day, all things will be made known to us, and everything will become clear. Some people have had to go through unimaginable heartache and had more than their fair share of pain, but no one knows why. All I can tell you is that all experiences, good and bad, shape us into the beings for which we were destined. You may be thinking, 'It's okay for her to say that because she hasn't had to go through what I have,' and perhaps you are right, but it is at these times that we have to have faith that all of our sufferings are part of a larger plan.

Because we are all blessed with free will, we can choose whether to use our experiences to learn and grow or allow them to drag us down. We have the freedom to use our experiences to help others by being lights for them to find their ways. Alternately, we can cast shadows and be prisoners to the darkness. The choice is entirely ours, but experience has taught me that, through suffering, we awaken from dormant states of living.

Some of us have experienced – or continue to experience – feelings that question what the point is of it all, going through the motions of life by eating, working, and sleeping, but never feeling truly alive. Looking back at my life, I do not doubt that every pruning I experienced preceded the most beautiful blossoming and abundant fruiting that nourished, lifted, and sustained me in some way. My experiences and the teaching I have experienced have taught me that suffering is a necessary part of our personal development, not as a way to test our faith or worth, but purely to ensure our growth and remind us of our humanity.

I think of life as if God has placed us in the middle of a jungle. We each have a vehicle (our body), a map (spiritual teachings), access to a walkie talkie (prayer and meditation), and our intuition (divine whispers), and the goal is to find our ways back to our sources. We are all here to learn and experience, to rediscover our divine natures and become fully aligned with our purposes and reasons for being. Each of us is a capable, worthy, and loving being, but it's up to us how we live our lives. There is teaching all around us, and we are free to seek out the truths of who we are for ourselves. That being said, some of the most influential teachings unexpectedly shows for us in the form of adversity, but they are all lessons to help us grow. On this journey back to our sources, we learn patience, empathy, humility, compassion, and love, but to truly understand them, we first have to experience them. Once we gain an understanding of these life lessons, we have two choices:

1. to be grateful for the lessons, learn from them, and share our knowledge and wisdom with others, reaching back and holding out a hand as a guide for them, shining lights on their paths, and

2. to allow the adversities and the difficult life lessons to destroy us, as we give up on life and sit around, waiting for our time here on Earth to come to an end.

I, for one, actively seek to enjoy my time here and choose to live with gratitude. In my darkest times, I felt powerless and thought that my only option was to accept my life by waiting it out. Thankfully, I was blessed with a wake-up call that took me down another path of learning and self-discovery, which led me here.

They say that where there's a will, there's a way, but perhaps, in my case, where there's a why there's a way would have been more accurate, as I did not possess much will. What I did have was a great love for my children and the need to set a good example for them. They needed a rock on which to build to support their foundations, but at the time, I had broken into so many pieces that I more closely resembled sand, and we all know what happens when we build on sand.

Even though I didn't value my life at the time, I cared immensely for my children and placed great value on theirs. They were my 'Why', and in recognising this, I found a 'Way'.

When we go through the pain, we feel as if no one knows what it feels like, but what I later discovered when I opened up to people about my feelings was that I was not alone. Since then, almost every person to which I speak has gone through similar experiences of deep personal suffering.

Because of my love for my children, I gathered the strength within my soul to sustain me, and I would not allow myself to surrender to the darkness. I found my way out, and now, when clouds come between me and my source of light, I know that they, too, will pass.

I continue to seek out the right teachers, either in person or through books and courses, and I understand that my life, like everyone else's, is a work in progress.

I love talking to older or wiser beings, hearing their stories, and gaining knowledge and understanding from their life experiences. Those who have walked this path before have so much to teach us, allowing us to make wiser decisions and avoid repeating our mistakes, not that we always listen.

I choose to share what I have learned, not only because I believe it is my moral obligation to do so but also because my soul longs to serve.

We all have something valuable to teach others through our unique circumstances. All we have to do is speak our truths in whichever way we can, simply by opening our hearts for others to see our souls, so we can learn from each other.

If I can ease the suffering in a handful of souls in my lifetime, even just a little, my past suffering and the countless hours I spend writing will not have been in vain.

I have been blessed with life for a reason, and so have you. My intention is not only to make my life count but to do so with abundant joy. Because I am no stranger to the dark, I know how it feels to suffer, but I also know there is a way out, and my work can light the path to pave the way for others.

You are free to use the lessons I have shared with you in this book, but equally, you may also discard them. All I ask is that you remember that all things are possible for those who believe, so have faith and trust that all will be well.

If my book does not speak to your soul, someone else's will, so don't stop seeking out life lessons and teachers, and never stop believing that you will find your way back to the warmth and light of the Sun. When you align with your source and trust, the right teachers will appear in your life.

Each of us takes the same journey, and we all do what we can to find our ways, not only enabling us to survive but to live the best lives we believe there are. Some of us know there are no limits to the kinds of life we can co-create, and others doubt that life can be anything more than it is, but if we can dream it, I believe we can create it. I have come to understand that if we can focus our energies on envisioning a brighter tomorrow, we can make it happen. Our only limits are our imaginations.

I have a big vision for my life and a steadfast determination to help others create emotional freedom by providing a way for them to get through the storms of life. Doing so allows me to feel as if I am playing my part in the world by sharing a part of myself.

TRUSTING OURSELVES

Subconsciously, we trust our bodies, even if we don't think we do. For example, if we cut or wound ourselves, we trust that, in time, our bodies will heal. We don't understand how we do it, but we don't become fearful or worry that our wounds will never heal. We do all we can to promote the healing process by taking appropriate action: cleaning it, covering it up, and maintaining cleanliness to ensure bacteria-free environments and avoid infections. We do what we can and then sit back and trust.

There is no point in worrying about something over which we have no control. We have to surrender to the invisible healing power within us.

If we are distrustful and continue to open our wounds to examine them, we can hinder the healing process, whether they are wounds of the body or spirit, so we generally trust our bodies, but do we trust our abilities to heal our emotional wounds? By trusting in our abilities to work through things no matter the outcome, we begin developing more peace within. Being aware of the things we tell ourselves is a vital component to living happier existences. Words have powerful energies and can damage us if we allow them to penetrate our psyches. The stories we tell ourselves influence our self-perception, so we must choose our words wisely.

When we tell ourselves that we are capable, resilient, loving, and confident beings who live lives of purpose, this is what we will be.

On the other hand, by calling ourselves weak, useless, and worthless beings, this is what we allow ourselves to become, regardless of our capabilities and purposes. Any self-talk heard enough times, kind or unkind, will become cemented in our minds and either support or impede our growth and progress.

So many of us are our own worst enemies and harshest critics. We sabotage our wellbeing without even realising that *we* are the ones throwing spanners in the works of our happiness. Regularly putting ourselves down and not trusting in our abilities can rapidly develop into habits without us realising, but once we begin to open our awareness and make conscious efforts to speak using kind and loving words, we can quieten the inner critics and begin to love and trust in ourselves more. Ralph Waldo Emerson said, 'Self-trust is the secret of success,' and I would have to agree. If we can't trust ourselves, who can we trust? The reality in life is that we can only truly rely on ourselves, but if we don't trust ourselves, then what?

I never used to trust my judgement, but I now recognise that I was just scared of making a mistake. Now I call it fear, but then I called it being indecisive, which seemed like an endearing character flaw I could not change. In reality, I was so insecure with myself that I doubted my ability to make my own decisions and ended up letting others choose for me. That way, others would not judge and change their opinions of me based on my choices, but in time, living this way led to a feeling of complete powerlessness.

As I write this book and explain how I felt at various points of my life, it sounds as if I am two people, one resilient, determined, and powerful being and another timid, insecure, and weak, depending on the situation – don't we all have these opposing character traits within us that can make life so confusing and challenging at times? This polarity is the constant conflict between our soul selves and our ego selves.

I talked about this earlier in the book, but let's clarify how to differentiate between our soul selves and our ego selves.

- Our soul selves are pure, loving, kind, and powerful beings. They do *everything* with love because they function in alignment with the source.
- Our ego is the frightened part of us that sits opposite to love. It seeks validation, wants to own, accumulate, be right, and succeed by worldly standards due to the fear of never being enough.

I believe our earthly goals are to connect and align with our soul selves and silence the overactive egos. We are humans, and egos are a part of our human forms.

However, *we* are free to choose how we live our lives, whether we feed and listen to our soul selves or our ego selves.

By feeding and listening to our soul selves, we will be free to live with inner peace and joy as we partake in life's true treasures, but if we only feed and listen to our egos, we trap ourselves in a cycle of never feeling quite good enough.

We can temporarily satisfy our egos through attaining worldly success, but as soon as the novelty wears off, we seek to achieve the next level of success, always striving but never quite arriving. We think we will be happy, have inner peace, and find that for which we are looking when we reach our goals. Whether it is winning awards, gaining qualifications, having X amount of followers, earning X amount of money, or looking a certain way, even if we succeed in reaching those goals, our egos will never be satisfied. We fail to fill our emptiness meaningfully, and self-worth slips through our fingers once more. All we truthfully seek is a deep inner connection with our true, loving soul selves which dwells not in fear but love.

To create love and peace within, we have to let go of the ego and develop self-love and self-trust. Letting go does not mean that we have to give up all of our possessions and live a pauper's life. It's about understanding that by trusting and aligning with ourselves as soul beings, recognising that we are divine, we become unattached to our material things and/or the lifestyles we live with, which we often use to validate our worth as humans. We understand that material things, such as titles and labels, exist independently, outside of who we are. We can still enjoy the material things, which undoubtedly enriches our lives while acknowledging that what we possess does not define us. We hear of rich and famous people taking their own lives, which seems ludicrous to us because, in our eyes, they have it all: money, success, fame, recognition, and respect. But if they are disconnected from their soul selves and lack a deep connection, peace, and fulfilment in their souls, they will still have a sense of emptiness within.

We choose whether to be prisoners to our egos or realign with our soul selves and fly freely.

When we do the inner work of learning who we are as soul beings, trust comes naturally. For most of my life, I was insecure and needed constant reassurance that I was loved and valued. Even when my life was going according to plan, I still felt empty inside because I was unaware of the ego/soul conflict going on within me, and there was always that inner void, the feeling that something was missing. Something *was* missing – it was self-love and self-trust.

After taking the journey I ask you to take here, I can stand proudly and say, 'I am whole.' I continue to strive to keep my ego-led thoughts quiet and recognise them as thoughts and not truths. They manifest themselves as judgements or insecurities. To counteract these thoughts, I continually remind myself that I am a divine spiritual being and that every person who crosses my path is my soul brother or sister.

When I remind myself that we are all one with the Universe and possess divine love within, I allow myself to live in a place of love and compassion instead of fear. When I experience fearful thoughts, I remind myself that I am a loving, compassionate being – not a frightened, ego-led being – which helps me realign with my soul.

I am stronger now than ever before, and I can promise you that if you take this journey and stay on this path, you will be more resilient, too.

Every small step is a step forward, which, in turn, is progress. You will learn to trust the whisperings of your soul that will lead you to the inner light, no matter how dark it gets. I know that I will still have to face adversity in my life, as will you, but the difference is that now I have all the tools at hand, not only to protect myself but also to dig my way back up to the surface if I ever fall into a pit of darkness again. I trust in God, my divine source of love, and I trust in my ability to work things out. With my strength, courage, and God's hand in mine, when I fall, I trust that I will always rise again.

Trust and Let Go

Letting go is an essential part of setting ourselves free and living happier lives. It takes a lot of faith and trust to let go, but once we build the courage, we can spread our wings and fly. If we continually hang on to people, things, the past, and all things detrimental to our growth, our loads will become so heavy they will weigh us down and stop us from soaring. It makes sense, right? If we allow ourselves to be weighed down or tie ourselves to the pain holding us back, how will we ever be free?

Letting go takes an element of trust because we hang on to all of these things for a reason. Perhaps it is the fear of moving on, fear of not being loved, fear of failing, or even fear of success. It sounds strange, I know, but with success comes change and perhaps more judgement. Those around us don't always like to see us change and succeed because it forces them to face their own insecurities. Letting go of the ego and trusting ourselves takes courage. The word courage itself comes from the Latin word 'cor', which means heart. By opening our hearts, we learn to let go, take leaps of faith and trust that all will be well.

As we grow through life, we have to learn to let go...

- When we leave our mothers' wombs, we have to let go and learn to breathe for ourselves. We don't hold on for dear life and refuse to come out, fearing the world outside (even though it may feel like that is the case for many mothers). We allow the change, and we naturally trust.

- When we take our first steps, we have to let go of our parents' hands and trust we will be able to walk. If we never let go, we may never learn to walk by ourselves.

- When we let go of our mothers' legs when we go to nursery or school, we trust we will be taken care of and feel safe.

- When we let go by attempting to ride our bikes for the first time without training wheels, we trust we will be able to ride without falling.

The process of letting go and having trust in our abilities naturally repeats itself; when we are young, we do not give it much thought, but as we get older, we begin to listen to our egos. By allowing self-doubt and fear to creep in, we inevitably stunt our personal growth, we stop listening to our souls and we stop trusting as we live within the confines of our zones of comfort. We become grown men and women, still hanging onto our mothers' legs, so to speak, as we fear stepping out into the unknown and facing uncertainty. As you work your way through this book, know that each step you take to let go and trust will not always be sure and stable. There may be a little uneasiness, a few tears, or wobbles at the start, but until we let go of our old ways of thinking and limiting behaviours, we will never know our full potentials. We will still fall at times when we take new steps or stumble upon the uncharted ground on our journeys through life, but the more we trust and keep going, the more likely we are to discover our wings, leap from the nest, and fly.

A Tidy Mind

Tidying our minds is similar to cleaning out our wardrobes. Some things have been there for years, serving only as reminders of the past. For this reason, we have to take stock once in a while. If we don't get rid of the old, we leave no room for the new. We can identify which items are valuable and will always serve us – these are never a waste of space – but we have to be picky about others and deliberate over whether they deserve to take up precious space in our minds.

When we open our wardrobes to see they are packed full of unnecessary items, we can become frustrated. All we see are untidy messes, so instead of facing the task of sorting through it, we often close the doors and go back to wearing the same old things, even if we feel horrible in them. In doing this, we essentially hold on to feeling bad, but we put it off for another day because it's easier to ignore than face, which is simply too much work.

Again, the same goes for our minds. When we delve in to sort things out, we open the doors, take one look at the mess, tell ourselves it's too hard, close the doors, and return to our old thought patterns. Despite making us feel bad about ourselves, we continue to fall at the first hurdle, ultimately perpetuating our feelings of powerlessness over our happiness.

I once heard Dr Wayne Dyer equate this process to carrying a massive bag of poo around with us through life. Now and then, we reach into it, smear it over ourselves, look around, and wonder why life stinks. This tongue in cheek scenario resonated with me, and it made me laugh because it is so true. It gets worse when we think that a lot of the time we not only carry around our poo, but we also carry around other people's, which weighs us down even more and increases the overall stench.

In any case, we have the power to change. We can keep hanging onto old thought patterns, old habits, or past pain that no longer serves us, or we can rid our minds and hearts of it for good by putting the bag of poo down and moving on without it.

We are fully responsible for the way we feel. We have the key and the map, so if we want to get to the treasure, we need to step into the unknown and trust. We are the answers to our prayers, and we are the only knights in shining armour that can save us.

Clearing out mental space brings more clarity to our lives as we rid ourselves of the futile thoughts that throw spanners in the workings of our minds. By tidying our minds, we will feel more at peace, and life will run with more ease and flow.

This book is a helping hand to guide you through the pile of junk that fills your heart, mind, and soul. It may take a bit of effort to get it cleared, but once it is tidy, the path ahead will be visible, and you'll see where you are and in which direction you are heading. Below, I have listed some of the things we need to examine so we can gauge how attached we are to them. By sorting through them, we can decide whether keeping them will serve us or weigh us down. As we look into each area, we can consciously let things go, setting ourselves free from the stink and pain of the past.

Possessions – Money and material wealth may make our lives easier and more enjoyable; however, if we fix our minds on the idea that possessions make us happy, we will feel a sense of inadequacy in our lives when we do not get everything we want. It's healthy to dream and desire nice things, but if we use them to define our worth or make us happy, we set ourselves up for disappointment and suffering.

Labels – We also use labels to define our worth at times. These can range from job titles, accolades, and achievements, to the clothes we wear, the shapes and sizes of our bodies, or where we live, but if we measure our worth and happiness on how others see us, what happens when we are no longer at the tops of our games or on the list of high achievers? Does it mean we are no longer worthy? Will we still lead happy, humble lives, or will it lead to emotional suffering?

Excuses – When we let go of them, we free ourselves from hiding the truth. We take responsibility for how we feel today instead of using excuses to justify why we can't succeed in our health, work, or life goals. By holding onto flawed reasoning, we validate our powerlessness and waiting for something outside of us to change to improve our lives, and we all know that is unlikely to happen.

Fear – This is no easy feat; it takes trust to let go of fear. One thing to remember is that fear isn't real. If you think about it, the fear we feel is about possible negative outcomes we make up in our minds and not the truth. The feeling of fear is real, but the stories we predetermine aren't – they are projections of what *could* go wrong in any given situation. We can choose to think fearful thoughts or let go and trust that whatever happens, all will be well.

Complaints – They can come pretty easily – trust me, I have done my fair share of complaining in my lifetime – but that all changed when I began living consciously. Once I became aware of my thoughts and behaviours, I realised that complaining served no purpose but to prevent me from growing. I said I wanted to be happy, yet I fed myself continuous negative thoughts and feelings. By focusing all my energy on everything that was going wrong in my life, I put my struggles in the limelight, unknowingly featuring them centre stage in my day to day life. Only when I chose to let go of complaining and make gratitude the protagonist of my life was I able to create peace of heart and mind.

Anger and Resentment – Letting go of anger and resentment removes the bitterness in our hearts and frees our souls to be happier and more carefree. We often feel resentment towards those who have hurt us in the past, but we forget that *we* decide whether we continue to give our thoughts the power to upset us or let them go. If we hang onto them, we keep the pain alive within us. On the other hand, if we trust that we have learned a valuable lesson from our challenging experiences and let them go, we free ourselves from carrying around the weight of the past.

People – Letting go of people who are no longer in our lives through death or broken relationships is never easy; however, we must allow ourselves time to grieve in either case. We can't just hold in the pain of loss; we have to release it and use the time to focus on gratitude for the love we once shared, for the time we had them in our lives, for the good times, and the love and connections we had with them. I am not saying it is easy to let go, but in time, we have to free ourselves from the pain of loss and hold tightly to the beautiful memories. The greatest gifts we can give our lost loved ones are living happy and fulfilling lives.

Negativity – At times, we all find ourselves caught up in a cycle of negative thinking, but where does that take us? By hanging onto negative thoughts and words, we will only spiral downwards as we allow negativity to suck the life, joy, and enthusiasm from us. Not only do we bring ourselves down, but we unwittingly drag others down with us. We focus our minds on all that is going wrong in life, but by making conscious efforts to look at ourselves and the ways we think and speak, we recognise the part we play in the way we feel. Negativity and happiness cannot coexist, as one counteracts the other. We have to choose whether to think more positive thoughts and words or keep hold of the negative ones.

Perfectionism – This one was hard for me to let go of because I had convinced myself it was a positive trait to possess. Before abandoning this belief, I took pride in my perfectionism, thinking of it as a reflection of my best efforts. However, by setting such high standards for myself, I found it difficult to shake the feeling that I was not good enough if I ever I failed to meet my expectations. I had put impossible pressure on myself to be perfect all the time, but I always fell short. I would beat myself up with criticism, which led me to doubt my ability and worth in everything I did. When I finally recognised that I was setting myself up for failure by holding on to my perfectionism, I let go and was content, knowing I had done my best. If I had held onto perfectionism, I would not have written any of my books because I am not perfect. In reality, there is no such thing!

Limiting Beliefs – We all have limiting beliefs, and we all too often listen to the voices of doubt in our heads instead of trusting our souls. As we grow up, our self-perceptions are shaped by those who mean well. They may share their opinions to manage our expectations, protect us from looking foolish, or feel the disappointment of failure. We might have been told by others that we do not have the right body shape to be dancers or that we have to be super smart if we want to be doctors. Instead of supporting our true desires, they were more likely to encourage us to pursue something more suited to our abilities. In other circumstances, these opinions may also have had an impact on our senses of self-worth. For example, others may have told us that we are unkind, and as a result, we grew up believing that we were unworthy of love and kindness. Whatever our limiting beliefs, we have to let them go and trust that we can be and do whatever our hearts desire. If we have desires and dreams, then whatever we want is within our reaches to some extent, but only if we learn to let go and trust in our abilities to work things out.

Judgement – We tend to care so much about what others think, but we have no idea what is going on in their hearts and minds. We can speculate, but the truth is that it is impossible to know unless they tell us outright. That doesn't seem to stop us, though, does it? We have great imaginations when it comes to the "s/he thinks" voices in our heads. We come up with all sorts of opinions as to what others think and say about us, most of which are incorrect. The truth is that people are generally too busy minding their own businesses to pay any mind to us. Some may have strong opinions, but it is not our business what others think about us, and it is not the truth, but just their opinions. When we know who we are and love ourselves for it, it does not matter what others think. The only people who need to love and accept us for who we are is ourselves.

The Past – The past is no longer today's reality. What happened yesterday cannot be changed. If yesterday was what it was, why do we keep going back to replay the horrors of the past when it doesn't serve us? In my book *Your Life Your Legacy*, I take the readers on a trip down memory lane, revisiting the trajectories of their lives, not to dig up the past, but to remind them how far they have come and how much they have grown. Often, the horrors of the past turn out to be some of our greatest life lessons that have shaped us into the people we are today. Without the wake-up call and lessons learnt, we would not have become the pillars of strength and resilience we are today. Holding onto the past and not letting go stops us from moving forwards.

As humans, we naturally grow and evolve when we trust in the intelligence of the Universe. In contrast, when we hold tightly onto the past, we stunt our development. The past is a memory of what has happened; the future is ours to write, so the only reality is now, in this very moment. When we live consciously in each and every moment, letting go of the need to control the past or the future, suffering subsides, and we begin to live fully, openly trusting in the beauty of our souls instead of attaching our happiness to ideas or thoughts.

Buddha said, 'Attachment is the source of all suffering,' and if you think about it, it makes a lot of sense. Happiness comes from within, so attaching ourselves to something outside of ourselves and beyond our control inevitably brings us suffering. Because almost everything we value in life exists outside of ourselves – from family, friends, relationships, and work to homes, lifestyles, and even our bodies – we have to let go of our attachments to them if we want to live happier and more carefree lives. Of course, we do not have to let go of *them* per se, but we must let go of our attachments to them. Our children do not belong to us. They are not our possessions. They are free souls who come into this world through us, but not for us. We need to learn life lessons from each other, but other people are not a part of our souls, even if we feel they are at times. Like us, our children are unique, loving, compassionate souls. We must acknowledge they are here on journeys of their own; our roles are to love and guide them. Often, they are our most profound mentors as they teach us patience, unconditional love, and selflessness. Life on Earth is temporary, but the lessons we learn through love are eternal.

If God has blessed us with enough years upon the Earth, we have probably experienced the pain of separation, whether through death, broken relationships or our families growing up and starting their own lives, but when we attach ourselves to those we love, we set ourselves up for suffering. We are here to love, serve, and share ourselves with others, but not one soul belongs to us – they are all as free as we are.

When we attach ourselves to people, material things, lifestyles, ways of thinking, or even religion, we act from places of fear and not from love. Despite the fear of not being loved, valued, having enough, or being enough, we have to remember that we are all whole, complete souls. As human beings, love, kindness, and compassion inherently reside at the very core of who we are.

- Attachment to religious beliefs may result in becoming biased, and we may refrain from opening our hearts to people of different faiths, creating division.
- Attachment to science and its theories can create closed minds that prevent progress and advancement.
- Attachment to people can produce a sense of ownership where fear and jealousy can grow.
- Attachment to material things can give us false senses of worthiness, valuing ourselves solely on what we have instead of who we are, preventing spiritual growth.
- Attachment to ideas or dreams can sometimes cause frustration if we lose our open-mindedness, preventing our life experiences from naturally unfolding.

Becoming aware of our thoughts and fears and recognising them as false truths is the first step to letting go. The past is so difficult to let go of as we all have so many beautiful memories, but we have to be picky and consciously choose which ones we keep, actively deciding what serves us and what doesn't.

I often revisit the past as both of my parents have passed on. If I want to feel their love, I allow my mind to travel back. However, it is essential that when we look back, we do so wearing our gratitude spectacles and not our shades, as, through them, we can only see the dark sides of our pasts.

Referring back to my 4xA system, I believe it is helpful to work through any major blocks...

1st 'Acknowledge' that the past happened, and we cannot change it.

2nd 'Accept responsibility' for the past and our own emotions. We have lived it, and it's our responsibility to let it go for our peace of mind and wellbeing. To understand that we cannot change what happened, but can change how we look at it and how it affects our future.

3rd 'Act on it' by actively laying our pain to rest, letting go and seeing it as a lesson to help us to reshape our lives for the better. Work out how we can grow from this experience and determine how we can use it to help others dealing with similar issues.

4th Looking at the possible 'Aftermath'. If we do not change the way we look at our past, how will it serve us to stay where we are on an emotional level? Seeing what our possible future will look like if we remain stationary will enable us to see a better path forward through change.

Holding on to a painful past can only hold us back and keep us chained to our suffering. We cannot fly high and stay on the ground simultaneously, so we have to choose. Ultimately, we are free to let go and choose happiness or suffering. I know this sounds crazy, and you may be thinking, 'That's not true, I don't choose to suffer' but we all too often get attached to our suffering and use it to prevent us from trying, in case we end up failing...yet again. We get stuck in a mental pattern of replaying our most painful moments over and over again in our minds like a broken record, even though we know that it hurts. As an example of this, in my early teens, my friends and I would innocently exchange boyfriends every few weeks. However, if I got dumped, that was another matter. I would play the saddest songs on repeat and cry in my bedroom, feeling sorry for myself. Unbeknownst to me, all I had to do to feel better was to change the record, but oh no, I had to torture myself over and over again, feeding the pain. Until the next boy came along, of course, and then I would instantly let the old suffering go.

I can laugh at that now, but many of us still live our lives that way. We play the victim because it is simply easier than taking control of our feelings. It gives us an excuse to give up responsibility for ourselves through blaming others for our unhappiness but, in doing so, we become trapped in a web of negativity and victimhood, making life a test of endurance instead of a joy.

Trusting in our life's journey is similar to a mother bringing a child into the world. For nine months, she carries a child in her womb, taking care of her diet, body, levels of stress and surroundings as she prepares to give birth to a new life. Despite these outward actions, she doesn't actively *do* anything to grow a baby in her womb. All she can do is trust in the process and allow nature to take its course, surrender and have faith that a force greater than herself will make a whole little person made of flesh and blood, bringing a beautiful and precious soul into the world. What a joy!

If she didn't trust and instead got stressed every day about whether the child was growing enough, whether it had fingers and toes or if its organs were forming, the stress would most likely hinder the natural process, not help it.

We don't understand the complexity of how we form life within ourselves, so we let it go and let it happen. We must have trust in our life experiences in the same manner; in the wisdom of a higher power that knows what is going on within us, even if we do not. We have to stop asking why and start trusting. In doing so, we align with our source, cease resisting and allow the blessing of life to naturally unfold, opening our soul to an abundance of life's beautiful treasures.

Nature does not force itself to grow; the loving energy within every tree, every flower, every bird and every living creature is at work. They trust that nourishment will be provided for them and don't seek recognition and praise from their peers. Trees don't compete or compare themselves with others – they just are. No two are identical, and each one is beautiful in its own way. All living things on the Earth have a reason for being, and all things are unique and beautiful, just like we are. Imagine if everyone was free from judgement, comparison, labels and fear – what a peaceful world we would inhabit. By laying down the burdens we carry, we free up our arms and hearts to open them wide and invite more love inside.

GROWING WITHIN

What do you need to let go of in your life to free you from being weighed down? Let's look into the wardrobe of your life, tidy up the mess and throw away old thought patterns, untruths and pains that are no longer serving you. If they are holding you down and preventing you from growing into the best version of yourself, they have to go.

I have shared some of the thought patterns that I needed to let go of, and now it is your turn. By doing this exercise, you will begin to unload the unnecessary and feel considerably lighter. When we ask the right questions, we uncover the truth for what it is, not as a confusing mess that clutters our minds.

Under each title, write down what you need to let go of in that particular area by asking the right questions…

1. What do you need to let go of that is holding you back?
2. What is your current mindset concerning this area?
3. What benefits do you gain from holding onto this particular mindset?

4. What benefits will you gain from letting go?

Let's use "Possessions" as an example to give you an idea of how to do this decluttering exercise of letting go.

Imagine that a person needs to sell their house because they can't afford to keep it but, emotionally, they are not ready to let it go. Their reluctance to let go of the past requires them to look deeper to understand what is holding them back. Once they begin to see things clearly, it enables them to let go...

1. – What possessions do you need to let go of that are holding you back?

– I need to let go of my attachment to my house. I have to move, but I don't want to.

2. – What is your current mindset concerning this area?

– My house is my home; I raised my family there and made many happy memories. I want to hang on to those memories, so I want to hang on to my house. I know that I have to let go, but it's so painful, and the reality is that I can't maintain a home this size anyway. It makes me sad to think of leaving the past behind.

3. – What benefits do you gain from holding on to this particular mindset?

– It made me feel as though my life was staying still, but I can see that it is not helping me in any way because my memories exist only in my mind and heart, not in the house.

4. – What benefits will you gain from letting go?

– I will be financially better off. I will have a smaller house to maintain, giving me more free time. I will be able to stop worrying about paying large house bills for heating etc.

Now it's your turn...

Possessions

1. *What do you need to let go of to help you to move forward? Are you holding onto old clothes, furniture or items that clutter your personal space and cause you unnecessary stress?*

_____

_____

_____

2. *What is your current mindset concerning the possessions you want to keep?*

_____

_____

_____

3. *What benefits do you gain from holding on to this way of thinking?*

_____

_____

4. What benefits will you gain from letting go?

_____

_____

Labels

1. What labels do you need to let go of that are not serving you? Are they concerning your insecurities about your body shape, age or self-image, or are they labels that others have placed on you in the past that you can't seem to shake off?

_____

_____

2. What is your current mindset concerning the labels you wear and how you use them to define your worth?

_____

_____

3. What benefits do you gain from holding on to this particular mindset, and is it helping you?

_____

_____

4. *What benefits will you gain from letting go of the labels that you have carried around with you that were weighing you down?*

_____

_____

Excuses

1. *What excuses or lies do you tell yourself that prevent you from taking responsibility for your life and hold you back? For example, do you say such things as, I'm big-boned, all my family are overweight – I cannot do anything about my size and shape, or my illness prevents me from trying?*

_____

_____

2. *What is your current mindset concerning this area?*

_____

_____

3. *What benefits do you gain from holding on to the excuses you tell yourself?*

_____

_____

4. *What benefits will you gain from letting them go and taking full responsibility for your actions?*

_____

_____

Fear

1. *What fears do you need to let go of that are holding you back? What false stories do you tell yourself that prevent you from stepping forward to claim the life of your dreams?*

_____

_____

2. *What is your current mindset concerning this area? What scares you? Looking foolish; failing; being judged by others?*

_____

_____

3. *What benefits do you gain from holding on to fear?*

_____

_____

4. *What benefits will you gain from letting go and facing your fears?*

_____

_____

Complaining

1. *What do you complain about regularly that prevents you from taking responsibility for the part you play in improving your life?*

_____

_____

2. *What is your current mindset concerning this area? Who or what are you blaming for the current state of your life?*

_____

_____

3. *What benefits do you gain from complaining about the state of your current circumstances?*

_____

_____

4. *What benefits will you gain from letting go of complaining and blaming?*

_____

_____

Anger and Resentment

1. *What thoughts of anger and resentment are you carrying around that you need to let go of to help you move forward and create inner peace?*

_____

_____

2. *What is your current mindset concerning this area? Are feelings of anger and resentment helping you or holding you back – why do you think this?*

_____

_____

3. *What benefits do you gain from holding onto anger and resentment? How does it help you?*

_____

_____

4. *What benefits will you gain from letting the anger and resentment go?*

_____

_____

People

1. *Who have you formed an attachment to that you need to release? Are you hanging onto a lost love or someone close to you that passed away? Who do you need to let go that is preventing you from moving forward in life?*

_____

_____

2. *What is your current mindset concerning this area? What are you telling yourself that prevents you from letting go?*

_____

_____

3. *What benefits do you gain from holding on to this person in your mind? How does your attachment to them serve you?*

_____

_____

4. *What benefits will you gain from gently letting go of your attachment to them?*

_____

_____

Negative Thoughts and Words

1. *What negative thoughts do you continually feed your mind with that you need to let go of to help you move forward? How do these negative thoughts make you feel?*

_____

_____

2. *What is your current mindset concerning this area? What unkind things do you tell yourself that hurt you or steal your peace of mind?*

_____

_____

3. *What benefits do you gain from holding onto negative thoughts and words?*

_____

_____

4. *What benefits will you gain from letting negative thoughts and words go?*

_____

_____

Perfectionism

1. *What are your ideas of perfection that you need to let go of to help you move forward? What areas of your life get you down, in which you think that you are not good enough?*

_____

_____

2. *What is your current mindset concerning areas in which you feel you are not excelling? How does your perfectionism hold you back?*

_____

_____

3. *What benefits do you gain from holding on to perfectionism?*

_____

_____

4. *What benefits will you gain from letting go of perfectionism and doing your best, regardless of the result?*

_____

_____

Limiting Beliefs

1. *What limiting beliefs do you need to let go of to help you to move forward? What mental blocks prevent you from trying new things or believing in yourself?*

_____

_____

2. *What is your current mindset concerning this area? What were you told by yourself or others that made you think you could not succeed in this area?*

_____

_____

3. *What benefits do you gain from holding on to your limiting beliefs?*

_____

_____

4. *What benefits will you gain from letting go of your limiting beliefs?*

_____

_____

What Others Think

1. *What are your concerns about what others think? Do you need to let go of other people's opinions of you and why?*

_____

_____

2. *What is your current mindset concerning what others think? Why does it matter to you?*

_____

_____

3. *What benefits do you gain from continuing to care about what other people's opinions are?*

_____

_____

4. *What benefits will you gain from ceasing to care what others think?*

_____

_____

The Past

1. *What do you need to let go of in your past that keeps you stuck and stops you from moving forward?*

_____

_____

2. *What is your current mindset concerning past events and the thoughts that you can't seem to shake?*

_____

_____

3. *How is holding on to this way of thinking about the past serving and helping you?*

_____

_____

4. What benefits will you gain from letting go of pain from the past?

_____

_____

COUNTING MY BLESSINGS

Trusting your soul means going back to the way you once were as a small child, free from doubt and concern for what others think, without past experiences to influence your next step and the weight of old conditioning and belief systems to cloud your judgement. It is about silencing the voice in your head and living from the heart in the same way you did as a joyful and carefree child, making choices that you know deep down are best for you. As adults and parents, in particular, we often put the wellbeing of others above our own. However, for us to show up as the best version of ourselves, we have to practice self-care first by following our natural intuition and trusting in the whispers of our souls.

That does not mean we have to disregard our duties as good human beings, as forces of good in the world, but it means that we do not live our lives being and doing what others think is best for us. We can take advice and consider other people's point of view, but ultimately, we have to listen to the loving voice within our souls. To let our soul be our guide. We all inherently know what is best for the growth of our souls. Through obtaining an extensive knowledge of our souls and following our guiding principles, we can develop that deep self-trust.

When we trust that everything in the past happened *for* us rather than *to* us, we can live with more peace as we ride out the challenges of life.

Every cloud has a silver lining, and the sun shines after every storm. It is the nature of life.

- **List ten blessings you have received in life – big or small – that came after, or as a result of, a challenge that you had to overcome.**

Some examples:

- Because I became ill and almost lost my life, I transformed my whole lifestyle, diet and outlook on life, and I now live a healthy life with more joy and enthusiasm.

- I was devastated after losing my job – but if I hadn't, I would not be doing my dream job now.

- If my relationship had not ended, I would never have met the true love of my life.

1. _____

2. _____

3. _____

4. _____

5. _____

6. _____

7. _____

8. _____

9. _____

10. _____

DAILY PRACTICE

Mindfulness

When we stop living in fear and begin to trust, we allow ourselves to live in the moment, the only reality that exists. The past is done and cannot be changed, and the future has not yet happened. We must live in the now. The tragedy is that we often miss out on the beauty right in front of us as we fixate on the past and future instead of grounding ourselves in the present moment.

Mindfulness is a practice that allows us to live in each moment, being fully present. This whole book, in effect, is about mindfulness and taking an honest look at where you are in your life and accepting it for what it is, but you can complete your daily practice of mindfulness at any time and in any place, as often as you choose. It's about being fully aware of what you are doing and how you feel with every breath and step you take.

We are so concerned with what is coming next that we are going through life mindlessly, missing out on the simple joys of life that create feelings of contentment, love and fulfilment. Let's use food, for example. How often do you sit down and consciously enjoy every mouthful of a delicious meal? We are all guilty of sitting down to a family meal without giving thanks or acknowledging the work that has gone into preparing it; without savouring all the flavours, textures and feeling the sensations in our mouths. We merely sit and eat. We may enjoy it, but we scoff it down without experiencing the delicious flavours or savouring the love that went into the preparation.

Do we stop and make eye contact with our child or spouse when they are talking to us? Or do we carry on with what we are doing without giving them our full and undivided attention? We may hear them but are we actively listening? Do our actions make them feel as though they are valued or heard?

When we go for a walk, are we thankful for the gift of our functioning legs, aware of every step and breath we take, our surroundings and what we can see, feel, smell and hear?

Once you begin taking notice of the here and now by being fully present, you will feel more nourished by life. With an absence of thought concerning the past or future, you are free to connect with the gift of life, resting your focus purely on the feeling of being alive. You will start to feel more connected with your soul and with all things as joy begins to flow naturally back into your life.

You can practice mindfulness in all that you do. When you eat your next meal or snack, activate your awareness. Take note of the flavour, texture, and sensations you feel without thinking of what you have to do next. When you cook, be aware of stirring the contents of the pot or kneading the dough. When you sit and admire a plant or flower, notice the colours and textures and scent without naming it or trying to understand it, purely enjoy it. When you go out for a walk, watch the leaves sway in the trees, listen to the birdsong and feel the breeze on your skin. Don't look at the complexity of life or focus on the naming or labelling whatever you see – practice savouring the moment.

Focusing your energy and attention on whatever we are currently doing calms a busy, overactive mind and helps us gain clarity and stillness. Live in the power of this very moment, taking in the beauty of the world and marvel at this gift of life.

The more we tune into *now*, the more peace we will feel as we let go of all the noise and confusion that we allow to enter our minds that prevents us from living in the present – a divine gift.

LIFE BEFORE DEATH

SHE PUT LOVE IN OUR HEARTS AND SMILES ON OUR FACES.

Many years ago, I came across a question that profoundly impacted my life. At the time, it caused me anxiety and many tears, but ultimately, it liberated me from the prison I had built around myself and was the answer to my prayers. What was the question?

"What sentence would you like to be written on your headstone that would capture who you were in your life?"

A simple enough question, but it touched a nerve deep within as it forced me to face my truth. It took me two days of deep contemplation, profound soul searching, and a waterfall of tears before I was able to answer with the words: "She put love in our hearts and smiles on our faces".

Even now, all these years later, these words ignite my soul and remind me who I am at my core. I had always known this truth, but for too long, I had allowed life to distract me from my reason for being. The reality was, *I* had gotten in the way, and it was my responsibility to stop holding myself back so that I could begin to live my truth.

It has taken me many years to get to where I am today, and I have had many challenges along the way, but because I have awakened to my reason for being, every step has been worth it. I know exactly why I was born and what my purpose is in life.

We all have the answers to life's questions within us. When we learn to ask revelatory questions, we will begin to receive answers equally as revealing. Knowing this, I ask that you dive deeply into the questions I pose and implore you to answer them honestly to unlock your awareness and to help you understand *your* reason for being. You don't have to be faced with tragedy or the threat of death to awaken your truth – you can choose today to open your eyes, mind and heart to see the path ahead with more clarity. To choose to feel truly alive.

You have a unique gift that you were born to embody and when you know what that is, and begin to share it, life will get a lot better. It may not feel like a life-changing gift to you, but even if you touch the soul of one other person in your lifetime, you are making a difference. Once you come to understand the truth of who you are and see life as a series of lessons for you to learn from, you will begin to give more, love more and serve with more joy. You will understand your worth in the world and live life with more enthusiasm as you come to know that your presence in this world truly matters.

As parents, for example, we know that it is our job to raise a well-rounded child by ensuring they are morally good, healthy and prepared for life; physically, emotionally and spiritually. We may get tired or frustrated at times, but we never give up on them. We may unwittingly make mistakes from time to time, but our intentions are good. We don't set out as a parent and say we want to screw up our kids' lives, health, mindsets and self-esteems, do we? But unfortunately, sometimes it happens. When we set a clear intention for our lives, even without a fixed life plan, somehow, somewhere, sometime, with focused action, we will get there. With a vision for our lives firmly in place, we can begin the journey of living a purpose-filled life. Whether we ever reach our final destination or not is irrelevant because the joy is in the journey. If I were to die tomorrow, I know that I have given life my all up until this very moment. I open my heart and soul to the world and allow it to pour out onto the pages of my books because I intend to use my time on Earth to teach people how to create more love, inner peace and joy in their lives, and that is what I am doing. My methods may change, and my teachings will evolve and grow as I do, but my intention for my life will always drive me forward.

A few years ago, I couldn't do what I am doing now as I was not yet ready. We have to trust in divine timing and that life will unfold intentionally at its own pace. There is a time for learning. A time for growth. A time to teach. A time for peace. And also a time to die. But before we die, we first have to make the very best of life.

We often go through the motions of life, but we do not truly live. Fear is our biggest obstacle as it robs us of living a life that we love. We allow doubts and fear to take over, but why? Do we fear failure? Ridicule? Humiliation? Do we fear not being good enough, attractive enough, young enough, qualified enough or loved enough? We all have so many fears, as we talked about earlier, but again, are we going to let them determine the quality of our lives, happiness, purpose and fulfilment?

Fear itself cannot harm us or hold us back. Ultimately, we must choose whether to side with fear or faith. We tend to listen to the false stories we tell ourselves as we cycle through all the possible scenarios – what could go wrong? How could we fail? But if that is the case, we can also make up optimistic scenarios that are equally likely to happen. I like to opt for the positive because I fully believe that we can have anything we ask for in life through faith. Although, we will only receive what we ask for if it serves the greater good.

"Ask, and you shall receive", will not work with good intentions alone. Faith, self-belief and focused action are paramount in the creative process. We can sit around and pray all day, but without focusing our attention on following our good intentions, all we have is hope. Imagine I dreamed about becoming a successful author but never tried to write a book. Or perhaps I did write one, albeit half-heartedly, but I got cold feet and decided not to send it to any publishing houses. How will they know of my work if I do not show them? No one will stop me on the street or call me out of the blue and say they want to publish my work – I have to be brave and put myself in a vulnerable position at the risk of being rejected. One of the most empowering things we can learn is that rejection does not equate to failure – it is proof that we are trying. If we never try, we can never fail, but is that even living? Failure itself has its benefits as it teaches us what does not work, essentially taking us a step closer to knowing what does. For me, the ultimate way we let ourselves down in this life is by refusing to try at all. I would rather fail a thousand times than live in fear and die with regrets.

As I contemplated what I wanted to have written on my headstone, I realised that I was not on track to where I wanted to be. I had a heart full of love and the passion required to promote positive change in others, but I wasn't doing anything to advance in that direction. At the time, I studied scriptures and personal development intensely in search of answers. But when I look back, I struggle to see how that helped anyone other than myself. Something had to change – I knew that I wanted to live a life before death.

Death is inevitable for us all but sadly, we rarely talk about it. I must admit that I have been a little obsessed with death, especially after my mum died so suddenly. My world fell apart on the day she died, and it took me four years before I could finally accept that she was gone from my life forever. But now, I see her passing as a blessing. She never wanted to get so old that she would need to be taken care of in any way or need any assistance at all for that matter. She was a strong and independent woman, and even at 70 years old, we had to run alongside her to catch up if we were out walking together. She was here one day and gone the next. An aneurysm took her life with no warning and with no heartfelt goodbye.

My mum talked about dying all the time, and she spoke of it with such joy as if she was looking forward to it, which was weird in my eyes. But she had a beautiful vision of heaven in which she believed she would reunite with her parents and family. She had great faith and spent a lot of time at the local cemetery as she seemed to find peace there.

I am not obsessed with death like my mum was, but I use it as a focal point for my life. As I mentioned before, I am not afraid to die when my time comes, but because I have so much work to do before I go, it's not on the cards for any time soon. But if fate had it that I die tomorrow, I would go peacefully knowing that I am truly living the best version of my life today.

I, like my mum, feel comfortable talking about death. I believe that if we all faced the reality of our mortality, we would live with more joy. Because as a society, we rarely discuss death, we are living as if we are immortal beings with no sense of urgency. But the truth is that OUR TIME IS LIMITED…and there is no avoiding it. No matter how successful, happy, faithful or rich and famous we are, our time will come to leave this physical world, and there is no escaping this reality. We can keep quiet about it and ignore that we will die one day but because we are 100% sure of our mortality, why aren't we living life more fully now? I know that people feel uncomfortable talking about death – I can see and feel their fear when I talk openly about it. They tense up and change their body language. Their uneasiness is evident as if someone was talking about the ins and outs of their sex life (no pun intended). But just because we don't talk about death, it doesn't make the reality of our physical fate disappear.

I know that you know this is your fate, but by choosing to be empowered by it rather than letting it engulf you in fear, you will find the courage to be your true self. By embracing the knowledge that your time is limited, you can begin to live your life to the fullest because you have nothing to lose. Now is your time, and this is your life, so live it with joy now.

Health

Although we know that death is inevitable, we might as well give ourselves the best opportunity to live a long life. Don't you think? What we put into our bodies and how we treat them counts – fact. I know this first hand because I went from being a smoking, drinking, sugar-loving, wheezy, medicine-filled chronic asthma sufferer to a medication-free, symptom-free, clean eating health nut who at one time couldn't walk up a flight of stairs but now runs three or four times a week. I can say hand on heart that if I had not changed my lifestyle and habits all those years ago, I would not be here to tell the tale. Even though I didn't fear death, I wasn't about to give up on life. In truth, my near-death experience was one of my biggest blessings, even though I did not see that at the time. If you are going through health challenges at

318

this moment in time, this could also be one of your greatest blessings. You may not see it right now, but you can either complain about it or use it as a pivotal point to turn your life around and get you moving in the right direction. It may seem like a mountain to climb, but every step you take is progress. Not everyone is born with a fully functioning body; some people spend their lives in physical pain while others may need full-time care and would give anything to have the freedom to choose good health. So I urge you not to waste the gift of your body by abusing it or neglecting to take good care of it. This truth isn't always easy for us to accept, but it opens our awareness. We have the option to choose a better quality of life before death.

We have so much more control over our lives and health than we think we have. We have gotten into the habit of putting labels on our ailments and accepting them as truth. The question is, are we using these labels to justify our poor health and surrender our responsibility? If we shed the labels and focus on what our bodies need instead of focusing on what is wrong, we can begin healing from within.

Pain has a purpose regarding both mind and body. It is there to tell us to stop, slow down and take a look at the problem. Taking a painkiller may kill the pain, but it is no different from coldly pushing down our soul selves and neglecting our genuine emotions by locking them away in an attempt to silence their cries. Our bodies are not steel – they are precious living vessels intrinsically designed to hold our souls. They can last a lifetime if we take good care of them and treat them with the love and respect they deserve, so why do we take them for granted? We wouldn't dream of feeding sweets or fizzy drinks to our precious little pets or our beautiful flowering plants, but we don't think twice about putting them down our throats and often those of our children too. I know I sound harsh, but tough love is needed here, and until *we* take full responsibility for our health, we will have to rely on luck to get us through life.

I don't know about you, but I am not prepared to leave my life and health to chance. I got a second chance at life, and I will not play Russian roulette with it.

Imagine that we were born immobile beings, each given a car at birth to last us a lifetime, which was our only means of transporting ourselves around. We cannot use anyone else's car when ours is run down or share our cars with others. If this was so, how would you treat that car? Would you run it to the ground without thought? Would you give it the right fuel and oil it needed to keep it running at its best? Would you pay attention to the red flashing lights that indicate if it needs water or is overheating, or would you ignore the warning sign, perhaps taking out the light bulb altogether to remove the distraction?

This metaphor may seem an overly simplistic way of illustrating the relationship we have with our bodies, but it is a clear one. Today, we care far more about how our cars (bodies) look on the outside than we do about keeping our engine (health) in perfect working condition. Again, I think this is a symptom of avoiding the reality of our mortality.

Taking full responsibility for how we treat our bodies is the first step. We must banish excuses, stop telling ourselves lies and face up to the truth. Only then can we develop a good relationship with our bodies and put an end to the abuse. I know it isn't always easy, but neither is living with a disease or debilitating illness for the rest of our lives, but that is the alternative. So many of us have body and health issues. In fact, I would bet that I don't know a single person that doesn't have a concern of some sort with their physical form. We compare, judge, self-abuse, torture, starve or overfeed our bodies and then wonder why we have issues.

- Are we eating for health and fuel, or are we using food as a desperate attempt to fill an emptiness in our souls?

- Are we obsessively dieting and working out to try to feel valued, accepted and loved on a deep level by ourselves and others?

- Are we using alcohol or drugs to quieten the cries of desperation to attain a life of purpose and meaning?

- Are we so insecure about who we are that we feel we have to present ourselves in a specific way to be valued?

- Are we so focused on work or having fun that we have been taking our precious bodies for granted?

My advice would be to focus on your health and how your body feels when you eat and work out, not how you look. When we listen to what our bodies want, we will hear the cries. Just as we must work to tidy our minds, it is also essential to clean out our bodies to gain clarity and forge a path forward. When we focus on health, we seek to gain strength, energy and vitality for life instead of admiration and validation from others for our looks. There will always be someone more attractive, younger, fitter, muscular and more radiant than us, so focus your energy on vitality and longevity.

Concentrate on being healthy by eating clean, fresh, healthy, organic, unprocessed foods. Find a sport or activity that you love, and enjoy moving your body to lift your spirits. Get out into the open air and take in the beauty of the natural world to gain energy and strength from the elements. Give thanks for the food you eat and enjoy every mouthful with no distractions other than chatting with your loved ones. Drink clean, fresh running water that hasn't sat in plastic bottles for months on end if you can. Even enjoy your favourite foods from time to time, but do so mindfully, and again enjoy every bite.

Good health isn't difficult; it's our obsession with perfection that holds us back. Women are not supposed to have six-pack abdominals – we were born to bear children. Men developed muscles from hunting, cutting wood, building shelters and fighting off wild beasts, but no predators are trying to eat us anymore. There is nothing wrong with the beautifully sculpted bodies of both men and women, but my point is we don't *have* to look that way. Some people need to look a certain way or maintain a particular fitness level to make a living, but we cannot compare ourselves with them. Healthy is being a healthy weight and being comfortable in our skin.

Don't waste all of your precious time trying to chase perfection or to look like someone else, as you will always come up short. The minute you stop the obsessive body sculpting, your body will return to its natural state and what then? Will that diminish your worth as a human being? Instead, focus on putting some of that energy into growing your heart, mind and soul, loving yourself and others, and living your life with passion and purpose.

By taking care of our bodies for health, energy, longevity, and vitality, we not only improve the quality of our lives, but we also give ourselves the best chance of avoiding suffering.

So, if you are having health challenges at the moment, take yourself through the Four- A steps to move you forwards. Instead of telling yourself you are ill, cementing this health challenge in your mind, remind yourself that you have the power within you to overcome every obstacle, including this one. Tell yourself that you are in the process of regaining your health and wellbeing through the flow of healing love, self-care, and focused action. Your health is in your hands, so 1. Acknowledge the challenge; 2. Accept responsibility for it; 3. Act on it to work in your favour; and 4. Contemplate the Aftermath before leaving it to chance.

Purpose

Why are you here, and what makes you the unique being you are? If you don't already know the answer to these questions, now is the time to delve deeper within. Establishing these two things will help you identify your life's purpose. When I ask people what their life's purpose is, no matter what age they are, the majority say they do not know. We go through our lives wishfully thinking that, in time, our purposes will reveal themselves, but I know people in their 60s and 70s who still haven't worked this out. Although they retain the desire to do something valuable with their lives, and they are not ready to surrender to old age, they still feel lost and confused about why they are here. I believe that, deep down, everyone knows their purpose, or they, at least, have a dream. While some give up on their dream lives, others keep them locked away because bringing them to the surface and acknowledging them demands confrontation. Instead, they suppress them and tell themselves the time is not right or their time has passed. Does this ring any bells? I hear people say things such as 'One day, I will write a book. One day, I will travel the world. One day, I will learn to play the piano. One day..." but the reality is that we do not know how many of these 'one days' we have ahead of us. We may have many, but that is out of our hands, so now is the time to spend our lives being truly alive.

If we ask ourselves the question 'If I could do anything in the world I wanted and I was guaranteed 100% success at it and could not fail, what would I do?' our reasons for being will reveal themselves.

We are all blessed with unique gifts, passions, and talents for a reason, and we create joy within ourselves when we develop and share them. When we work on living our purpose, we feel fulfilled and fully alive with the knowledge that we are what we are born to be, doing that which we were born to do.

Having no enthusiasm for life or feeling as if we have no purpose creates a life of 'just getting by', trudging through life until we reach the end, and that is not why we are here. We are here to experience all aspects of life and not just endure it. Happiness is our birthright, and by not following our dreams or living up to our potentials, we deny ourselves the great gift of life. Living that way doesn't necessarily mean we will be unhappy, but we run the risk of living without passion, surviving but not thriving, and worst of all, feeling a sense of regret when we pass away.

Just the thought of feeling that way saddens me. We don't need to be highly successful, respected, or even earn livings at pursuing our purposes. Above all, having a purpose and reason for being is what gives us the energy and enthusiasm to jump out of bed in the morning. In my mind, living a successful life is less about achieving and gaining external rewards and more about having a deep sense of inner peace, love, and meaning. It doesn't have to be a grand, worldly life purpose but something that makes our souls sing and puts smiles on our faces.

How do we know if we are living our life purpose? The best way to find out is to gauge your level of enthusiasm about what you are doing or what you want to do. What excites you? What ignites your soul? What job would you do, even if you didn't get paid? What makes you sit upright in your chair or gives you the courage to speak up? What is it about the world that gets under your skin that needs to change for the better? Once we identify that about which we are passionate, we can figure out how to use our innate enthusiasm to make the world a better place for all of us. When you are genuinely excited about something, you find a way to push through the self-doubt and fear, knowing this is your calling.

You feel that way for a reason, and it is your moral obligation to do something with your passion, to develop your knowledge and understanding and seek ways to use that passion to live up to your potential. You may only be 20 years old or 70 years young, but it's never too early or late to begin. For example, at 20, you may have a passion for politics but fear you do not have the life experience to speak up about your ideas and vision of a better world. On the other hand, you may be in your 70s and have a passion for saving animals but think you are too old to start something new. Your only block is your limiting belief, so step aside, stop holding yourself back, and start living today. By taking a step forward, no matter how small, you begin to move in the right direction towards making a difference in your life and the lives of others. Be true to yourself, and let your light shine through.

We may look at others and wish we had their lives, or perhaps even think they have been lucky, but in reality, we have no idea what obstacles they have had to overcome to get them to where they are today. They may have had to overcome tremendous blocks, be they spiritual, emotional, or physical. Perhaps we look at the offspring of the rich and famous and disregard the success in their lives. We may conclude that they would not be in the same position if not for their financial and social privilege. In assuming this, we minimise the time and effort they put into perfecting their craft and overlook the possibility they had to work even harder for others to recognise their talents and reward them for their accomplishments, independent of their parents. We have no idea what emotional traumas they may have faced by having rich and famous parents. Are they successful because their parents have provided for them, or because they emulate their parents' mindset? Yes, they may have had access to better education and more opportunities, but *they* had to do the work. They also had to do the inner work to know their souls and live life with meaning and purpose. No amount of money or worldly success can give these individuals a sense of purpose and meaning in life. We are all created equal, and we are all responsible for our happiness in life, no matter our families. We all have fears, doubts, and feelings of unworthiness at times, and we all come from the same divine source of love. It's not what we have that matters but what we do with what we have that counts. It all depends on how we choose to spend our valuable time and energy and what our intentions are for our lives.

Life without intention is like a journey with nowhere to go – we end up going around in circles, feeling lost, and end up asking ourselves, 'What is the point of it all?' We may take a few steps forwards and even a few backwards, but without a reason to move forwards, we won't get very far and end up living monotonous lives, missing out on so many of life's true treasures. When we stay in one spot for too long without change, movement, or growth, our energy stagnates. At that point, stress or depression can start to creep in, making every step a challenge, so it is paramount to our health and wellbeing to keep moving forward.

My husband is a Chinese medicine practitioner and acupuncturist, as I said before, and it is his job to identify the blocks and stagnation in the body's meridians. The treatment is to strategically place acupuncture needles at certain channel points for specific lengths of time to wake up and unblock stagnation to allow the energy – the Qi (vital life source) – to once more flow with ease. When our bodies become imbalanced due to stress, diet, lifestyle habits, or illness, the Qi energy is blocked and trapped and needs to be released before the body can heal itself naturally. It is neither the needles nor my husband that does the healing – the unblocking of Qi energy allows the body to regain its natural flow and balance to heal itself.

Why am I telling you this? Because our minds and souls need the same kind of treatment, but thankfully, without having to stick needles into ourselves. We need to identify the blocks and focus our good energy on them as this will cause them to release and allow our lives to flow with ease again. When we were children, most of us had no mind blocks, and we acted in line with our souls, but as we grew, so did our doubts and fears, and we created these blocks out of fear. We openly told people what we wanted to do with our lives without fearing judgement or ridicule. Free from doubt, we were happy to dream up incredible lives ahead of us, but over time, we allowed fear to stop us from dreaming.

If you don't already know your purpose, make that your mission, and take that first step. The fact you are here and have stepped through this last door is proof that you want to be here, that you are looking for improvement and willing to step up and start living, but where should you start? One way is to 'reverse engineer' the kind of person you desire to be. When we reverse engineer products, we carefully deconstruct them to fully understand how they work and create new versions of the products. We can also do the same with people who inspire us by understanding who they are and how they think. Whether we desire to be more like our grandparents, world leaders, or the cheerful lady who works in the charity shop who always has a big smile on her face, by looking closely at why we admire these people, we can identify and emulate their qualities.

Think about three people you admire who are making a difference in life –

– What are their top attributes?

– What do you admire most about them?

Work on attaining these attributes within yourself.

We are all here to grow, progress, love, serve, and contribute, so any step in that direction will bring you more clarity and give your life more meaning. As you take these steps forward, your path will unfold before you, revealing happier ways.

Unhappiness usually enters our lives when we feel we are not living the lives we think we should or we don't have the relationships we hoped to have. We, perhaps, had dream lives mapped out for ourselves in our minds when we were younger, and then, one day, we looked around to see that we were not living the lives we wanted for ourselves. To remedy this outcome, we must either change our visions of the lives we once wanted to something more attainable or change ourselves and start working for what we truly desire. One thing is for sure – our dream lives will not just land in our laps with no effort on our part. 'I am not saying this will never happen, but our chances that the loves of our lives – be it a dream job, partner or lifestyle – will fall into our laps are relatively slim. We have to reach up to meet them. The intentions we have for our lives also have to be clear, but the outcome doesn't necessarily have to be. Let me explain. For example, say I was writing this book with the fixed idea of reaching millions of souls throughout the world with the hope of becoming an international best-selling author. If I held only that goal in my heart, mind, and soul, what would happen if my dream did not materialise? How would I feel? I would most likely feel as if I have failed in my mission, but because I do this work intending to reach millions of souls and become an international best-selling author with the overarching purpose of making a difference in the world and lift up as many people as I can through my books and writing, I cannot fail. Does that make sense? I feel as if I am winning just by doing the work, and I trust that whatever will be will be. If I can touch ten million, ten thousand, 100, or even ten souls, I know my work is valuable. I am living my purpose, and I surrender my will to the source of my being. It is, of course, wise to do all we can to fulfil our destinies, but we also have to make sure we do not attach ourselves to rigid final results.

Being flexible, staying in flow with the rhythm and beat of your heart, living with an open mind and soul means that all things are possible and not just what we think is possible. Going with the flow of our hearts and souls through staying soft opens our worlds to countless possibilities. Gentle flow signifies life is open to change and growth. Trust that life will unfold for you when you reach up to meet it, forever seeking that which lights up your soul. If you have gone deep within yourself and opened up by working through this book, your purpose will readily emerge when you begin to know your soul and listen to your heart.

Your purpose was always within you, but you may only hear the whisperings of your soul now that you have unlocked the doors to let in more light to enable you to see your true self. Every one of us has a purpose, and we can embrace our reasons for being, or we can equally keep them locked away. The choice is entirely ours, but by freeing ourselves from the fear and leaning into the flow of who we are, we can play the parts that destiny foresaw us playing and feel at one with the universe. When we suppress our natural longings and desires, we imprison ourselves and risk coming to the ends of our lives filled with regret. Each of our lives is truly valuable, and all of us matter, but to fulfil our lives' purposes, we first need to exercise our free will and decide to shine in our own ways by being true to ourselves.

Regrets

My biggest fear in life is not failing, or being alone, unloved, or dying – it is reaching the end of my life with regrets. Mark Twain reflected this sentiment when he said, 'We regret the things we don't do more than the things we do.' Yes, we can make mistakes as we ultimately learn from them, but imagine being on your deathbed, looking back at your life, wondering what if? Now, when I have a decision to make, big or small, I use the deathbed scenario to help me decide.

Imagine coming to the end of your life and wishing you had done things differently – wishing you had written that book, mended that relationship, been brave enough to speak up and live your truth, been true to yourself and pursued the love of your life – if we try and fail in all of our life's endeavours, we know we have tried and given ourselves the best chance at living happy lives. We will then be able to leave the Earth with peaceful souls, knowing we have truly lived.

If we do not want to come to the end of our lives filled with regret or haunted by words left unsaid, it is of the utmost importance that we take the time, here and now, to decide what our priorities are in life and to live our lives accordingly.

Some of us live as if we are immortal beings judging by how we treat our bodies and put up with less than what we believe we deserve, but can we afford to settle? Again, OUR TIME IS LIMITED. There is only one today. There is only this moment right now.

Knowing this, why do we so often choose to spend our time dwelling in the past or the future?

We very rarely take each moment as it comes to enjoy it for what it is. We hold onto anger and resentment of past wrongdoings or pain and illness and use it to influence our choices today. We also worry about the future and what lies ahead, but the reality is there is only now. Living in the present moment is essential. Tomorrow is not guaranteed, and neither is 12 hours from now, so why wait for some future event to bring you happiness when you could live with joy now?

If you have dreams within you that you suppress – fear of being too old, too young, not good enough, not confident enough, or not smart enough – you are doing yourself an injustice. The very fact that you have the dream means it is yours. If you can dream up an image of yourself being or doing anything in life, you have already created it in your mind, and it stems from within you. For example, I have friends who are actors and who love nothing more than performing in public. They feel like they are truly alive when they are performing. Conversely, I have no desire whatsoever to become an actor, so the thought doesn't even enter my head. It is not that I don't think I could do it, but that I have no desire. I may change my mind in the future (never say never), but at this moment in time, being an actor or performer does not light me up inside. Expressing my truth through writing, on the other hand, lights me up. It feels natural, and the words flow smoothly and readily. Speaking in public, however, means I have to step out of my comfort zone, but because I refuse to live a life of regret, I know that when the time comes, I will step up to the challenge because I will regret it if I do not. Does it scare me? Absolutely. Does it stop me? No way! I know who I am and what I was born for, and I am ready and willing to step up and meet my destiny. I owe it to myself and the world to do what I was born to do and be who I was born to be. If life had no challenges, we would have no opportunity to grow, and we could reduce all we do to a series of monotonous actions. As humans, we need growth and progress to feel truly alive, and when we step out of our comfort zones, we step out into a world of endless possibilities.

Only two years ago, while taking the first steps towards writing the first of my books, I was terrified. I was overwhelmed with self-doubt and paralysed by fear. I made up stories in my mind about not being good enough, smart enough, or popular enough, and I wondered why anyone would want to know what I had to say or teach. But do you know what? I felt the fear and did it anyway, and I found this new love of my life. I had all this love bottled up inside of me, and writing became an outlet for the loving energy to spill out from my soul, filling myself up and refuelling my soul as I went.

Because I refuse to die with my dreams still in me, I will do all I can to make them a reality. I have received the gift of life, and I am not prepared to sit around, waiting to die, and neither should you. The question is, 'Are you willing to step up to proclaim your reason for being, or are you waiting out your days merely surviving?'

If we silence the longings within due to fear of failing or looking foolish, the only people we betray are ourselves. By undervaluing who we were born to be, we go against the natural order of life's purpose. If you were to come face to face with your ten-year-old self, would you tell her that she does not matter or that she should not follow her heart, or would you tell her that she can be and do whatever her heart desires? You are that child within, and you deserve the best chance at life, so do justice to your soul and live fully.

In doing this work, I have freed myself from the restraints of outside opinions and accepted that I only obtain genuine happiness when I am true to myself, rather than conforming to societal expectations. I live my life as if no one is watching because it makes me happy and frees me from the blocks that once imprisoned me. We often get sucked into other people's ways of thinking, wasting precious time on superficial hang-ups, but what if we cast their thoughts aside and started living by our own rules, ideas, and values? Would we behave in the same way?

For example, I am a 50-year-old mother with teenage kids, but when I visit the beach in the summer, I like to play in the sea. Whether I am with my family or on my own, I can pretty much guarantee that I am the only middle-aged woman doing handstands and rolls under the water. I sometimes see others my age swimming with their heads sticking stiffly out of the water. Do they behave this way because they don't like to put their heads underwater, or is it an attempt to protect their hair? I know that my hair can get dry and be ruined, but if I think about being on my deathbed, will I say that I am glad I kept my hair in good condition or that I wish I had fun while I had the chance? Whilst my body allows me to do handstands in the water, I will continue to do so. I know this sounds simplistic, but every choice I make in life stands trial against the deathbed scenario first. After that, my answers come freely.

Before implementing the deathbed scenario test in my life, I used to be indecisive but not now. Now, I am happier, more confident, and absolutely sure of the choices I make, regardless of how scary they may seem.

Priorities

Many years ago, when I was in my 20s, I was invited to the home of a family. The family unit was composed of a husband and wife and their six beautiful children who were kind, cheerful, helpful, and really friendly. I was in awe of their mother – she was gentle and kind, and it was clear they were a happy family – but what I noticed most about my visit was the state of their home, which was untidy and disorganised, which, quite frankly, threw me a little. It wasn't just unkempt – there were clothes, toys, blankets, and towels strewn everywhere throughout the house, in the living room, kitchen, bathroom, bedrooms, and hall. It was so messy that it was hard to find a place to sit down or even walk without stepping on something, but what the mother said to me stuck in my heart and soul forever. She said that as a mother of six children, she could either dedicate her time to feeding her family healthy foods and nourish their souls by spending time with them one-on-one or keep her house clean and tidy, so she made a choice. I was blown away by her way of thinking, and suddenly, all my assumptions of her melted away, and she was so right. That day, she taught me a valuable lesson – the importance of getting my priorities in order.

I hadn't given it much thought before that day, but I came to realise that how we spend our time here on this Earth counts. No matter who we are, how much money we have, or how privileged we are, each of us has the same 24 hours a day, 168 hours a week, and 8,760 hours a year. It's how we choose to spend our time that determines the quality of our lives. For example, if we spend 40 hours a week working and 56 hours a week sleeping (eight hours a night), that leaves us 72 hours every single week to spend how we choose. We hear ourselves make excuses for not getting stuff done or not having the time to eat healthily or exercise, but with 72 hours a week, surely we can do better than that. We drag ourselves through life being pulled along by the crowd, but how we manage our time should be the first thing on our to-do lists. I am, by no means, claiming to be a master in the area, but I am very aware of the distractions in life that steal our time, energy, and relationships. If, for example, you have a habit of watching TV in the evening, for how long do you sit? Four hours a day equates to 28 hours a week, roughly 120 hours a month, or 1,460 hours a year, staring at the TV screen. How crazy is that? Once we track how we spend our time, we realise how much we waste on things that do not light us up. I am not here to tell you to stop watching TV or doing any activity you love but to open your eyes to how you spend your precious time. We do not have unlimited credit when it comes to time, so it is paramount that we spend our time wisely. As you answer the questions at the end of this chapter, you will begin to open your eyes to see how precious your time is. All too often, we go about our lives without being fully aware of the gift of life itself. We get sucked into a life and a world that does not bring us joy, and we feel powerless to do anything to change that, but we have more power over our lives than we think. Today is a good day to start, and because you have reached the last door on this particular journey, you have demonstrated to yourself that you are worth it. Every step you take in any direction is movement. Even a wrong move is a right move in the end, as you will discover what you don't want. By imagining yourself on your deathbed and looking back at your life, you will know what is truly important to you. Have you lived your life to your full potential? Have you made the most of your gifts and talents? Have you made a difference in the lives of others? Have you played your part by being a light and a helping hand in your life? Have you lived with an open heart and mind? Have you loved as you wanted to be loved? Have you put smiles on faces?

Falling in Love with Life

The simple truth is that love is the energy and vitality of life, and if we spend our lives focused on embracing and sharing that love in any way we can instead of being focused on fear, we can live our lives with joy, no matter what it throws at us. Fear drains energy and vitality from our lives and hearts, but the beauty of knowing this truth is that we understand we can choose love over fear in every step and move we make. When we meet the loves of our lives, we do not let fear hold us back – we let down our guards and open our hearts without thinking. It is in overthinking that we allow fear to enter through the false stories we tell ourselves. Imagine reaching the end of your life and being able to look back and say that you loved life, you opened your heart, and you truly lived by letting love be your driving force instead of fear.

We live for love; it is the very essence of who we are, and the closer we stay aligned to that truth, the happier our lives will be. It is only when we allow fear to take over our thoughts and dominate our choices that we end up veering off track, lost, and disconnected from our reasons for being. I write this book with love and imbue everything into it with the hope of sharing it with all of you who join me on life's journey. I feel personally responsible for the wellbeing of my fellow travellers. While I come to you as a teacher, I am also a student, and it is my responsibility to learn all I can to enable me to share my knowledge and understanding with you. I have so much to give, but I also have so much to learn. Although I am writing this book, it does not make me an expert, only a speaker expressing my truth and spreading love over the world and all who inhabit it.

I believe that every one of us has this same love within ourselves, but we often allow fear to cloud our visions and suppress the longings in our souls. When things happen to us that we feel are unfair, we shut off the loving parts of ourselves, replacing them with feelings of fear, anger, resentment, bitterness, and envy. These feelings are counter-intuitive – as we let them eat away at us, they busily attract more of what we want to avoid, leaving us broken, alone, fearful, and bitter. The only way to remedy this is to break the pattern and start injecting love wherever we go. Yes, we have to expose our soul selves and perhaps, feel vulnerable in the process, but we can only leave the room we are in by opening the door and stepping outside of our own spaces. When we step into our lives with open and loving hearts, we begin to reap the rewards of life and fall deeply in love with it. Love is the remedy, the medicine, the healing, and the cure for all ailments of the heart, mind, and soul; it is the source of who we are.

Love is the essence of heaven on Earth.

Acceptance

The hard truth is that the death of our bodies is inevitable. We can ignore this truth, or we can embrace it and use it as a reason for living the best possible lives right now. Each passing day we walk this Earth is a gift, so perhaps it is time to start treating life as something to be cherished and fully embraced. By accepting that our bodies are vessels that age and will one day release our souls, we can motivate ourselves to make our time on the Earth count. No one knows for sure what lies ahead or what death has in store, but whatever it is, I believe it will be beautiful. As I mentioned before, my mum was a loving, faithful soul who did not fear death; it was something she looked forward to experiencing. She even seemed somewhat excited when she talked about death. I imagine that she knew she was a virtuous person as she had lived her life according to her religion, and therefore, had earned her place in heaven. She was unafraid to die because she had spent her life, like so many others, living and preparing herself for acceptance into heaven. I am also unafraid of death, but I do not live my life with the hope of being granted eternity in the presence of God. I honestly do not know what lies beyond death. Even though I have ideas, I do not believe I have to live my life following one particular religion to view myself as 'worthy' of entering into an eternity of peace. My heart being full of love not only brings me peace of heart and mind, but it also sparks joy within me. I do not behave in such a way to impress God or feel I deserve a place at his table; I share my love because I care for my fellow beings and want to be a guiding light for them. For you. This passage may make me sound like a new-age hippie, but I am just me, Nadia Wong, born into this world filled with love for all. Whether I am loved back is irrelevant. Before I awakened to my reason for being and my calling in life, I never felt truly loved. I had so much love for all people, but I still felt empty. Only when I began loving and accepting myself for who I was, regardless of how the people around me treated me, that I started feeling like a whole, loving, and complete being.

I am now unafraid to live fully and to die. I live my life for each moment, and I surrender my soul to the divine love that is the source of my being. I live my truth with every word I write and every step I take. I accept my imperfections and know that I am and always will be a work of art in progress, forever growing. I am a child of the divine love that is the source of all life on the Earth, and I fully accept who I am in each moment that I live and what will become of me in death. I believe that each soul born into this world is divine love and has a vital part to play. I know, with all my soul, that it is my calling to share my findings with whoever needs to recognise that they are not only loved, but they *are* love.

GROWING WITHIN

A Life Well Lived

Imagine yourself in your golden years, sitting outside on the veranda of your home. It is a beautiful evening, and as you sit in your rocking chair watching the sun set gently on the horizon, you think back over the marvellous life you have lived. Nothing has been left undone, no words have been left unsaid, and you feel happy, complete, and content with the way you have spent your time here, on Earth. You have lived a full and happy life, and your heart is full of gratitude for the blessings of life and the lessons you have learned, which enable you to feel a deep satisfaction within your soul.

As you sit, rocking peacefully in your chair with a smile on your face and pure peace in your heart, ask yourself these questions:

1. What aspects of my life am I most proud of and why?

_____

_____

_____

2. *How did I make a difference in the world and other people's lives, even by the smallest degree?*

_____

_____

3. *Who have been my greatest cheerleaders, those who have supported and loved me through everything?*

_____

_____

4. *For what will I be remembered when I pass on?*

_____

_____

5. *What sentence would I like to be written on my headstone that would capture the essence of who I truly am?*

_____

_____

_____

Soul Satisfaction

The objective of life is to experience things that expand and grow our souls as human beings. We face wide ranges of formative encounters, from fears and challenges to unconditional and unshakeable love, for us to experience the whole spectrum of emotions. The challenges we face are not punishments but lessons from which we can only learn by experiencing them for ourselves.

We can only know the devastating pain of emotional loss through which others go when our hearts are broken by people we love with all our souls. We can only understand grief and the pain of losing loved ones when we lose those we love through death. Through this suffering, we learn and develop empathy, humility, compassion, and a deep connection with each other. Without suffering, we would feel no joy. We cannot completely know the pain that each of us suffers, and we certainly cannot compare our physical or spiritual suffering. However, when we know pain and heartache for ourselves, we can begin to know each other as spiritual beings and expand our souls.

Through our deepest fears and doubts, we can begin to understand each other more deeply as soul beings as they empower us to connect with each other, learn from each other, and grow.

The questions here, in Door #10, may be tough to answer – they were for me when I took the journey myself, but take time to meditate over and contemplate your answers. There are no right or wrong answers because we are all unique and diverse beings, but be true to your soul self, and the answers will open your heart, mind, and soul to the endless possibilities ahead.

- *If you could do anything in the world you wanted, and you were guaranteed 100% success and could not fail, what would you do? What impact might you have on the world?*

_____

_____

_____

- *Without using excuses (such as a lack of time or blaming others for your life choices), what truthfully stops you from pursuing your dreams, holding you back?*

_____

_____

_____

_____

- *Who are the three people you aspire to be most like in the world, be it parents, relatives, influencers, artists, celebrities, and so on and why?*

1. _____

2. _____

3. _____

- *How much of your free time do you spend on average daily on...*
1. *Improving your health and wellbeing through daily exercise, preparing healthy foods, getting fresh air out in nature, and the like?*

_____

_____

2. *Life's distractions such as TV, social media, mindless gaming, and so on?*

_____

_____

3. *Your personal growth and improvement through reading, studying, or listening to audiobooks and/or podcasts to improve your knowledge and develop your talents and passions?*

_____

_____

4. *Improving the quality of your relationships by spending quality time with your family and friends?*

_____

_____

- *What are your top five priorities in life, and why are they so important to you?*

1. _____

2. _____

3. _____

4. _____

5. _____

- *What adjustments do you need to make, starting now, to help you live in accordance with your life's main priorities instead of allowing distractions to lead you off track?*

_____

_____

_____

_____

_____

_____

- *What ten things do you hope to accomplish or experience during your precious time here that will satisfy the longing of your soul?*

1. _____

2. _____

3. _____

4. _____

5. _____

6. _____

7. _____

8. _____

9. _____

10. _____

COUNTING MY BLESSINGS

As this is the final door of this book, let's take another look at our lives, on the whole, to seek out the many blessings we have that have made our lives so memorable. We have counted our blessings throughout this book, but we also have to continue to do so as we go through life, keeping our eyes and hearts open to all we already have and are.

The seemingly insignificant areas of our lives are what give them the most meaning in the end. For example, the fact you are reading this book means you have been blessed with eyes to see, and you experience this beautiful world through sight. You are fortunate to have had an education that has allowed you to learn to read, enabling you to understand what I have written. You have been blessed with a curious heart, mind, and soul as you seek out personal growth and fulfilment. Lastly, don't forget that you have been lucky enough to have me as your guide! All jokes aside, we often take the blessings of our physical form for granted, but they *genuinely* are blessings. Not everyone benefits from the simple things in life that we all too often overlook, so let's regularly remind ourselves of the gifts that we *do* have. They do not make us better than anyone else, but there is no denying that our health and physical abilities make life so much easier for us.

The next time you feel like complaining about being overweight, your job, your spouse, or your bank balance, remind yourself how fortunate you are to be here and focus on all you have rather than what could be improved. If you hear yourself moan about getting older and ageing, remember those who have passed on early in life who will never experience the ageing process. Let's stop complaining and start focusing on gratitude instead.

Your life is a blessing, and whether you believe it or not, you are a precious, divine soul who was born for a reason. It's your job to learn, love, live, and lift yourself and others as you journey through life.

You, my friend, are a blessing.

Again, imagine yourself sitting in that rocking chair in your golden years, looking back at your life's journey, counting the blessings you have received. List them below.

My Life's Greatest Blessings:

1. _____

2. _____

3. _____

4. _____

5. _____

6. _____

7. _____

8. _____

9. _____

10. _____

DAILY PRACTICE

To complete this book and bring it all together, review the daily practices, pick three that resonate with you, and stick to them. Some will feel naturally uplifting; others, not so much. Do what feels right for you. Building new and life-changing habits can take time and effort to begin as we exercise new ways of being. It's a workout for the soul that sustains you for your entire life. If you become tired of the same daily practices, review this book again, and go back through the door you feel you need most at any given time. Life can be challenging at times, so instead of trying to keep ten plates spinning at the same time, work on whatever you feel you need at the moment. I do suggest that you never stop seeking gratitude and stay mindful at all times. It is in the small, seemingly insignificant moments that you will reap the most benefits and feel love, inner peace, and joy.

The lessons in this book may not be the easiest of paths to take in life as they require dedication and focused action while taking a bit of an uphill climb, but once you reach the summit, I promise that the views will be breathtaking. Taking this route will increase your peripheral vision of possibilities and teach you the lessons you need to apply to live a full and meaningful existence. It is *the* key!

CONCLUSION

My heart is full of gratitude and love for the honour and pleasure it has been to guide you on this journey of opening the doors to your life's true treasures, just as I have. Five years ago, I couldn't have imagined I would be where I am now, sharing my life's journey with you, but here I am, happier and more secure than ever. I face life with joyful optimism, a heart full of love, and a complete and nourished soul. I see divine love wherever I go, and I know that all is as it should be. I may fall from time to time and have my moments of doubt and fear like any of us, but because I use my tried and tested tools to get myself out, I do not live there, which is why I share them with you.

If this book has enriched your life in some way, I ask you to please share it to help others to reignite the flame of their inner light.

My parting words to you as I leave this book in your capable hands are about making a Personal Promise to sign and regularly review. It will serve as a reminder of your worth, inner beauty, and reason for being, allowing you to live in alignment with your soul self. I have taken the liberty of writing out a Personal Promise for you, but I invite you to write a version of your own, specific to your hopes, dreams, and aspirations, as a commitment to yourself for your time here, on Earth.

As you use *The Key to a Happier Me* to open doors and take responsibility for your life and happiness, I promise that you will tap into life's true treasures. Although you can use this book as a tool to guide you, you will find the highest wisdom, clarity, and peace of heart and mind not in my words but in *yours*. For that reason, it is paramount that you take the time to write down your answers to the questions and apply *your* truth to your life. I am your guide, but the power is all yours. You are worth more than you can ever imagine.

May you be blessed with infinite love, grace, light, and truth.

May you know your true self, love your true self, and be your true self.

May your heart and soul expand exponentially to feel the essence of divine love.

My wish and my prayer are that your eyes, heart, mind, and soul are now open to enable you to create a bright and beautiful inner world, full of love, light, joy, and an abundance of happiness and infinite possibilities – this is your birthright!

With love, from my heart to yours,

Nadia

XXX

MY PERSONAL PROMISE

I promise to treat myself and others with love, kindness, and respect.

I promise to dedicate time for myself every day to nourish my heart, mind, body, and soul.

I promise to seek out my soul self, begin to know myself and be true to myself.

I promise to be open and willing to see the best in myself and others.

I promise to use positive and kind words when I talk about myself and not to put myself down.

I promise not to compare myself to others but to be the best I can be for myself.

I promise to develop, use, and share my gifts and talents.

I promise not to follow the world but to follow my soul.

I promise to take control of my life and not allow life to control me.

I promise to be true to myself and love myself for who I am.

I promise to approach life's challenges with grace and understand that I will learn and grow from them.

I promise to look for the good in all people and all things and hold back my judgement.

I promise to forgive myself and other people for their mistakes as I keep in mind that no one is perfect.

I promise I will always follow my heart and do what is right.

I promise to make the most of my life and look for things for which to be grateful every day.

I promise to love and respect my body and take care of the life I have.

I promise to treat others as I wish to be treated by them.

I promise to be faithful to my guiding principles to allow me to live in peace with who I am.

I promise to keep my heart and eyes open to seek out and do all I can to lift those within my reach.

I promise to be the person I wish to see in the world.

I promise to be the very best version of myself and to spend my life continually growing, learning, and improving.

I promise to remind myself often that we are all of equal worth, and we each have a divine purpose on the Earth.

I promise to love openly and see the beauty in myself and others.

I promise to spend my life doing that which I was born to do and listening to the whisperings of my soul.

I promise to believe in myself and know that I deserve to live a life of joy.

I promise to love, cherish, and honour myself until death do I part.

I promise to be my own best friend.

I am a loving soul being, and I deserve to be treated with love and respect, especially by myself!

Signed:

ABOUT THE AUTHOR

 After a near-death experience in her twenties, Nadia Wong understands the true gift of life and the value of our relationships with ourselves and others. Nadia is a mother to her two teenage children and the author of four published books, a certified life coach and Mind Tools for Kids coach, and a lifelong seeker of love, light and truth.

Nadia was born in the UK to an Italian mother and Chinese father and moved to Italy in 2001 to live her dream life and start a family. She has been living there ever since.

She now spends her life teaching valuable life lessons and lovingly guiding others to create happy inner worlds to ignite their inner light, joy and enthusiasm for life.

She says, "It is my Divine calling to help people to see the truth and beauty of who they are deep within; to help them to develop self-worth and self-trust, giving them the confidence to create their very own happily ever after".

Other Books by Nadia Wong

Your Life Your Legacy

A parent's guide to writing their own piece of personal history. Using her own stories, Nadia helps to guide you through writing your own beautiful legacy for your family, bringing more meaning and purpose to your life, and theirs.

My Life My Legacy

An accompanying journal to 'Your Life Your Legacy' – containing 101 questions to answer. This journal is designed to open your heart, mind and soul to the blessings of life as you write, to leave your own legacy for your loved ones.

My Growing Heart

A life guide for teens and young adults to help them to navigate themselves through life with greater joy and clarity, for them to create their own happily ever after.

 Nadia Wong Author

 @Nadiawongthehappinesscoach

 www.nadiawongauthor.com

NADIA WONG

Love is always the answer

Conscious Dreams
PUBLISHING

Be the author of your own destiny

www.consciousdreamspublishing.com

info@consciousdreamspublishing.com

Let's connect

Lightning Source UK Ltd.
Milton Keynes UK
UKHW022242171221
395825UK00009B/626